For Foreign Office use only—not to be Circulated.

THE CASE

OF

CAPTAIN BURTON

LATE H.B.M.'S CONSUL

AT

DAMASCUS.

N.B.—All the Private Letters contained in this Case (not addressed to Captain Burton) have been forwarded to him by the writers to make what use he pleased of. Signatures are only omitted in cases where the writers might be subjected to persecution by Turkish local authorities, and so forth.

London:
Printed by CLAYTON & Co., Foreign and Parliamentary Printers, Temple Printing Works,
17, Bouverie Street, Fleet Street, E.C.

For Foreign Office use only—not to be Circulated.

THE CASE

OF

CAPTAIN BURTON

LATE H.B.M.'S CONSUL

AT

DAMASCUS.

N.B.—All the Private Letters contained in this Case (not addressed to Captain Burton) have been forwarded to him by the writers to make what use he pleased of. Signatures are only omitted in cases where the writers might be subjected to persecution by Turkish local authorities, and so forth.

Martino Publishing
Mansfield Centre, CT 06250 USA

&

Voyager Press Rare Books
West Vancouver, BC Canada

&

Wayfarer's Bookshop
West Vancouver, BC Canada

2005

Martino Publishing
P.O. Box 373,
Mansfield Centre, CT 06250 USA

&

Voyager Press Rare Books
West Vancouver, BC Canada

&

Wayfarer's Bookshop
335 Southborough Drive
West Vancouver, B.C.
V7S 1L9 Canada

ISBN 1-57898-541-2

© *2005*

All rights reserved. No new contribution to this publication may be reproduced, stored in a retrieval system, or transmitted, in any form or by any means, electronic, mechanical, photocopying, recording, or otherwise, without the prior permission of the Publishers.

Library of Congress Cataloging-in-Publication Data

The case of Captain Burton, late H.B.M's consul at Damascus.
   p. cm.
Documents in English, French, or Italian.
Originally published: London: Clayton & Co., [1872?].
ISBN 1-57898-541-2 (cloth: alk. paper)
   1. Burton, Richard Francis, Sir, 1821-1890. 2. Syria--Foreign relations--Great Britain. 3. Great Britain--Foreign relations--Syria. 4. Diplomatic and consular service, British--Syria--19th century.

G246.B8C375 2005
327.4 105 6'092--dc22   2004061067

Printed in the United States of America On 100% Acid-Free Paper

FOR FOREIGN OFFICE USE AND FACILITY ONLY.

NOT TO BE CIRCULATED.

The recall from my post at Damascus on the 15th August, 1871, may, by many, be considered to imply that it resulted from something that went wrong, or that I have incurred official displeasure; at least, it might be so understood by those whose duties did not oblige them to read my despatches. With the view, therefore, of retaining the confidence and good opinion of my Chiefs, I have put together such papers and despatches as will give an account of my stewardship in Syria, and the state of that country during my time (1869-70-71). They are for the use of the Foreign Office only.

My appointment was conferred upon me by the Earl of Derby, then Lord Stanley, in November, 1868. I was absent in South America on sick leave, after a severe illness. As soon as the news of my appointment reached me I hurried back, and on arriving was desired by Lord Clarendon, who was most considerate about the unhealthy season, to arrive at Damascus in October. This I did, and took charge on 3rd October, 1869.

During my absence on sick leave, a few persons who disliked the appointment, and certain missionaries who feared that I was anti-missionary, and have since handsomely acknowledged their mistake, took measures to work upon Lord Clarendon on the plea that I was too fond of Mahometans, that I had performed a pilgrimage to Mecca, and that their fanaticism would lead to troubles and dangers. On becoming aware that I had lived in the East, and with Moslems, for many years after my pilgrimage, Lord Clarendon, with that good taste and justice which always characterized him, refused to change my appointment until that fanaticism was proved. I had the pleasure of reporting to him a particularly friendly reception.

RICHARD FRANCIS BURTON,
Late H.B.M.'s Consul of Damascus.

London, March, 1872.

The following despatches show—
    1. (June 19, 1869) Lord Clarendon's caution.
    2. (June 21, 1869) My answer.
    3. (Oct. 29, 1869) My report of reception.

[SEPARATE.]

FOREIGN OFFICE, June 19th, 1869.

SIR,

With reference to your separate despatch of the 14th instant, I am directed by the Earl of Clarendon, in communicating to you his Lordship's sanction of the arrrangement therein proposed for your procceding to your post, to take this opportunity of repeating to you what his Lordship has already verbally stated to you, that very serious objections to your appointment at Damascus have reached him from official quarters, and that although Lord Clarendon has allowed that appointment to go forward on receiving from you assurances that the objections raised were unfounded, his Lordship has warned you that if the feeling stated to exist against you on the part of the autnorities and people at that place should prevent the proper performance by you of your official duties, it would be his Lordship's duty immediately to recall you.

I am, Sir,
Your most obedient humble Servant,
(Signed)   JAMES MURRAY.

Captain Burton,
    Howlett's Hotel,
        36, Manchester Street,
            Manchester Square.

HOWLETT'S, June 21st, 1869.

SIR,

I have the honour to acknowledge the receipt of a despatch, marked separate, of the 19th instant, and to express my gratitude for the sanction with which his Lordship has favoured me.

I now renew in writing the verbal statement, in which I assured his Lordship that neither the authorities nor the people of Damascus will show for me any but a friendly feeling; that, in fact, they will receive me as did the Egyptians and the people of Zanzibar for years after my pilgrimage to Mecca. But as designing persons may have attempted to complicate the situation, I once more undertake to act with unusual prudence, and, under all circumstances, to hold myself, and myself only, answerable for the consequences.

I have, &c.,
(Signed)   RICHARD F. BURTON.

James Murray, Esq.,
    Foreign Office.

HER MAJESTY'S CONSULATE, DAMASCUS,
October 27th, 1869.

MY LORD,

I had the honour to inform you, in my despatch of the 6th inst., that though I had not received my Barat (Exequatur) and Firman, I exchanged friendly unofficial visits with his Excellency the Wali (Governor-General) of Syria.

Since that time I have been honoured with the visits of all the prelates of the Oriental Churches, as well as by a great number of the most learned and influential Moslems, and of the principal Christians. Amongst them were his Highness the Amir Abd el Kadir, his Excellency the Greek Catholic Patriarch, his Excellency the Bishop of the Greek Orthodox

Church, the Syrian orthodox and the Syrian Catholic Bishops, Archimandrite Jebara of the Russian Orthodox Church, the Shayhh el Ulema, Abdullah Effendi el Halabi, the Shayhh el Melawíyyeh of Koniah, Ali Pasha el Aazam, and Antun Effendi Shami, the latter a member of the "Shaury" Council for Syria in Constantinople, Said Effendi Usturwáneh, President of the Criminal Court of Damascus and its dependencies, Mohammed Effendi el Minnini, Vice-President of the Criminal Court of Appeal, the Mufti Mahmud Effendi Hamzeh, Ibrahim Effendi Tannus, head of the Greek community, and member of the Principal Court of Administration, Shayhh Mohammed Effendi el Halabi, member of the Lower Court, and several others.

All these dignitaries evinced much pleasure and satisfaction at my being appointed H.M.'s Consul in their City. Some of them, indeed, earnestly requested me to interest the English public in forming a company for making railways through Syria, that being the sole means of bringing about the civilization of their country.

In conclusion, I have the honour to draw your Lordship's attention to the fact that notwithstanding Abdullah Effendi being the most learned, influential, and orthodox Moslem, and though it is not consistent with his principles to call upon any Christian before being visited, he first came to the office in company with his brother, and after an interview of fifty minutes departed, with a promise to renew the visit.

On the 23rd instant I returned the visit of this Shayhh el Ulema at the great Mosque el Amawi. On the 26th instant I received a duplicate copy of H.M.'s commission, together with the Barat and Firman of H.I.M. the Sultan, directing the local authorities to recognize me as H.M.'s Consul, This day (Oct. 27) I assumed charge of the Consulate, and exchanged the usual official visits.

I have, &c.

(Signed) RICHARD F. BURTON.

The first unpleasantness that occurred (June-July, 1870) was with Mr. Mentor Mott, Superintendent of the British Syrian School at Beyrout. Mr. Mott would come up and distribute Christian tracts to the Mahometans in Damascus. Damascus was not then in a temper for such proselytizing. It was an excitable year, and it was necessary to put a stop to proceedings which, however well meant, could not fail to endanger the safety of the Christian population. I was very sorry for this, as Mr. Mott is a kind, humane, and charitable man, but with an enthusiasm in his religious views which makes him dangerous out of a Syrian Christian town. I resolved upon reporting him to the Embassy. Mrs. Mott wishing to be beforehand with me, at once sent several complaints upon the subject to the Embassy, and I need not detail her proceedings with the Foreign Office. She accused me of writing against her husband in the "Levant Herald," which the editor subsequently contradicted. When Mr. Kennedy arrived at Beyrout, in January, 1871, Mr. and Mrs. Mott expressed a wish to become reconciled to me. Hoping it was in sincerity, I permitted Mrs. Burton (who was very anxious for an amicable settlement), through Mr. Kennedy, and after several invitations and advances on the part of Mr. and Mrs. Mott, to arrange that we should go to their house for a school distribution of prizes, and several courteous notes passed between Mrs. Mott and Mrs. Burton during our stay at Beyrout. Mr. Mott was sincere, but Mrs. Mott, as soon as Mrs. Kennedy departed, came to Damascus, and in the presence of a large party affirmed that Mr. Kennedy had read out to her certain instructions from the Foreign Office, that I was either to make her an apology or be dismissed the service; and ten or eleven other similar histories too trivial to repeat. The whole party informed me of this, and I desired Mrs. Burton to write and ask her if it were true, whereupon she wrote to Mrs. Burton an unqualified denial of all their statements. This called forth from all those who knew Mrs. Mott in Damascus, and many persons in Beyrout, a condemnation which was embodied by the Rev. W. Wright (Senior Missionary in Damascus), in a letter which I print with the despatches. The whole correspondence which I possess is too trivial and lengthy to lay before the Foreign Office —unless desired—to prove how impossible it is for any person living in Syria to avoid trouble with Mrs. Mott.

Not content with this, Mrs. Mott has, since my departure, spread a report that Mr. C. F. Tyrwhitt-Drake promised her "if she would head a memorial to get Captain Burton back to Damascus, he would undertake that Captain Burton would suppress all her past misdeeds." Mr. Drake's letter in reply is also added thereto.

To my surprise, Mr. Consul-General Eldridge, *officially*, openly espoused her cause.

I beg leave to add that I never allowed any unpleasantness between Mr. and Mrs. Mott and myself to interfere with my unceasing endeavours to promote the interests and business of the British Syrian Schools, and I shall presently show that even Mrs. Mott was obliged to acknowledge this justice on my part.

My conduct in the above case was, I believe, approved of by my Chiefs.

Despatches belonging to this case (and letters):—

Damascus, June 29th, 1870. Mrs. Meshaka to Captain Burton.
Damascus, June 30th, 1870. Captain Burton to Mr. Mott.
Beyrout, July 1st, 1870. Mr. Mott to Captain Burton.
Damascus, July 10th, 1870. Captain Burton to Mr. Mott.
August 17th, 1870. Mrs. Mott's letter to the Embassy, Constantinople.
August 11th, 1870. Sir Henry Elliot to the Consul-General Eldridge.
August 11th, 1870. Sir Henry Elliot to Captain Burton.
August 31st, 1870. Mr. Odo Russell to Captain Burton.
September 1st, 1870. Sir Henry Elliot to Captain Burton.
October 4th, 1870. Captain Burton to the Earl Granville.

October 4th, 1870. Captain Burton to Sir Henry Elliot.

Damascus, March 1st, 1871. The Rev. W. Wright to Mrs. Mott.

March 17th, 1871. The Rev. W. Scott to Captain Burton.

Damascus, March 15th, 1871. The Rev. William Wright to Mrs. Mott.

Jerusalem, Feb. 18th, 1872. Charles F. Tyrwhitt Drake to the Rev. Dr. Jessop, of Bayswater.

[1. OFFICIAL.]

DAMASCUS, June 29th, 1870.

DEAR SIR,

Last Sunday, without my knowledge, Mr. Mott visited the prisoners, seventy in number, gave them to drink lemonade, and small religious books to read. Holo Pasha has complained that the distribution of books has excited the people, and desired that the fact should be represented to you for prevention in future. Miss James being unwell, I spoke on the subject with Salim Kassab, a schoolmaster, who told me that Mr. Mott was about to start for Beyrout, and left yesterday by the diligence.

I am, Sir,

Your obedient Servant,

NASEEF MESHAKA.

To Capt. Burton.

H.B.M.'s CONSULATE, DAMASCUS,

June 30th, 1870.

SIR,

I have the honour to state that on the 29th instant I received a letter from M. Naseef Meshaka, the Protestant Dragoman of H.B.M.'s Consulate, Damascus, informing me that last Sunday you visited, without his knowledge, the prisoners of that city, seventy in number, and distributed amongst them small religious books. His Excellency Holo Pasha, Acting Governor-General of Syria, has complained that your proceedings have excited the Mussulman population, and he has desired that they should be represented for prevention in future.

When offering you a Kawas to visit the prison, I understood that you were going on some errand of charity to one of your own flock. I regret your proceedings the more, as I have hitherto warmly supported the Protestant missions and schools in this province. It is my duty to inform you that those living in security at Beyrout will not suffer by displays of indiscreet zeal; they may, however, imperil the whole Christian population of Damascus and is environs, who live amongst fanatical Mussulman communities, and on the borders of the desert.

Copies of this letter will be forwarded to Her Majesty's Foreign Office, and to H.M.'s Ambassador at Constantinople.

I have the honour to be, Sir,

Your most obedient humble Servant,

RICHD. F. BURTON,

H.B.M.'s Consul, Damascus.

To Mr. Mentor Mott.

BEYROUT, July 1st, 1870.

SIR,

I am in receipt of your letter of June 30th, respecting my visit to the prison of Damascus. In compliance with your instructions, I applied to the Kawas to accompany me, but he replied that as he was in charge he was unable to leave the Consulate. I accordingly proceeded to the prison, and was informed by the keeper that admittance would not be obtained without permission from the Colonel. A soldier went with me to Mustapha Bey, who sent an officer to attend me. Concluding that everything was *en règle*, I gave the prisoners some lemonade, and to those few who could read a copy of one or two of the enclosed papers. May I request you to do me the favour to read them. This is the first time I have heard any objection raised against them. Had I been aware that any Moslem at Damascus would object, I should have abstained from giving them.

As you have considered it necessary to send a copy of your letter to the Foreign Office, and also to our Ambassador, I must avail myself of the same privilege.

I am, Sir, your obedient Servant,

MENTOR MOTT.

Captain Burton,
H.B.M.'s Consul, Damascus.

DAMASCUS,
July 10th, 1870.

SIR,

I have the honour to acknowledge the receipt of your explanation relative to your visit to the Damascus prison, and must express my surprise that after so long a residence in this country you should be unaware that Protestant tracts are unacceptable to fanatical Moslems. To give you some idea of it I may inform you that the Mufetish sent round to collect all you had circulated both in and out of the prison during your few days' visit to Damascus, for the purpose of making a bonfire of it. For the sake of the English name I sent my Dragoman, Hanna Misk, to request the acting Wali to stop such a proceeding; and he, with great good taste, spared us this mortification.

I have the honour to be, Sir,
Your most obedient humble Servant,
RICHARD F. BURTON,
H.B.M.'s Consul, Damascus.

To Mr. Mentor Mott.

Copy of Mrs. Mott's letter to the Embassy at Constantinople.

DEAR SIR,

I have this morning received a communication from H.M.'s Consulate-General in Syria, in which Mr. Eldridge advises that I should immediately send your Excellency a copy of the letter addressed to my husband by the Wali Rashid Pasha, on the subject of the charge brought against him by Captain Burton, respecting his visit to the prison of Damascus.

We concluded that the Wali's letter had set the matter at rest, but Captain Burton has seen fit to publish a most injudicious and insulting article in the "Levant Herald" (July 13), which our Consul-General advised should be submitted to you.

I feel how safely we can leave it in your hands to protect us against this and similar charges, which might so easily stir up the angry feelings of the Moslem population, with whom we are living on terms of mutual confidence.

I deeply regret being obliged to trouble you on this subject,

And remain,
Your obedient humble Servant,
(Signed) AUGUSTA MENTOR MOTT.

[COPY.]

Sir Henry Elliot to Mr. Eldridge.

SIR,

Mr. Consul Burton has reported a circumstance which lately occurred at Damascus upon the occasion of Mr. Mentor Mott's visiting the prison of that place.

From the explanations which have been sent to me on the part of Mr. Mott I am led to believe that the Mutessariff had greatly exaggerated any indiscretion that Mr. Mott may have committed upon that occasion, although from his own showing he seems to have acted inconsistently.

I am fully aware of the important services which Mr. and Mrs. Mott have rendered to the cause of education in Syria, and I should be sorry to see their usefulness impaired by any misunderstanding with the Turkish authorities—such as could not fail to arise from any attempt to proselytize the Mahometans, which would, moreover, too probably lead to the repetition of the disastrous outbreaks of fanaticism which have been seen on former occasions. It would be advisable for you to point out to Mr. Mott, when he visits such a fanatical place as Damascus, the necessity of confining his intercourse to such of his own people as may happen to be there, or at least abstaining very carefully from giving grounds for a belief that he went for purposes of proselytizing a Moslem population.

I am, &c.,

(Signed) HENRY ELLIOT.

[No. 3.]

FOREIGN OFFICE,
August 31st, 1870.

SIR,

I am directed by Earl Granville to state, in reply to your despatch circular No 8, of the 11th ult., that his Lordship cannot avoid the conclusion that Mr. Mott's proceedings, as therein described, however well intended, were liable to misconstruction. His Lordship, at the same time, is of opinion that you should have forwarded a copy of Mr. Mott's letter to you. And I am to instruct you to report whether you were aware that a letter of apology, which that gentleman addressed to the Governor of Damascus, was accepted by his Excellency as satisfactory.

I am, &c.,

To Captain Burton. (Signed) ODO RUSSELL.

[COPY, No. 2.]

THERAPIA,
August 11th, 1870.

SIR,

I have received your despatch No. 5, of the 11th ultimo, enclosing the copy of a letter which you had addressed to Mr. Mentor Mott, on the subject of some proceedings of his when he visited the prison at Damascus. I have likewise received from Mr. Mott a copy of his reply.

It is of the utmost importance to prevent anything being done at Damascus that may seem likely to excite the fanaticism of the population there, and it is your duty to interfere if you see a British subject acting in a manner which in your judgment tends to provoke it, and more especially to set your face against any attempt to proselytize. With regard to this particular case, it appears from the information which has been sent to me that the Mutessariff took an exaggerated view of it, for the Governor-General, after receiving Mr. Mott's explanation, returned him a very courteous reply.

Mr. Mott appears to have committed an indiscretion upon the occasion in question, but he is represented to me as a kind, well-meaning person, and ready to listen to any remonstrance. I have therefore requested Mr. Consul-General Eldridge, by the despatch of which a copy is enclosed, to point out to him the necessity, when he visits such a fanatical place as Damascus, of abstaining very carefully from giving ground for a belief that he went for purposes of proselytizing or distributing Christian tracts among a Moslem population.

I am, Sir,

With truth and regard,

Your obedient and faithful Servant,

To Captain Burton. (Signed) HENRY ELLIOT.

[Copy, No. 3.]

Therapia,
September 1st, 1870.

Sir,

With reference to your despatch, No. 5, of the 11th of July, and mine in reply to it, No. 2, of the 11th of August, I have now to enclose the copy of a letter which I have received from Mrs. Mott, transmitting one which her husband had received from the Governor-General in reference to the occurrence which formed the subject of them.

You will see that Rashid Pasha is far from attributing the same importance to it as the Caimakám, and takes the opportunity of bearing witness to Mr. Mott's benevolent exertions, which I hope may in no way be interfered with by the exaggerated alarm which any ill-advised proceedings may have caused to some subordinate authorities.

I am, Sir,

With truth and regard,

Your obedient and faithful Servant,

To Captain Burton. (Signed) HENRY ELLIOT.

Damascus,
October 4th, 1870.

My Lord,

I have the honour to acknowledge the receipt of your official letter (No. 3) of August 31st, 1870. The reason why I did not furnish a copy of Mr. Mentor Mott's letter to me is, that that gentleman informed me in writing that he would himself send in a copy of his reply to the Foreign Office. In accordance to orders I have to report that I was not aware that any letter of apology had been addressed by Mr. Mentor Mott to the Acting-Governor of Damascus, or that it had been accepted by His Excellency as satisfactory. Nor do I believe that anything of the kind took place. I have been provided by Her Majesty's Embassy, Constantinople (Sept. 1, 1870) with a copy of the reply of His Excellency Rashid Pasha, Governor-General of Syria, dated July 6th, 1870, and accepting Mr. Mentor Mott's excuses. Of this, also, I was not aware; moreover, His Excellency Rashid Pasha was far distant from Damascus at the time, and I am better acquainted with the state of the capital than he could be. The Governor of Damascus at once closed three Protestant schools, one of 13 or 14 years' standing, and was persuaded to re-open them only by the influence of this Consulate. I have done my duty in reporting that Mr. Mentor Mott's visits to Damascus may be, in times of excitement, dangerous to himself and to others.

I have the honour, &c.,

Earl Granville. RICHARD F. BURTON.

DAMASCUS,
October 4th, 1870.

SIR,

I have the honour to acknowledge the receipt of your Excellency's despatch (No. 3) of September 1st, 1870. With respect to the enclosed copy of His Excellency Rashid Pasha's letter to Mr. Mentor Mott, dated July 6th, 1870, I have the honour to observe that the Governor-General was, at that time, far distant from Damascus, and that he could not be as well acquainted as I was with the effect produced by Mr. Mentor Mott's proceedings. I have done my duty in reporting the danger of this gentleman's visits to this capital, especially in times of excitement; and after this I can no longer hold myself responsible for what may occur in case his visits are repeated. I have also received through H. M's. Consulate-General, Beyrout, the copy of a letter addressed (August 17th, 1870) by Mrs. Augusta M. Mott to your Excellency.

This letter contains the following words :—" Captain Burton has thought fit to publish a most injudicious and insulting article in the " Levant Herald " (July 13th), which our Consul-General advises should be submitted to you." Mr. Eldridge has distinctly denied that he advised anything of the sort. I published nothing of the kind. Mrs. Augusta M. Mott alludes to an anonymous news letter dated from Beyrout, and by her attributed to me. It is well known here that what I publish in the " Levant Herald " is signed with my own name, and that that paper has other correspondents at Beyrout and at Damascus besides myself.

I do not deny that Mr. Mentor Mott's exertions have been with a benevolent object. But I beg to call your Excellency's attention to the fact that since the decease of Mrs. Bowen Thompson, who established the British Syrian Schools, and in whose hands these establishments did great good to the country, the management at head-quarters has changed—not for the better.

It is hardly my office to warn the Home Committee of the change; but I consider it right to bring my statements to the notice of your Excellency.

I am, &c.,

Sir Henry Elliot. RICHARD F. BURTON.

The affair ended here till January, 1871, when a reconciliation took place during Mr. Kennedy's visit, and after his departure the *animus* was kept up by Mrs. Mott, as the following letters show:—

Copy of a letter from the Rev. Wm. Wright to Mrs. Mott.

DAMASCUS,
March 1st, 1871.

DEAR MADAM,

When in Damascus you called upon us one night, and, with other information on the same topic, you told us—

1. That Mr. Kennedy told you his instructions were to compel Captain Burton to apologize to you, or else to resign his office.

2. That you said a visit to the British Syrian School from Captain Burton would be accepted as a full apology.

3. That that visit was made by Captain Burton, and you considered the apology complete.

That there might be no room for misunderstanding among those present, I interrupted the conversation with this question: "Am I to understand that Mr. Kennedy told you that his instructions from the Foreign Office were to get an apology for you from Captain Burton, or else to get his resignation?" And you replied with deliberation—

4. "Yes, yes;" and charged us not to speak of it.

When I expressed doubts as to the treatment of an English official in the way you described, and said I heard that Mr. Kennedy's mission had reference to the fees in three of the Consulates at the sea-ports, and that I understood so from Captain Burton himself, you replied—

5. "Do not believe it. We know. He was sent out expressly with reference to the British Syrian Schools."

Of *minor matters which you emphasized*.

That on Mrs. Burton attempting to deny the authorship of the "Levant Herald" letters on the part of Captain Burton, in the presence of Mr. Kennedy, you said—

(a) "Do not tell a falsehood, Mrs. Burton. Captain Burton told me himself he wrote the letters; and you added, "And I put in the spice."" Whereupon Mrs. Burton made a scene, kissed you, and the "Levant Herald" letters were no more referred to.

I understand that these statements in substance, with certain modifications and limitations (such as that Mr. Kennedy read you a statement from a letter, in which he was instructed to ascertain if Captain Burton were the author of the "Levant Herald" letters, and if so, to demand from him an apology or his resignation), were repeated several times, and to different parties, during your stay in Damascus.

Some of us have heard with astonishment that you have denied having made the statements. Will you enable me to say whether or not; and I shall place these questions and your answers before the seven or eight of our colony who heard the words.

Yours faithfully,
(Signed) WILLIAM WRIGHT.

Mrs. Mott,
    British Syrian School,
        Beyrout.

[COPY.]

BEYROUT,
March 8th, 1871.

DEAR SIR,

I am at a loss to understand the drift of your letter. I have already replied fully to Mrs. Burton on this subject. "In a multitude of words there wanteth not sin;" and I believe you will agree with me that Christian missionaries have something better to do than to stir up strife.

Yours faithfully,
(Signed) AUGUSTA MENTOR MOTT.

Rev. W. Wright,
    Damascus.

DAMASCUS,
March 17th, 1871.

DEAR CAPTAIN BURTON,

During her late visit to Damascus, Mrs. Mentor Mott made certain statements regarding you of a nature calculated to injure you in your character of British Consul in Damascus. Those statements she has since, in a correspondence with Mrs. Burton, either entirely denied having made, or explained them away to certain ambiguous phrases, capable of being interpreted in two senses. I wish to lay before you the substance of her remarks, as made to me.

I had one short interview with Mrs. Mott while she was in this city. At once, and without any provocation on my part, she forced on my reluctant ears her account of the object of Mr. Kennedy's visit to Beyrout. His mission was, according to her, from first to last, to inquire into the relations between Mr. and Mrs. Mott and Captain Burton, and, if possible, to resettle them, Mr. Mott having been offended and injured by a severe criticism of his conduct which had appeared in the "Levant Herald," and which was supposed to be the production of Captain Burton. Mr. Kennedy was instructed, *and he read his instructions to this effect to Mrs. Mott*, to give Captain Burton his choice between an apology for the supposed wrong, or a resignation of his office. Owing, however, to Mr. Kennedy's kindly remonstrances, Mrs. Mott did not insist upon a formal apology, but accepted a visit from Captain Burton instead.

All this implied that Captain Burton was the acknowledged author of the letters in the "Levant Herald," and I asked Mrs. Mott what evidence she had on this point, and the same time freely admitting that there had been a general impression that Captain Burton *was* the author, and that I had myself shared that impression. In reply, Mrs. Mott assured me—

1st. That Mrs. Burton had herself told her, "Captain Burton writes the letters, and I put in the spice;" and that, on Mrs. Burton's attempting, in Mr. Kennedy's presence, to deny that Captain Burton wrote the letters, she had promptly quoted against Mrs. Burton her own words, to the utter confusion of the latter, and Mr. Kennedy's complete conviction on the subject.

2nd: I was assured that "Captain Burton told Mr. Barker so." In a letter to Mrs. Burton, Mrs. Mott denies ever having conversed with Mr. Barker on the subject. This I entirely believe; but it in no way affects my veracity. I am not concerned as to *how* Mrs. Mott gets her information, whether directly or indirectly. She certainly declared to me that Captain Burton made the above admission to Mr. Barker.

You may well imagine that I am performing no pleasant task in making this communication to you. It distresses me to have to expose the self-contradictions and prevarications of one who claims to be considered a Christian lady, but I feel I should ill deserve the position in which I stand as a missionary in Damascus, and forfeit all right to the name of gentleman, if I remained silent. Had Mrs. Mott's words been mere idle gossip, or keen, though unfriendly, criticisms of character, I should never have referred to them—such things every one expects, and every one makes light of—but I have been long enough in Syria to know that an attack on a Consul's character concerns us all; for it tends to tarnish the superior lustre of the British name, and to weaken the legitimate influence of Britain in this land. I feel it doubly incumbent upon me to defend the good name of a Consul, who, as far as I can judge, has brought to the discharge of his office the two essential, but not always associated, qualities of integrity and energy.

I have the honour to be, Sir,

Your obedient Servant,

(Signed) JAMES ORR SCOTT.

P.S.—You are welcome to use this letter in any way you think fit.

Copy of a letter from the Rev. Wm. Wright to Mrs. Mott.

DAMASCUS,
March 15th, 1871.

DEAR MADAM,

Your letter, in which you profess not to understand the drift of mine, has reached me, and, according to promise, I have shown it to those who heard your statement in Damascus, which you have since denied.

The honour of an English lady, and your high position as the deputy of Christian philanthropy, called for a suspension of judgment till you should have an opportunity of re-affirming the statement which you circulated so sedulously in this city.

My questions, which were plain and direct almost to insult, you profess not to understand; and our conviction is now complete that those stories which you told so musically, and with such evident zest, were entirely of your own invention. I was not one of those who were surprised when we heard you had contradicted your statements, for I knew several of your statements that night were untrue when you were repeating them—such, for instance, as that you "Saw Miss Dales' girls' school in Damascus, and that it was a very insigificant affair;" though Miss Dales had left Damascus, and the house in which the school had been held was destroyed, seven or eight years before you ever saw Damascus. We have, however, been so much accustomed to your misrepresentation of mission work in Damascus, that I just followed our ordinary rule of denying your statement when I heard it.

I most cordially agree with your statement that missionaries have something better to do than to stir up strife; but I fear you failed to profit by the maxim.

I am no advocate of Captain Burton, for he needs not my advocacy. We move in different spheres; but he is our Consul, and we need his help, and we have always found his help prompt and effectual when solicited. I have nothing to do with Captain Burton's private opinions, nor do I know them, but he has never by word or act said or done in my presence anything disrespectful to Christianity. Captain Burton's official acts in Damascus have been rigorous and just. Especially has he endeavoured to shield and help the oppressed, even to incurring the wrath of the rich and influential. From the beginning we have taken Captain Burton as we found him, and our relations have been cordial.

You came to Damascus, and instantly you met the Rev. Mr. Scott you commenced your narration. You forced your stories on his reluctant ears, though he protested that he had not heard from the Consul any account of Mr. Kennedy's mission. You came to our house night after night *expressly to contradict* what Captain Burton told me was the object of Mr. Kennedy's mission. You told your stories in the presence of my wife's neice, Miss James, and your sister, with a glow of inexpressible satisfaction, though the truthfulness of your assertion was challenged by me at every pause, and you well knew that had I believed what you said, I must have for ever doubted the veracity of Captain Burton, and our social relations must have come to an end. Then you wrote a letter to Mrs. Burton, giving as your representation in Damascus of Mr. Kennedy's mission the very statements that you stigmatized as absolutely false *" as the Burton's lies."*

Then you represented those whom you obliged to hear your words as "whisperers" and "slanderers," and prayed in your own maliciously pious way that we might have "a better memory and more truthful lips." Then your character as a Christian missionary did not prevent you from stirring up strife by these words to Mrs. Burton :—"I heard stray stories about what you had said about me, but I did not credit them, and now less than ever;" though you prudently abstained from giving any of the statements when challenged, doubtless remembering that there were a number of witnesses to all our interviews. When I remember that saddening exhibition in which you used so dramatically the death of Jessie Jago, and yet continued to prop up invention by invention—when I look at your note before me, and see the attempt to cover over your malignant untruths by a pious assertion of Christian piety—I fear that your sense of right and wrong is too indistinct to enable you to profit by any advice of mine. I shall, however, discharge my duty to you by reminding you that a series of accidents has placed you in a position where your example may be most baneful. Young English ladies of high purpose and devoted zeal enter your establishment as workers. What must be the effect on their impressionable natures, should they find that your gushing words and high pretensions are backed up by a false and hollow life? There are numbers who will be ready to condemn missions altogether when they find missionaries assuming great piety, and yet neglecting to speak the truth. The children of the country that you are entrusted to elevate will be quick to see you through and through, and if your life is false and hollow they will catch your tone.

With respect to our present relations, I have hitherto carefully shunned you, not being able to believe your statements, and not wishing to contradict you in this disagreeable business which you have forced upon us. I have given you an opportunity of acknowledging your fault, which you have not had the courage to accept; and until you do so, according to the Christian rule, you must be to me as " an heathen and a publican."

I shall, however, as heretofore, carefully distinguish between the head of the B. S. School, and the schools themselves, which are the product of the faith and love of generous England.

I shall assist the teachers and the schools to the best of my ability; but I shall beg to be excused from having any communication with you directly or indirectly, till I know that you have repented of your past falsehood, and learned to speak the truth.

Yours faithfully,

Mrs. Mott,   (Signed)   WM. WRIGHT.
Beyrout.

Thus ended the second attempt of Mrs. Mott to injure me. The third she commenced after my departure from Syria, which called forth the following letter from Mr. Tyrwhitt-Drake:—

Copy of a letter from Mr. Tyrwhitt-Drake to Dr. Jessop.

Sir,

Yesterday I received a letter from Damascus, informing me that *you* said that I had written a letter to Mrs. Mott, of Beyrout, engaging to get Captain Burton to suppress what he had to say against her, on condition that she would head a memorial in favour of his return to Syria.

This is a lie. Therefore, as I have always been led to believe that you are a clergyman acting upon just and conscientious motives, I ask you not only, *not* to propagate this false report no further, but to contradict it directly.

Had you known me personally, I trust that you would never have given credence to such a report. If Mrs. Mott has told it to you, I cannot imagine how a Christian woman in her responsible position can have gone out of her way to spread such an astounding falsehood about a person so utterly removed as I am from her sphere of life, and who neither has, nor ever had, and certainly never will have, any connection with her doings.

As far as I can remember, I never wrote a single line to Mrs. Mott in my life; and it would be very odd if I were to have forgotten having done so, as I have only seen her on three occasions, viz., twice in March, 1871 (once at Mr. Eldridge's house, where I was introduced to her, and secondly at Basoul's Hotel), and thirdly, and lastly, at B'hamdoon, in September, 1871. On this last occasion she pressed me (in the presence of Miss Seely) to pay her a visit, though I was almost a total stranger, at Suk el Gharb. This invitation I did not accept.

In September last I was more than once requested by a lady resident in Syria connected with the schools—*not* Mrs. Mott—to write a *copy of a letter* (as she thought I should perhaps be able to word it better than she could) *for her to rewrite* and sign and send to her friends to do likewise; the purport of this letter being that Captain Burton's return to Syria would be most desirable, &c., &c. At last I consented, and wrote the letter (of which I still retain a copy), and if it has fallen into Mrs. Mott's hands it was never meant for her, but written simply for the use of the lady who asked for it.

As it in no ways emanated from me, I purposely tore (or cut) the bottom of the sheet of paper on which it was written (a *large*-sized sheet of foreign letter paper, which also contained a private note on the second page to the lady at whose request I drew it up) in order that it might be rewritten.

I write this fully to show that, if this letter is in Mrs. Motts hands, I have suffered from a most unworthy breach of confidence.

I am perfectly aware that many people at Beyrout have, even though personally unknown to me, and without any proof at all of other offence, chosen to give me an ill name for my upholding the cause of Captain Burton, who has been most disgracefully treated. This tittle-tattle of course affects me no more than the reeking fumes of the dunghill at its base, affect the tower which stands before the windows of the room in which I write.

It is curious that every one at Damascus speaks well of Captain Burton, while those at Beyrout speak most evilly of him behind his back, thus fulfilling their duty as pious Christians. I would to God that I had some real power to aid Captain Burton, whom I know to be an honourable man, and one who never feared to do his duty as an English officer and a gentleman.

In conclusion, Sir, I beg you to write and inform me what has been your reason in spreading this report about me, at the same time telling me, that that which emanated from you has also been contradicted by you.

I remain, Sir,

The Rev. Dr. Jessop,
Beyrout.

Your obedient Servant,
CHARLES F. TYRWHITT-DRAKE.

CASE No. 2.

MR. CONSUL-GENERAL ELDRIDGE AND THE DRUZES.

THE Druzes applied early in 1870 for an English School. I was on very friendly terms with them, and as two missionaries wished to travel amongst them, I gave them the necessary introductions. They were cordially received and hospitably entertained by the Shaykhs, but on their road home they were treacherously followed and attacked, they were thrown off their horses, their lives were threatened, and their property was plundered.

Such a breach of hospitality and violation of good faith required prompt notice: firstly, to secure safety to future travellers; and, secondly, to maintain the good feelings which have ever subsisted between the Druzes and the English. To pass over such an act of treachery would be courting their contempt. I at once demanded that the offenders might be punished by the Druze chiefs, and 20 napoleons, the worth of the stolen goods, were claimed by me for the missionaries. The Druzes sent down to Beyrout to try to pit Consulate-General against Consulate, and refused to pay the claim. I then applied for their punishment to the Turkish authorities, knowing they would at once accede to my first demand—a proceeding approved of by Her Majesty's Ambassador at Constantinople. After three months the Shaykh el Akkál, head religious chief, brought down the offenders, who were recognised by the missionaries. To my surprise Mr. Consul-General Eldridge ordered me to release them, and wanted to give them a present of 250 piastres each, saying he had pledged his word that they should not be punished. He also declared openly that I was applying for the punishment of the wrong men, although the missionaries had recognised them. They confessed their guilt, and the Shaykh, who was staying as a guest in my house, assured me that I was perfectly right in acting as I had done, and that every Druze was heartily ashamed of the conduct of these two men.

I asked for an official order in writing from Mr. Eldridge. He declined. The case was referred to Constantinople. My proceedings were found just. I have lived so much amongst Easterns that I know how to treat them as they should be treated, whilst pursuing the orders laid down for me by Her Majesty's Government.

I regret that I have not a single official letter from Mr. Consul-General Eldridge to put in. He wished that we should be on the friendly terms of corresponding privately, and although I have received and possess more than a hundred private letters I do not like to make use of them, in order to show that I was on the best of terms with him, and that I always endeavoured to act in concordance with him whenever it was possible: and my surprise was extreme, when I found that he had been officially opposed to me on every great occasion.

Documents—

Mr. Eldridge to Captain Burton, July 9, 1870.
,,   ,,   July 16, 1870.
An abstract of Captain Burton's reply, July 17, 1870.

ALEIH,
July 9th, 1870.

MY DEAR BURTON,
I have received no end of letters from the Druze Chiefs of the Hauran, expressing their regret at the robbery of Mr. Pritchard, and now I have a whole deputation of the Druzes of the mountain, who tell me that the guilty parties are at Jeremanah, ready to come to Damascus, to throw themselves at your feet, ask your forgiveness, and restore the stolen property, on condition, however, that you are *not* to hand them over to the Turks, but to accept their apologies and promises of good behaviour, and to these conditions I have acceded, as I wanted to settle the affair *en famille*. At Stamboul I explained the matter to the Eltchi, and that I hoped to arrive at this result without an appeal to the Turks, and H.E. agreed with me in the views I expressed to you in my letter on the subject shortly before I left Beyrout; therefore I hope you will be satisfied with the apologies, return of the things stolen, and promises of good behaviour in future, as I believe the latter will be sincere,

I am overwhelmed with congratulatory visits. I have received six parties to-day, and have now two parties waiting to see me, which will explain the haste in which I write. Hope to see you soon.

Yours most sincerely,
(Signed)   G. JACKSON ELDRIDGE.

ALEIH,
July 16th, 1870.

MY DEAR BURTON,
Your letter of 13th (just received), in answer to mine of 9th, rather upsets me, so I take a big sheet to try to prove that you are in the wrong in imposing, or trying to impose, a fine on the guilty Druzes, supposing always that they have given up the property stolen, have begged your forgiveness, and promised to behave better in future. 1st. *We* have no right to impose a fine upon any subject of H.M. the Sultan—and the Druzes are un-

doubtedly subjects of the Sultan—and I have always laboured and still labour to render them faithful ones. 2nd. Supposing we had the right to levy the fine, to whom is the amount to go? Not to us, certainly, nor to the Queen—the Turks would naturally object to that. To the party robbed (as you say Mackintosh, whoever he is, claims twenty napoleons—for what I don't know)? This, at best, would be accepting a bribe to compromise a felony, which, I believe, in England is an indictable offence, although, perhaps, not here—though it must not be forgotten that we are here to uphold English principles as far as we can. 3rd. By insisting on this *fine*, which you have no right whatever to impose, you break *my* pledged word to the chief Druzes of the mountain, without whose assistance we should never have arrived at the results we have in this matter, and you can hardly compare your experience of this people to mine of seven years; and it was for their sakes that I accepted the conditions of a restoration of the stolen property, an apology to you, and a promise of better behaviour for the future, on condition that we should withdraw from the prosecution, while the fine you wish to propose has all the air of a bribe to compromise a felony, and will put you wrong with the Turks, the Government at home, and destroy the confidence of the Druzes, not only in the Hauran, but in the mountain, in us; and once that gone, we may look for serious troubles, as the Druzes will make a hard fight for it when they are once persuaded that we are against them. At Constantinople I explained to the Eltchi this affair, and said I should be satisfied with a restoration of the property, &c,, and he agreed with me. Now we appear to have obtained that object, you impose other conditions that cannot be upheld; therefore I hope you will let them go according to my terms, otherwise it is difficult to say where the matter may end. When you are here I will go fully into the matter with you, and explain more than I can in a single letter. The connection between the people here and those in the Hauran is closer than you think it is, and the robbers would never have been brought to book at all, had it not been for the influence I brought to bear from here. Glad of what you have done with Stambouli. I send this to Bludan by messenger, who will bring your answer back.

In haste, yours most sincerely,

(Signed) G. JACKSON ELDRIDGE.

Bludan,

Sunday, July 17, 1870.

My Dear Eldridge,

Yours of the 16th arrived to-day at 2.45, and mine will leave at 4 p.m.

I think the best thing you can do is to send me, as Consul-General, an order, on your own responsibility, to let the robbers go. It is entirely against my conviction; but your arguments are good as regards the fine. I was wrong to use the word "*fine*." But I merely advance the missionary's claim, and of course the money would go to *him*. So far from compounding the felony I would have pushed the affair to the utmost with the Government, and would have sent the two men to the galleys. I had no idea that you had *pledged your word* to the Druzes of the mountain. In your first note you put it much more mildly. I cannot believe that these men would not have been in my hands without any assistance but the Wali's. I do not doubt your experience of the people in the mountain, but the Hauran has seen many late changes which it is the interest of the mountaineers to keep hidden from

Beyrout. We will talk the rest of the matter over when we meet. I will at once send and have the fellows released, but *don't forget to let me have the order*. The rascals have indeed got off cheap. They have plundered and threatened the lives of two Englishmen enjoying their hospitality; they have escaped with an apology, and they have not returned the plundered articles.

Believe me, dear Eldridge, in haste,

Yours most sincerely,

RICHARD F. BURTON.

CASE NO. 3.

THE JEWS AND THE RUMOURED DANGERS IN DAMASCUS.

In June, 1870, I prepared a despatch for Sir Henry Elliot on the system of defrauding the poor and of ruining villages, quoting the case of one Yakoob Stambouli. I submitted it to Mr. Consul-General Eldridge, who disapproved of it, and it was not therefore forwarded to H.M. Government until November, 1870. The three persons chiefly concerned, however, heard of it. On August 26th, I received a letter from the Rev. Wm. Wright, which will be found in this case, and likewise one from the Chief Consular Dragoman, Mr. Nasíf Meshaka, which induced me to ride at once to Damascus (from Bludan, the summer quarter). I found that half the Christians had fled, and everything was ripe for a new massacre. I sought the authorities, and woke them up to the sense of their danger, and induced them to have night patrols, to put guards in the streets, to prevent Jews or Christians from leaving their houses, and all measures needful to convince the conspirators that they would not find everyone sleeping as they did in 1860. The Wali and all the chief responsible authorities were absent. The excitement subsided under the measures recommended by me, and in three days all was quiet, and the Christians returned to their homes. Mr. Consul-General Eldridge denied the report of danger. The fact is he has lived for nine years as Consul-General at Beyrout. Damascus, within his jurisdiction, is only fourteen hours from him, and he has never seen it. I affirm that, living in safety upon the sea-coast, no man can be a judge of the other side of the Lebanon, nor, if he does not know some eastern language, can he be a judge of Orientals and their proceedings. Certain Jews have been accused of exciting these massacres, because their lives were perfectly safe, and they profited of the horrors to buy up property at a nominal price. It was brought to my notice that two Jewish boys, servants to British protected subjects, were giving the well-understood signal by drawing crosses on the walls. Its meaning to me was clear. I promptly investigated it, and took away the British protection of the masters temporarily, merely reproving the boys, who had acted under orders. I did not take upon myself to punish them. Certain ill-advised

Jews fancied it was a good opportunity to overthrow me, and with me my plan of seeing fair proceedings on the part of British *protégés*. So they reported to Sir Moses Montefiore and Sir Francis Goldsmid that I had tortured the boy. My proceedings were once more proved just. The correspondence hereto attached is worth attention. It consists of—

Despatch to Sir H. Elliot from Captain Burton, November 21st, 1870, concerning the Jews' pecuniary transactions.

The notice Captain Burton wished to post at the Consulate door.

Mr. Eldridge's objections, November 30th, 1870.

Letter from Mr. Nasíf Mcshaka on Christian alarm, and one from the Rev. W. Wright, August 25th, 1870.

Sir Moses Montefiore to Earl Granville, complaining of Captain Burton, October 25th, 1870.

Ditto Sir F. Goldsmid, October 24th, 1870.

Mr. Odo Russell to Captain Burton, November 3rd, 1870, enclosing three complaints—

One signed Aaron Jacob and Jacob Perez, to Dr. Adler, Chief Rabbi, London, September 13th, 1870;

One S. W. Weiskopf, September 12th, 1870; and

One also from Aaron Jacob and Jacob Perez to Sir Moses Montefiore, September 13th, 1870;

Captain Burton's reply, No. 16, Damascus, November 28th, 1870.

„ „ No. 17 „ December 6th, 1870.

„ „ No. 18 „ December 15th, 1870.

The evidence of the chief of police, Ismail Agha, concerning the Jews and the crosses.

A letter from the English missionaries, showing their feeling on the above scandal, and also one from the Hon. Mrs. Digby El Mezrab (Lady Ellenborough) to the same effect, speaking for the tribes.

One from the Greek Patriarch (Orthodox), on the part of his people, and

One from the Greek Catholic Patriarch, signed by the Syrian Catholic Bishop, the Maronite Patriarch, and the Armenian Patriarch, on behalf of their respective peoples.

A Letter from Mr. Kennedy, enclosing further Jew complaints, January 14th, 1871.

M. Yakoob Stambouli's appeal to Mr. Kennedy during his visit, January 14th, 1871.

Ditto, Ishak Tobi.

Captain Burton's reply to Mr. Kennedy, dated January 24th, 1871.

The Defence and Certificates of the Dragomans, Mr. Hanna Azar and Mr. Nasíf Meshaka, accused by the Jews.

And, lastly, a letter from a Mr. Netter, a Jew, showing that his co-religionists at Damascus are paid to abstain from such actions as putting up crosses, &c.

Captain Burton's reply to Mr. Netter, October 4th, 1820.

H. B. Majesty's Consulate, Damascus,
November 21, 1870.

Sir,

I have the honour to draw your Excellency's attention to the following state of affairs at Damascus.

In former days, when not a few European Consuls were open to certain arrangements which made them take the highest interest in the business transactions of their clients, a radically bad system, happily now almost extinct, was introduced into Syria. The European subject, or protégé, instead of engaging in honest commerce, was encouraged to seek inordinate and usurious profits by sales to the Government and by loans to the villagers. In such cases he, of course, relied entirely upon the protection of a foreign power on account of the sums to be expended in feeing native functionaries before repayment could be expected. Thus the Consuls became, as it were, huissiers, or bailiffs, whose principal duties were to collect the bad debts of those who had foreign passports.

Damascus contains a total of forty-eight adult males protected by Her Britanic Majesty's Consulate, and of these the three principal are Messrs. Daud Harari, Ishak Tobi, and Yakoob Stambouli. Most of them are Jews who were admitted to, or whose fathers acquired, a foreign nationality given with the benevolent object of saving them from Moslem cruelty and oppression in days gone by. These protégés have extended what was granted for the preservation of their lives, liberties, and property to transactions which rest entirely for success upon British protection. The case of M. Yacoob Stambouli, whose family, as his name denotes, is from Constantinople, and whose affairs must be known by repeated representation to Her Majesty's Embassy, will explain what I mean. He has few dealings in the city, the licit field of action. But since the death of Shahadeh, his highly respectable father, in 1854, he has been allowing bills signed by the ignorant peasantry of the province to accumulate simple and compound interest till the liabilities of the villagers have become greater than the value of the whole village. Arneh, for instance, on the eastern skirt of Mount Hermon, owes him 106,000 piastres, which were originally 42,000. He claims 5,000 purses from the Jumblat family upon a total debt of 242,000$\frac{1}{2}$ piastres in 1857. I have not yet passed through a single settlement where his debtors did not complain loudly of his proceedings; and to Arneh may be added Adra, Zebadani, and Mejdel-el-Shams, a stronghold of the Druzes. Some villages have been partly depopulated by his vexations, and the injury done to the Druzes by thus driving them from the Anti-Libanus to the Hauran may presently be severely visited upon the Ottoman authorities. This British protégé is compelled every year in his quality of Shubasi (farmer of revenue) to summon the village Shaykhs and peasantry, to imprison them and to leave them lying in jail till he can squeeze from them as much as possible and to injure them by quartering Hawali, or policemen, who plunder whatever they can. He long occupied the whole attention, though it has other and more important duties of the Village Commission (Kumision Mahasibat el Kura), established in A.H. 1280 (1863). For about a year a special commission (Kumision Makhsus) has been sitting on his case, whose intricacies, complicated by his unwillingness to settle anything, weary out all the members. At different times he has quarrelled with every person in the Court—from the Defterdar, who is its President, to the Consular Dragomans, who compose it. Even felony is freely imputed to him. He is accused of bribing the Government Katibs (secretaries) to introduce into documents sentences of doubtful import, upon which he can found claims for increased and exorbitant interest; of adding lines to receipts and other instruments after they have been signed, and of using false seals made at home by his own servants. But lately one of the latter publicly denounced him, but was, as usual, paid to keep silence. He is reported again and again to have refused, in order that the peasants might remain upon his books, the ready moneys offered to him for the final settlement of village liabilities. I have attempted to bring these charges home to him, but in vain; his good management has baffled all my efforts, whilst leaving me morally certain that the charges are founded on fact. He corrupts, or attempts to corrupt all those with whom he has dealings. I was compelled to dismiss, shortly after taking charge, a Dragoman, who was his paid agent. M. Stambouli and his son openly state that they secured for a sum of £100 the good offices of my immediate predecessor, Mr. Acting Consul Wood, and that Mr. Rogers, whom he relieved, was also open to such arrangements. In my own case they proceeded, till summarily stopped, to throw out direct hints touching Arab mares, and indirect concerning diamond rings.

These scandals, which do not, however, exhaust the list, make me desirous of placing M. Yakoob Stambouli, and the two other Jewish protected subjects, upon a footing which will prevent them from breeding mischief in this Consulate.

With your Excellency's permission I would inform them that British protection extends to preserving their persons and property from all injustice and violence; but that it will not assist them to recover debts from the Ottoman Government, or from the villagers of the Province, and that it will not abet them in imprisoning or in distraining the latter. To such general rule of course exceptions would be admissible at the discretion of the officer in charge of Her Britannic Majesty's Consulate; in cases, for instance, when just and honest claims might be rejected, or their payment unduly delayed. The sole inconvenience which can arise to such creditors from their altered position would be the necessity of feeing the Serai more heavily than at present; and even now they openly communicate with the local authorities, reserving this Consulate as a forlorn hope. The change may possibly direct their attention to a more legitimate commercial career. Such a measure would be exceedingly popular throughout the country, and will relieve us from the suspicion of interested motives—a suspicion which must exist where honesty and honour are almost unknown; and from the odium which attaches to the official instruments of oppression. Finally, the almost universal corruption of Damascus renders me the more jealous of the good name of this Consulate, and the more desirous of personal immunity from certain reports which have been spread about those in office.

I have the honour, &c.,

(Signed) RICHD. F. BURTON.

To Sir Henry Elliot, H.M.'s Ambassador, Constantinople.

The Notice which I purposed to post on the door of H.M.'s Consulate, Damascus.

DAMASCUS,

June 20th, 1870,

Her Britannic Majesty's Consul hereby warns British subjects and *protégés* that he will not assist them to recover debts from the Government or from the people of Syria unless the debts are such as between British subjects could be recovered through H.M.'s Consular Courts. Before purchasing the claims, public or private, of an Ottoman subject—and especially where Government paper is in question—the *protégé* should, if official interference be likely to be required, at once report the whole transaction to this Consulate. British subjects and protected persons are hereby duly warned that protection extends to life, liberty, and property, in cases where these are threatened by violence or by injustice; but that it will not interfere in speculations which, if undertaken by Syrian subjects of the Porte, could not be expected to prove remunerative. British subjects and protected persons must not expect the official interference of the Consulate in cases where they prefer (as of late has often happened at Damascus) to urge their claims upon the local authorities without referring to this Consulate, and altogether ignoring the jurisdiction of H.B.M.'s Consul. Finally, H.B.M.'s Consul feels himself bound to protest strongly against the system adopted by British subjects and protected persons at Damascus, who habitually induce the Ottoman authorities to imprison peasants and pauper debtors either for simple debt, or upon charges which have not been previously produced for examination at this Consulate. The prisons will be visited once a week. An official application will be made for the delivery of all such persons.

(Signed)   R. F. BURTON,
H.B.M.'s Consul, Damascus.

BEYROUT,
November 30, 1870.

MY DEAR BURTON,

The messenger arrived, I think, on Friday last, and in the packet was the enclosed envelope, unsealed, in the state I now send it to you. It contained your Nos. 11 and 12 to *Embassy* and the Jewish Despatch in copy for F. O., so there must have been a mistake in making up the packet, which Iscander declares arrived with the seal broken as I now send it to you. All this puzzles me, as your private letter came intact, and I was surprised at your asking me to open the despatch which came with the seal already broken. I don't think Iscander would have pluck enough to break the seal of a despatch, or impudence enough to send it to me afterwards, open; he would have re-sealed it, sent it on, and said nothing had he opened it. I should like to have the matter cleared up, even at a little expense, so try to find out what you can and let me know the result.

I can't say I admire the Hebrew Despatch, which is vague and contradictory in my idea, and is not likely to produce the result you want to attain. Your sweeping charges against all European subjects and *protégés* in Syria is a libel, as I know of many who have never resorted to the practices you denounce. Money-lending is a perfectly legitimate trade, though in some cases it is a difficulty to know where to draw the line when the prefix of *dis* should be added to honest transactions. I have no sympathy with practices of Stambouli and his confrères, which I think scandalous, and while they reflect discredit on us they tend to injure greatly the country; but they have always been a part of the Turkish system of Government.

Yours most sincerely,
(Signed)   G. JACKSON ELDRIDGE

DAMASCUS,
August 25th, 1870.

(From our Dragoman in charge, M. Nasif Meshaka.)

DEAR SIR,

Some of the christians in Damascus are in great alarm; some of them left for Saidnayah, and others are about to leave elsewhere. Their alarm was occasioned from the following facts:—Signs of crosses were made in the streets in the same way which preceded the massacre of 1860. On the 23rd instant a certain Mohammed Rashid, a government inspector (Teftish), being in disguise, caught a young Jew, twelve years old, in the service of Solomon Donemberg, a British protected subject; making signs of crosses in a watercloset of a mosque at Suk el Jedid. Yesterday another young Jew, in the service of Marco, a French Jew, was caught also. Both of these two boys were taken to the Government: being under age they were at once released by order of Mejlis Tamiz Hukúk. It is believed that the Moslems are the authors of these signs, either directly or indirectly, to stop the Government from taking the Redif, which is managed in a very oppressive manner, that is, leaving many families without males to support them. Such kinds of Redif prefer rather to be hanged than seeing their hareem without support or any one to maintain them in their absence. A certain Nicolas Ghartous, a Protestant from Ain Shara, reported to me yesterday that while waiting or Mr. Anhouri, near the barracks of the Christian quarter, being dressed like a Druze, three soldiers of the same barracks came to him, and said, "Yakík el 'ijl," a technical term used for the Druzes meaning, "Are you ready for another outbreak?" Ghartous replied, "We are at your disposal." The soldiers replied, "Prepare yourself, and we will reap our enemies from here to the Bab Sharki" (the Christian quarter), and thus they departed. Hatem Ghanem, a Catholic member in the Hauran, came here to recover some money due to him by Atta Zello of the Meidán Aghas. While claiming the money he was beaten, and his religion and cross were cursed by his debtor, who was put in prison at the request of the Catholic Patriarchate. Twenty to thirty Redifs of the meidán ran away to the Lejaa, to take refuge there. The Redifs will be collected next Saturday, the 27th instant, some of them say at the Castle of Damascus, others at Khabboon and Mezzeh. The report is current that on that day there will be no work in town, and that there may be an outbreak. I am told that Serour Agha is now in service, and is patrolling during night, and sometimes with Holo Pasha. Although Ibrahim Pasha, the new Governor, arrived on the 22nd instant, he will not undertake his duties till the return of the Wali. The Government, as well as some Frenchmen, through Mr. Roustan, who is now at Jerusalem, intend to propose to the Wali to leave Holo to continue occupying his present function under the present circumstances. The Mushir left on the 19th instant. The Wali is absent. The Muffetish, whom you know his inefficiency, is the Acting Governor-General. Consuls are absent (that is the French and English). The presence of the high functionaries, and especially the consuls, is a great comfort to the Christians in general.

I do not see for the present any possibility of an outbreak, but I find it my duty to send you this report by a special messenger, in order not to be blamed in future.

Nothing further, but I remain,

Dear Sir

Your obedient and faithful servant,

(Signed)   N. MESHAKA.

From The Rev. Wm. Wright, Missionary, to Capt. R. T. Burton, Her B. M. Consul, Damascus.

Damascus, August 25th, 1870.

My Dear Sir,

I have just got in from Rasheiya, and before I sat down several Christians and one Moslem came in to ask if I knew what was coming. They seemed to be very much afraid; but, except that people don't act logically, I see no reason for fear. The fear, however, seems *very* great. I know nothing. Any English of us here should be ready at the worst to fight our corner. Many thanks for your prompt action in our affairs. It is something to have

"One firm strong man in a blatant land,
Who can act and who dare not lie."

Yours, most truly,
(Signed)   WM. WRIGHT.

[COPY.]

7, GROSVENOR GATE, PARK LANE,
October 25th, 1870.

My Lord,

I venture to solicit your Lordship's perusal of the accompanying translation of a Letter which has been addressed to me by the R. R. of the Jews of Damascus.

Your Lordship will perceive that the Jews complain that the attitude assumed towards them by Her Britannic Majesty's Consul at Damascus (Captain Burton) is such as to occasion them much injury and considerable anxiety.

I am deeply sensible of the powerful aid and protection which Her Britannic Majesty's Government has uniformly afforded whenever intervention has been sought on behalf of my co-religionists in foreign countries. I feel convinced that in the present instance the exercise of the good offices of Her Majesty's Government would save my co-religionists in the East from much unhappiness. The Rev. Dr. Adler, Chief Rabbi of the Jews of this country, has received a communication similar to the one above referred to, and from the same parties, a copy of which I likewise hand your Lordship.

I therefore beg that your Lordship will be so good as to take such measures in the matter as your Lordship may think fit.

I have, &c.

(Signed)   MOSES MONTEFIORE.

The Earl Granville, K.G.

[COPY.]

RENDCOMB PARK, CIRENCESTER,
24th October, 1870.

DEAR MR. HAMMOND,

The letter of which I enclose a copy, though dated 12th September, did not reach me till two or three days ago.

I have no means of ascertaining the truth of the statement respecting Captain Burton made by Mr. Weiskopf, but, as I believe him to be a respectable man, I have, after some consideration, thought that I ought not to withhold from your knowledge the information he sends me, especially as I hear from another quarter that the lady whom Captain Burton has married is believed to be a bigoted Roman Catholic, and to be likely to influence him against the Jews.

It has occurred to me as possible that Lord Granville may think it proper to give Captain Burton some general instructions, from which he would perceive that he would incur the serious displeasure of the Government by countenancing any acts of injustice or persecution.

I remain, &c.,

(Signed)   FRANCIS H. GOLDSMID.

The Right Hon. E. Hammond.

[COPY.]

FOREIGN OFFICE,
November 3rd, 1870.

SIR,

I am directed by Earl Granville to transmit to you the enclosed copies of correspondence communicated to his Lordship by Sir Moses Montefiore and Sir F. Goldsmid, in which most serious complaints are made against you, for the hostility which you are said to have shown towards the Jewish community at Damascus, and especially in the case of a Jewish boy, whom you are accused of having forced, by beating and threats of torture, to confess to a charge of having marked a cross upon the walls of a Turkish school.

Lord Granville desires that you will furnish him with detailed answers to every point of complaint in the enclosed papers.

I am, Sir,

Your most obedient humble servant,

(Signed)   ODO RUSSELL.

Captain Burton,
    Her Majesty's Consul,
        Damascus.

[COPY TRANSLATION.]

DAMASCUS,
17th Elul, 5630.
(September 13th, 1870.)

To the Venerated and Renowned Doctor Nathan Adler, Chief Rabbi at London.

We, the ecclesiastical representatives of the Jewish community at Damascus, after sending you our hearty greetings, find ourselves impelled by necessity to place before you what has occurred with respect to the British Consul of this place, whose name is Captain Burton. He has now been in this city one year, but from his arrival here he showed no friendly feeling to the Jews who are under British protection. Indeed, he is the very reverse of his predecessor, Consul Rogers, whom we remember with gratitude.

He has shown his bad feeling towards the Jews who are under British protection in the following matter :—The Mahometans have a school in an open place, which is chiefly inhabited by merchants or tailors. Among the latter is a Jew named Sim'an Ashkenazi, whose English passport is at the British Consulate. About a month ago it was reported that images of crosses had been seen on the walls of the school. Captain Burton, when he heard this, knowing that Sim'an's shop was close to the school, sent for his sons, two young men, also tailors in their father's shop. He also sent for two little boys, aged respectively seven and eight years, who were apprenticed to this tailor.

He asked them, "Why have you made these crosses?" The children replied, "We know nothing about them." He then terrified them, struck the little one, had their hands and feet tied with ropes, and said, "I say, you have made these crosses. Now, who prompted you to it, for grown-up people among your nation must have planned this." They answered, "We have neither made these crosses nor has any Jew told us to do so."

In consequence of this we, the ecclesiastical authorities, went to the Consul, and remonstrated. Then he, in a great passion, said, "This is all your doing."

We thereupon said, "After you have terrified and ill-used these children, so that out of sheer fright they may answer as you wish, it looks much like the Father Thomas affair, thirty years ago, when the Jews were so long ill-treated till, in their agony, they said all the things which their accusers wished them to say, without there being the slightest foundation to such statements.

Upon this Captain Burton rejoined, "True, this circumstance of making crosses is like the former affair—both are your doings." Then the interpreter, Hanna Azar, said to the Consul, "Mark what they say—they would assert that the Father Thomas accusations are really false."

We asked the Consul, "Who is the man that actually brings the accusation?" He answered "It is I that accuse you." We then went away in great distress of mind. On the same day he took away from the two sons of the tailor Sim'an the document which certified that they were under British protection, and told them that henceforth they were no longer so.

One of the children, who was a Turkish subject, he had brought before the Turkish authorities, that they should imprison it; but they declined to proceed against the child, much less to lock it up, on account of its youth.

The other boy, a Persian subject, returned to his home. Now, it is our duty to lay before you the origin and the cause of the Consul's animosity against the Jews. There are two interpreters connected with the British Consulate, whose names are Hanna Azar and Nasif Meshaka, and belong to the families who, thirty years ago, brought those horrible accusations against the Jews.

Consul Rogers, seeing the hatred they constantly evinced towards the Jews, dismissed them from the Consulate. Consul Burton, however, doubtless on account of the similarity of their sentiments to his own, appointed them interpreters to the Consulate, and ever since it has been the endeavour of these men to wrong us, and to sow hatred between us and our neighbours of different creeds.

We have also ascertained that Consul Burton has written to the English Government most grievous things concerning the Jews here that are under British protection. He wrote that the transactions between the Jews of Damascus and the Mahommedans as well as Christians are not in accordance with justice and truth; that there are Jews who get bills and bonds executed at usurious rates of interest, and that afterwards, as being under his protection, they apply to him to have those bonds enforced through the Turkish authorities; that by these means unpleasant relations arise between him and the Turkish officials, and he therefore applies to the British Government for authority to withdraw British protection from those who have hitherto enjoyed its benefits.

Now all the allegations that he makes are devoid of truth. The facts are these:—

Eight years ago the Turkish Government appointed a Commission in this city, consisting of three Turkish members and one member for each consulate, who meet twice a week at an appointed place, and whose duty it is to regulate and judge all matters connected with bill and other monetary transactions between Mahommedans, Christians, and Jews

This Commission has to sign and seal all such bonds and bills, and without their sanction no man can realize even the smallest debt of this description. As the rate of interest is regulated by the Commission, it is moderate, and what is customary in the cities of Syria. Now no Consul hesitates to authorize the enforcement of these bonds, as they are public and well known transactions, requiring in each case the sanction of the Commission. It will be seen, therefore, that what the Consul has written is devoid of foundation, but that his allegations are merely raised to do injury to the Jews.

We think it right that we should acquaint you with some further doings of the Consul Burton. Unlike the other Consuls, he does not make Damascus his permanent abode. He makes a journey of one or two days away from the city, stays away about a month, and then returns for two or three days. It is most difficult for persons who are under British protection to obtain an interview. If an appeal is sent on to him it does not for a long time meet with any attention, and if the petitioners appeal to the interpreters it is of no avail. When at last an audience with the Consul is obtained, instead of entering into the matter, he will not listen to the applicant, but reviles and mocks him. Indeed, we cannot recount the many instances of injury and oppression that the people who are under British protection have suffered.

We do not particularize them, as the aggrieved parties do not wish their complaints made known, for fear that they will be brought home to them, and they may suffer all the more. But it is an established and well-known fact that Consul Burton and his assistants do their utmost to afflict the Jews, and to sow discord between them and their neighbours.

We, therefore, beseech you to intercede for us, and to awaken the compassion of one who is the ornament of Israel and its glory the ever ready helper Sir Moses Montefiore, that he may once again come forward on behalf of his brethren at Damascus, and obtain the recall of Captain Burton, so that he may be replaced by a discreet and faithful man, who will not employ these two hostile interpreters, Hanna Azar and Nasif Meshaka, as there are many able and clever interpreters who are friendly to Israel.

It will readily be understood that the protection afforded by Great Britain to some of the members of the community is no small matter for the whole congregation, for it is through the benevolence and liberality of these men that the learned and the poor amongst us are maintained.

Now we put our trust in thee, father and shepherd in Israel, so that we may soon receive happy tidings, and that the community will be sheltered and protected.

(Signed)   AARON JACOB.
JACOB PEREZ.

[COPY.]

BAYREUTH,
le 12 Septembre, 1870.

MONSIEUR LE BARONET,

Votre profond amour pour le Judaïsme et votre zèle pour l'humanité me garantissent votre pardon de ce que j'ose vous importuner par cette lettre que j'ai l'honneur de vous adresser pour solliciter votre haute bienveillance en faveur d'une communauté renommée par ses malheurs. Je veux parler de Damas, cette antique cité où nos co-religionnaires ont constamment à souffrir d'une population ultra-fanatique.

Par malheur les autorités consulaires, quoique représentant la justice et le droit moderne, contribuent à entretenir les sentiments haîneux contre nous au lieu de combattre les préjugés d'une autre époque.

Parmi tous les Consulats celui de Sa Majesté Brittanique avait maintes fois défendu les Israélites contre des fausses accusations que nos ennemis parlent journellement contre les membres de la dite commune.

Par des motifs inexplicables le consul actuel, le célèbre Capitaine Burton, le compagnon de Speek, paraît avoir délaissé les traditions de sa chancellerie. Depuis son arrivée à Damas il prête l'oreille à ses drogmans, des Chrétiens indigènes, qui produisent à tout instant des calomnies contre les Israélites, dont plusieurs jouissent de la protection anglaise. Un de nos plus acharnés adversaires est le premier drogman du Consulat Anglais, Hanna Azar, Damasquin, qui inspire au consul une attitude hostile vis-à-vis de ses protégés israélites, preuve l'événement que je vais avoir l'honneur de porter à votre connaissance.

Il y a peu près vingt jours un Zaptié turc (policeman) prétendait avoir vu un garçon israélite faire des croix dans les lieux communé d'une école mahométane. Le garçon faussement inculpé fut traduit devant le Consulat Anglais comme étant au service d'un tailleur israélite qui a passeport anglais.

Le consul, M. Burton, le fit interroger par le nommé Hanna Azar, son interprète, mais le garçon persistait à prétendre qu'il n'avait pas fait la croix sur le mur. On l'intimida; le drogman frappa le pauvre jeune homme, et finit par faire apporter des cordes pour le garrotter. La vue de ces préparatifs l'effrayait, et le pauvre avouait. On fit appeler un autre garçon israélite, l'intimida comme son camarade, et voulut lui extorquer le double aveu d'avoir fait ces croix et de les avoir tracées sur le mur du précité édifice. Sur l'instigation des chefs de la communauté, nonobstant les coups donnés à ce malheureux, ce ne fut que le plus jeune qui avait cédé à la peine, tandis que l'aîné protesta énergiquement contre tout ce qu'on voulut lui avouer par la violence.

Alors le consul fit appeler les deux patrons de ces jeunes gens israélites, leur prit le passeport anglais, et leur adresser des paroles fort dures, prétendait que les deux apprentis n'avaient agi que sur leurs ordres, et qu'eux-mêmes étaient les instruments des chefs de la communauté—accusation aussi fausse qu'absurde.

La communauté consternée députe alors son Grand Rabbin chez M. Burton pour lui expliquer que de pareil faits ne pouvaient émaner des Israélites, que les deux garçons n'avaient avoué que sous des coups, et qu'un pareil procédé était peu digne du Gouvernement Anglais, qui avait, à tout temps, montré la plus bienviellante sollicitude pour les Israélites orientaux. On présenta au consul tout le tort qu'il portait à la réputation de la communauté, car déjà les Chrétiens et les Musulmans nous insultent publiquement en nous reprochant d'avoir tracé des croix sur des maisons musulmanes.

La croix a pour signification un triste souvenir de 1860, époque des massacres que les Musulmans avaient marqué d'avance par une croix les maisons chrétiennes vouées au pillage et au carnage; c'est donc une accusation bien grave que M. Burton voulut soutenir contre nos frères Damasquins.

La démarche du Grand Rabbin n'eut aucun succès; au contraire, M. Burton lui assurait qu'il porterait l'affaire à Londres et à Constantinople. En attendant, il la divulgue partout, et vous concevez qu'une calomnie sortant d'une bouche si autorisée ne manquerez pas de soulever contre nous les Musulmans et les Chrétiens à Damas. Il faut très-peu pour allumer la flamme du plus cruel fanaticisme ; une étincelle suffit pour faire éclater l'incendie.

Je viens donc, au nom de notre sainte religion, au nom de la liberté et de l'humanité et au nom de l'alliance israélite universelle, vous implorer votre intervention auprès du Gouvernement de sa Majesté Britannique en faveur de nos co-religionnaires à Damas, et vous prier d'éclairer votre Gouvernement sur la fausseté des accusations que la haîne seule dut produire.

Veuillez, M. le Baronet, prendre en considération que toute une communauté est menacée par l'intolérance d'un Consul Anglais, et par les machinations de ses drogmans, qui, s'abritant derriére leurs fonctions, ne font que méditer la ruine des nôtres.

Dans l'espoir que Dieu favorise vos démarches d'un plein succès, je vous remercie d'avance monsieur, de tout ce que vous daignerez faire pour Damas, et vous supplier d'agréer l'expression, &c., &c.

(Signed)   S. W. WEISKOPF,

Professeur au service du Comité Central de l'Alliance Israélite Universelle, Ancien Directeur de l'Ecole Israélite Française de Damas, actuellement en la même qualité à Beyreuth.

Mr. Francis Goldsmid, Baronet, Membre du Parlement, Londres.

[COPY TRANSLATION.]

To the Captain of the Lord's hosts, the glory and the crown of Israel, our shield and our buckler, our refuge and tower of strength, the mighty Prince in our midst, &c., &c.

Sir MOSES MONTEFIORE.

May his light shine resplendent till the coming of the Redeemer, the Anointed of the God of Jacob. Our prayers are directed unto God on high that He may lengthen thy days, that greatness and honour may not depart from thee, and that in thy days Judah may be delivered, and Israel dwell in safety. The complaints which we, the children of Israel, dwelling in the City of Damascus address, to thee have, alas! been wrung from us by the straights and distress in which we find ourselves.

About ten days ago an untoward occurrence took place. There is a school where the Turkish youth is instructed, which is close to a street inhabited by tailors and clothiers. Now there was a Jewish boy, about seven years old, apprenticed to a Jewish tailor who was under British protection. This boy went, for necessities of nature, to the closet of the school, where a Gentile was at the same time. At that time a policeman entered, and looking at the walls of the closet he found a cross drawn on the walls. When the policeman entered the Gentile fled, and the Jewish boy was left there. Instantly the policeman seized him and brought him before the authorities, saying, "I have seen this boy make a cross on the wall of the closet." However, the authorities would not entertain a charge brought against so little a boy.

After four days, the British Consul had the boy brought before him at the Consulate, and his interpreter, Hanna Azar, said unto the child, "Who has done this thing?" And the boy answered, "I do not know who did it." The interpreter asked, "Do you not work with another boy?" "There is another boy at the brother of the man to whom I am apprenticed, also a tailor." The interpreter thereupon said, "Then say the other boy (who is older than I am) taught me to make the cross." Then they had the other boy brought, and the interpreter said unto him, "See, this boy says you taught him to make a cross." Thereupon both cried out, "It is not true, we have not done it, nor do we know aught of it." The interpreter proceeded to frighten them and to beat them. They also brought ropes to tie their hands and feet. Then the little boy in his fright said, "This companion of mine has taught me to do this." Then the interpreter said, "Of a certainty this thing is not of your own devices, but grown-up people prompted you to it." Upon this the second boy cried out loudly and swore positively that he neither saw nor knew anything of this. Thereupon they sent for the two brothers, the tailors, who were under British protection, and the Consul and the interpreter spoke to them very roughly. On their denying having any knowledge of how the thing occurred the Consul flew in a rage, took their passports from them, and said, "Now, you must find out within four days who did this, and who taught the boys to make crosses." He then had the boys locked up. After a quarter of an hour, on the intercession of a Jew staying at the Consulate, they were given up to the two brothers, and the further hearing was adjourned for four days.

And when the authorities of our congregation knew of this terror seized upon us, and forthwith one of the undersigned, taking an interpreter with him, waited upon the Consul and said, "We have heard that you assert that the boys have made a cross, and that it was at the prompting of some grown-up persons. Now, we say that such things are not done in Israel, and could not possibly have happened in this manner. You say that the boy has confessed to it; but you must know that he spoke out of fright, as you did beat him, and had ropes brought to tie his arms and legs therewith."

The Consul answered, through the mouth of his interpreter, "What have we done? We frightened them a little, but I am convinced that they made the cross, and that some grown-up people have prompted them to it, and you must find out who has done this and taught the boys.

Then we said, "From your language we must gather that you think we know of this. Now, we cannot conceive why you attribute this wicked thing to us Jews, and bring an evil repute upon us, who are as innocent of it as you are."

The Consul replied, "I don't know." Then the undersigned reminded the Consul that the English Government had given special instructions that their Consuls should watch over the interests of the Jews in the city, and that there was such a despatch deposited at the Consulate; also, that if he wished it, we could obtain fresh instructions that he should be a help unto us.

The Consul said, "It is true there is such a despatch, but I feel certain that the boys have made these crosses, and that grown-up people have prompted them to it." The Consul also spoke of writing to Constantinople about it; and report says that he has already written to Constantinople.

Now, be it known that the interpreter is a wicked and worthless man, an enemy to the Jews, whom he has been seeking all the days of his life to injure.

Under the former Consuls he had no opportunity of doing so, as they were merciful and just men, who loved truth; but he has at last found a master under whom he thinks he can execute his designs of bringing us into evil repute, and of crushing Israel.

The Consul also, from the day he came here, showed hatred to Israel. He has shown his hatred in this very affair, where he meddles in a dispute which is not his. Who has required this at the hands of this man? And he did not investigate this matter in public, but at his own house, so that he might the easier launch accusations against us, create animosity, and place a sword in the hands of our enemies to slay us; and he has succeeded, for he has roused the spirit of hostility against us on the part of both Christians and Turks— the one reviles us, another scoffs at us, a third insults us; they would fain swallow us up altogether.

And, besides this, yesterday the Consul himself, with the interpreter and certain policemen, proceeded to the closet to inspect the cross—all for the purpose of evincing their revengefulness and fomenting ill feeling.

Now we know not what to do; to thee we turn our eyes. Arise for our help, and gird on thy strength for our salvation. We ask thee to procure the removal of the Consul and his interpreter: and that thou art our deliverer, that there is none like thee to rescue the innocent from the hand of the oppressor.

Oh! bring forth our righteousness as the light, and our judgment as the noon-day.

(Signed) AARON JACOB.
JACOB PEREZ.

Damascus, in the month of 13 (Sept., 1870), 5630.

[CONSULAR No. 16.]

DAMASCUS, November 28th, 1870.

MY LORD,

I have the honour to acknowlege having received this day a despatch (No. 5 of November 3, 1870) from the Right Honourable Odo Russell, transmitting copies of correspondence by Sir Moses Montefiore and Sir Francis Goldsmid, with enclosures, and directing me to furnish your Lordship with detailed answers to every point of complaint contained in these communications.

I proceed to make answer in order of date, deeply regretting the necessity of troubling your Lordship with so voluminous a despatch.

The letter of Sir Francis Goldsmid (October 24th, 1870, with enclosure from M. Weiskopf) apparently assumes that I have been guilty of "injustice and persecution" before any explanation has been required of me. The uncalled-for assertion touching "the bigoted Roman Catholic" I shall leave to be dealt with by the person whom it most concerns : I will merely remark that my official proceedings are not influenced by domestic interference. The charge of religious intolerance is to me a novelty; the world has generally given me credit for something too much of the reverse.

I cannot describe the letter of M. Weiskopf, except as a tissue of misstatements founded upon the false reports forwarded by his co-religionists at Damascus, and unhesitatingly, unscrupulously retailed, as if he had personally ascertained the facts of the case.

I distinctly deny that any consul at Damascus "contributes to keep up feelings of hatred against the Jews." Most, if not all of us, have to protect Hebrew subjects, and we protect their interests as if they were Christians or Moslems. I emphatically deny that any of the Dragomans of this Consulate have inspired me with hostility against the Israelite protected subjects. The senior Dragoman, M. Nasif Meshaka, so unjustifiably accused by MM. Aaron Jacob and Jacob Perez of "evincing hatred against the Jews," is the son of the well-known Doctor Meshaka. He had, and I believe he still has, business transactions with one of the Hebrew community, and both he and his father are trusted and respected by the whole Israelite body. Of M. Hanna Azar (who is not, and has never been, "First Dragoman of the Consulate") I positively affirm that during fourteen months intercourse with him, he has never shown the least symptom of unfriendly feeling against the Hebrews as a community; but he, and with him all Damascus, is perfectly aware of the reprehensible practices with which certain members of that estimable body are charged, and he has only done his duty in reporting to me their wicked and cruel conduct. Moreover, it is not my habit to be influenced in such matters by the opinions of my Dragomans.

The case of the boy Yusuf Alfiyyah, to which my attention is especially drawn, will at once prove to your Lordship what amount of confidence is to be reposed in the circumstantial statements of M. Weiskopf. The boy was arrested by a policeman and by a detective in plain clothes while in the act of drawing with a nail crosses in and about the privy of a Moslem mosque. This mosque is the Jami el Ahmediyyah, not a "school," as is stated by M. Weiskopf, and is confirmed by the letter of the two chief rabbis, who certainly know that they assert an untruth. It is not "in an open place," but in the great and crowded bazaar, the Suk el Jedid, and opposite the shop in which the boy was employed. I was unusually careful to ascertain the facts of the case. I went to the mosque and saw the crosses, not, however, as wilfully affirmed, in order to "evince my revengefulness and to foment ill feeling," but simply with the view of taking every precaution. I examined the policeman, and found his statement confirmed by the highly respectable and respected colonel of police, Ismail Agha, in whose presence the lad confessed that he had drawn the crosses. I then sent for the boy to the Consulate, and directed M. Hanna Azar to find out the names of the persons whom I suspected, with strong reason, of having sent him to draw the crosses. I strictly forbade all ill-treatment, and I sat in the next room to be certain that no violence was offered. M. Hanna Azar, to my full knowledge, never struck the boy, who began by owning that he had drawn the crosses, and who ended by denying the fact. He named, however, as his instigator a fellow servant, Yusuf Tashtash. Not knowing the latter to be a Persian protected subject, I sent for him and addressed a few questions to him; when seeing that no satisfactory reply was to be expected, I dismissed both the lads with a caution not to repeat the offence. Yet the Chief Rabbis assert that I had the boys locked up. Moreover, there is no "Jew staying at the Consulate," nor did anyone intercede in the matter. I then sent for the two masters of the lads, MM. Aaron Wolf Donemberg and Meyer Donemberg, Hebrews under British protection, and originally from Russia. Their father, Sim'an Ashkenazi, had given me, shortly after my arrival, some trouble by his fanatic feeling against certain Moslem neighbours. The affair was investigated by me at the Consulate, not at my own house, as is unjustifiably declared by the two Chief Rabbis. M. Meyer Donemberg began by stating a falsehood, namely, that he had dismissed the boy Yusuf Alfiyyah, who was still in his house and in his employment. This naturally strengthened suspicions which had before been aroused. I informed the brothers that I should apply for the opinion of Her Majesty's Ambassador at Constantinople about their remaining under British protection, and that in the mean time they would be protected by their father's passport. Accordingly I reported the case in detail on September 1st, 1870. The Right Hon. Sir Henry Elliot in reply (September 22nd, 1870) informed me that the charge must be brought home to the brothers Donemberg before they could be permanently deprived of their protection. I at once returned to them their passports, without using any "harsh language," but with a strong warning of what would happen in case of ill-conduct being proved against them. I may add that the "accusation, as false as it is absurd," was amply justified by popular opinion at Damascus.

On the next day M. Yacub Perez, political Chief Rabbi of Damascus, called upon me at the Consulate. He did not represent that he was deputed by the community, nor was he accompanied by the religious Chief Rabbi, M. Aaron Jacob, who has very improperly affixed his signature to what he personally ignores. The manner and the language of M. Yacub Perez were equally objectionable; in fact he addressed me as though I had been his servant. He insisted that the Jewish boys should not be punished, under any circumstances, simply because they were Jews. He was offended when it was pointed out to him that I looked to the high ecclesiastical authorities for aid in keeping order and in noticing misconduct. He accused me of wishing to revive the persecution which followed a certain murder committed thirty years ago. His age and his sacred vocation prevented my taking further notice of words and gestures, which I should have resented coming from a layman. The tone of his letter (Elul 5630) accusing me of "meddling in a dispute which was not mine," and asking "who has required this at the hands of this man?" will explain what I mean. I must also mention that M. Perez habitually shows anything but good will towards Christians. He has, within the last few days, threatened to excommunicate any of his co-religionists who may attend the school opened by the Reverend Mr. Frankel, Missionary to the Jews of Damascus. I must also point out that M. Weiskopf's lamentations over the "misfortunes" of the Jews, and his assertions of their "constantly suffering from a bigoted population" of "a spark being sufficient to light the flames of the most cruel fanaticism," and of their being "subject to false accusations," are inventions pure and simple; he must be aware that he is referring to days which ended in 1840. At present they are the merest *ad captandum* common places. I utterly deny that any spirit of hostility has been roused against the Jews of Damascus on the part of both Christians and Turks. It is a wicked and wilful calumny to assert "the one reviles us, another scoffs at us, a third insults us; they would fain swallow us up altogether."

During the awful massacre of 1860, not a Jew was even wounded, not a Hebrew house was plundered. On the contrary, certain of the Jews are universally accused of having pointed out the hiding places of the wretched Christians, and of having made fortunes by the spoils of the victims. Unfortunately they escaped punishment by the influence of their supporters in England. There is no one in Damascus who does not know this fact, which is characterized as an "idle charge" by Sir Moses Montefiore in a late letter to the "Times" (November 1, 1870). If your lordship desire it, I can, though very unwilling to revive memories which should lie in oblivion, confirm my statement by the highest testimony in Damascus. At the time when the crosses were drawn upon the walls of the Mosque, the city was in abnormal state of excitement owing to the calling out of the Radif or Militia, and rumours of a Russian advance upon Constantinople, I determined, in the absence of their Excellencies the Governor-General and the Commander-in-chief, to repress incendiary acts with the utmost energy, and my proceedings on that occasion are, I believe, looked upon with favour by every friend of order. The dispute *was* mine, at least if it be my duty to protect the lives and property of the large Christian population of Damascus.

I now proceed to the communication of Sir Moses Montefiore (October 25, 1870), and enclosure from MM. Aaron Jacob and Jacob Perez, the latter being the Chief Rabbi before alluded to. That venerable philanthropist has very properly forwarded the complaint addressed to him, and I have no reason to object to the tone of his letter. Sir Moses Montefiore also sent a telegram and a note to Mr. Eldridge, Her Majesty's Consul-General for Syria, and he was, I believe, informed that the Hebrews of Beyrout had heard no complaints about my proceedings. Mr. Eldridge, has, moreover, had occasion lately to tear up an anonymous communication addressed to him from Damascus, and purporting to be "signed by all the Jews."

The letter forwarded by MM. Aaron Jacob and Jacob Perez to the chief Rabbi of London contains exaggerations, misstatements, and inventions similar to those of M. Weiskopf, but even more reprehensible, because they are written upon the spot by men who well know the truth. I again distinctly deny that I have shown unfriendly feeling to any of the Jews beyond refusing to abet a small clique in proceedings which will presently be alluded to. The boys questioned at the Consulate were not seven and eight years old, but ten and twelve, an age which here represents fifteen or sixteen in Europe. I neither "struck the little ones," nor allowed any one to strike them, nor did I "tie their hands and feet with ropes." At first the junior boy owned, I repeat, that he had drawn the crosses, and was about to tell the name of the person that induced him so to do. Emboldened, however, by seeing that no violence was offered to him, he presently denied the fact. It is utterly untrue that I "in a great passion" said (to the ecclesiastical authorities) "*this is all your doing!*" I do not "fly into a rage" when on duty. What I said was that the Chief Rabbi should not demand the non-punishment of a Jewish offender simply because he is a Jew; but that he should rather assist me in maintaining order and in noticing misconduct. M. Hanna Azar certainly never uttered the expressions, "Mark what they say" et cetera. This is an invention which I abstain from characterizing. The boy had been brought before the local authorities before I saw him: he was not sent by me. It is untrue that I appointed M. Hanna Azar to the office of Consular Dragoman — in that capacity he had worked under my two immediate predecessors. Both he and M. Nasif Meshaka will forward their own refutations of these and other scandalous charges ("wicked and worthless man," for instance) so wilfully circulated against them.

The account of my "further doings," forwarded in the same letter, is as intentionally incorrect as the rest. I do make Damascus "my permanent abode." But I spent the hot and unwholesome months at Bludan, in the house which my respected predecessor, Mr. Consul-General Wood, built as a summer residence. It is four or five hours, not "one or two days away from the city," and whenever my presence was required I was at Damascus. I have also made a practice, whenever a complaint against the wretched peasantry was brought to the Consulate, of riding out, no matter what the distance might be, and of personally investigating the case. I have found villages in ruins, homes empty because the masters had been cast into jail, and women in tears at my feet. I found these things done in the name of England. Of course, there are men who complain of my absence, and even more of my presence. There is no difficulty in "forwarding to me an appeal," nor in "obtaining an interview with me." I sit with open doors, and any janissary or other *employé* denying me to a visitor without my order would be severely punished. I distinctly contradict the statement that I ever "revile and scoff" applicants; that anyone can complain of suffering through me or my assistants "injury and oppression;" that there has been any "attempt to sow discord between the Jews and their neighbours;" or that I have any wish to " crush Israel."

In noticing the translation of the letter (Elul 5630) forwarded to Sir Moses Montefiore by MM. Aaron Jacob and Jacob Perez, I have merely to repeat my refutations of their former reports. They begin by accusing me of torturing a boy seven years old, a charge probably never yet advanced against a British officer. They end with the modest request for the removal of the whole Consulate. They declare that only one cross was drawn upon the mosque walls. I saw four, of which one was outside the privy. M. Hanna Azar, whose voice I could hear, never told the boy to accuse his fellow servant. I carefully informed the Chief Rabbi that to my certain knowledge the lad had not been beaten, tied up, or otherwise maltreated. He has preferred to believe the Jewish boy, and to disbelieve the British officer.

I am aware, my Lord, that you will be surprised and shocked by the recklessness of assertion, by the baseless calumnies, and by the utter disregard of truth coming from two men of venerable age and of high ecclesiastical position. No Hebrew gentleman in England would believe such things to be possible. Unhappily, however, this total want of conscientiousness, of honesty and of honour, is here the general rule of man's conduct. As a public servant of twenty-eight years standing, and after a career patent to all men, I might expect my mere assertions to be received as valid; but far from wishing to avail myself of such privilege, I will, at the earliest opportunity, supply your Lordship with proof positive of all the assertions advanced by me. I would also draw attention to the fact that these high ecclesiastics, who justify their co-religionists in all matters, when they should assist a British Consul with their advice and authority, certainly ignore their own interests. The true way to disarm fanaticism is to act with justice and mercy: nothing can be gained by unscrupulously abetting the usurers who have so unmercifully ground down the faces of the poor.

In the letter of the Chief Rabbis (Elul 5630) the cause of my animosity " is skilfully stated so as to conceal the truth of the case." I had informed certain members of the Jewish community that their malpractices should be reported to Constantinople and to London. They resolved to be beforehand with me, and to make, in common parlance, a clean sweep of the Consulate: even the sex seldom alluded to by gentlemen in official correspondence was not to be spared. The Jews of Damascus may number 4000. Of these 26 are under British protection, and of the latter three have formed a cabal, which, by forwarding false accusations, by writing anonymous letters, and by fabricating reports and telegrams, hopes to substitute for me a " discreet and faithful man," and for the Consular Dragomans " able and clever interpreters who are friendly to Israel:" in other words, persons who will take their bribes and do their work.

The names of the three are as follows:—

1. M. Daud Harari. This person came a few days after my arrival to my private rooms and begged me to decoy into Damascus two peasants of Helbon, a neighbouring village, and to throw them into prison till his claims were satisfied. He hinted that I should " see good " from him—in other words, be well paid for the treacherous act. I shall not forget his look of mingled surprise and wrath when I thanked him for his kindness, but declined to avail myself of it.

2. M. Ishak Tobi. I am at this moment investigating the case—to quote one of many reported to me by an unhappy Moslem—Mohammed Jamur, who has been repeatedly imprisoned, and at last turned out of house and home by this merciless creditor. M. Jamur's papers are, according to Moslem law, perfectly *en règle*, but M. Ishak Tobi, by his British protection, caused that small point to be completely overlooked. I was writing to consult Sir Philip Francis upon the legal points of the case when your Lordship's despatch reached me.

3. M. Yakub Stambuli. Of this person, I may state that in one case (the Jumblat affair, well known to Mr. Consul-General Eldridge) he lent in 1857 the sum of 242,000½ piastres (about 2420 Napoleons) to the deceased Said Bey, and he now claims, I am told, from the family 5,000 purses, or 35.000 Napoleons. Only to-day I have released from jail two ragged

and half-starved peasants from Telfita, whom he threw into prison under the false charge of their plundering his granary. He has repeatedly assured both the Consular dragomans of his friendship and confidence when working every means against them.

Such are the men who do so much injury to the fair name of England!

It is true, as the Chief Rabbis assert, that eight years ago the Turkish Government appointed a village commission; but the measure did not work well. Moreover, certain commissioners were open to arrangements, and the recognized twelve per cent. per annum often, by some peculiar process, became eighteen per cent. I have lately investigated a case of the kind forwarded to me by the villagers of Zebdani.

The fact is, my lord, that many of the generation which became British *protégés* in 1840 have passed away, and have given place to another of a different stamp. M. Shahadeh, the father of M. Yakub Stambuli was a highly respectable man; but no one respects his son, and much less his grandson. The idea that the Jews are still persecuted may linger in England; here we know better. There is no branch of community more powerful at Damascus than this which Mr. Erskine terms (No. 3, of February 12th, 1864,) the "money-lenders under British protection." They enjoy the confidence of influential friends in England—they are leagued together by the "Alliance Israélite universelle"—and they are by no means scrupulous, as their writings prove, when they determine to gain a point.

The Chief Rabbis "remember with gratitude" Mr. Consul Rogers, about whom, however, their co-religionists have spread the most damaging reports. Without intending any unfriendly allusions to my predecessor, I may state that on arriving at Damascus I found our position as Englishmen far from satisfactory. The claim of certain "money lenders" had been advanced with such pertinacity, in private as well as in public, that feeling ran high against us. Throughout the country the villagers had been impressed with the idea that the usurer's word was law to the British Consulate: even the Bedouin shunned us, as though they expected harm at our hands. Under these circumstances my task has not been light. The many reforms which I have introduced were necessarily unpopular with the few interested in keeping up the normal state of affairs. Strict views of duty are not likely to prepossess in their favour men who live in luxury and even splendour by beggaring their neighbours.

The complaints forwarded against me, my Lord, are simply a trumped-up case concealing the true giste of the "money lenders'" grievance, namely, the injured feelings of a small cabal, whose bribes I have refused, and whose evil work I will not do.

But the Chief Rabbis have wholly neglected to say how hard, and how successfully I have laboured in the cause of the Jewish Community. The Hebrews of Safat applied to me for assistance in mediating with their kaimakam (governor) and thanked me publicly when it was freely given to them. The Israelites of Tiberias have also acknowledged my efforts in their favour. The case of M. Zelmina Füches, a Jewish protected subject, has occupied me for the last fourteen months. On the morning after the cabal met at the house of M. Jacob Perez, one of the most influential Jews reported to me all their proceedings. I could quote many other instances as to prove that I have treated Jew and Gentile alike, and to disprove the unjustifiable charge of intolerance or of hating any respectable and influential body of men.

My conduct at Damascus as elsewhere, my Lord, has been carefully regulated so as to deserve the approval of Her Majesty's Government, and to uphold the honour of the British name. The general voice will, I believe, pronounce that I have not been unsuccessful. The abuse of British protection has been duly reported to your Lordship. I venture to hope that for the future, it may be limited, especially in the case of the "money lenders" to securing their persons and properties from injustice and violence, and not be used, as unhappily it has been, to the effect of depopulating villages, of ruining an industrious peasantry, of filling prisons with indigent debtors, of leaving women and children to starve, and of making the name of England a reproach.

I confidently appeal to your Lordship's sense of justice in disposing of this scandal, and in notifying to those who have not hesitated to report calumnies and untruths of their own invention, that such statements will do more harm to those who make them, than to those against whom they are made.

         I have the honour to be, &c,

           (Signed) RICHARD F. BURTON.

[Consular No. 17.]

          Damascus,

           December 6, 1870.

My Lord,

   In continuation of my official letter (Consular No. 16, of November 28, 1870), I have the honour to forward to your Lordship the replies to the libellous charges brought against the Dragomans of this Consulate—MM. Nasif Meshaka and Hanna Azar—by the chief Rabbis of Damascus—MM. Aaron Jacob and Jacob Perez.

   I am personally answerable for the accurateness of the documents enclosed. As regards the Bimbashi (Colonel) of Zabtiyyeh or Police—Ismail Agha—I have been personally acquainted with that officer for upwards of a year. I can testify to his being a man of property, an excellent public servant, very friendly to the English nation, and wholly unprejudiced against the Jews, or against any section of the community in Damascus.

   I shall dissuade Messrs. Nasif Meshaka and Hanna Azar from taking legal steps in this matter until the decision of your Lordship be received. But I would earnestly request that some measures be adopted to prevent the constantly-recurring nuisance of false accusations, of trumped-up charges, and of anonymous letters of complaint, a never-failing weapon in the hands of the small section of the Jewish community interested in removing public servants who do their duty honestly and honourably. It is generally believed at Damascus that Mr. Acting Consul Wrench, an officer who, since the days of Mr. Consul Richard Wood, had the moral courage to oppose the "money-lenders" in their career of extortion, was removed by the cabal which has not hesitated to demand my recall.

   Hence the reason why (as Sir Moses Montefiore states in his letter to the "Mail," Nov. 7, 1870) he never heard of the "cruel accusations brought against his co-religionists" by Messrs. Palmer and Drake ("Mail," Nov. 1, 1870). The fact is that a Consular officer, especially if he be a person without private means and with a family, can hardly be expected to do his duty, to the extent which his conscience demands, with such a weapon perpetually suspended over his head. It will not escape your Lordship's perspicuity that the tone of the complaints written by the two Chief Rabbis is one that shows how much the Hebrews of Damascus are accustomed to command. Whilst Sir Francis Goldsmid and the venerable Sir Moses Montefiore suggest precautionary measures, the Chief Rabbis unhesitatingly demand my recall and the dismissal of the two Dragomans of this Consulate; they evidently expect that, on their simple assertion, an officer of 28 years standing should be disgraced, and that similar dishonour should be extended to two Syrian Christian gentlemen of high local standing, who have long served the British Government. The attack upon the Meshaka family is the more unjustifiable, as the head of that house not only served fourteen years in H.M.'s Consulate, Damascus, with unblemished reputation, but he also was sorely wounded and nearly lost his life in the massacre of 1860.

   In my own case, I do not think that Sir Francis Goldsmid will, as an English gentleman, refuse to make an acknowledgment that his letter of Oct. 24, 1870, was written under erroneous impressions. I feel the more injured by it as he and his family have known me and might have asked for my explanation of the case. Sir Francis Goldsmid simply " believing M. Wieskopf to be a respectable man," has virtually endorsed his defamatory charges against me, one of which was that I struck and bound hand and foot with ropes two little boys aged respectively 7 and 8 years. So calumnious a libel was probably never yet circulated against a British officer—certainly never against one of my length of service and well-known antecedents.

The insinuations about "the bigoted Roman Catholic" should, I venture to remark, never have been produced in official correspondence. And, in the last paragraph of Sir Francis Goldsmid's letter, it is virtually assumed that I require "general instructions" to prevent my "countenancing any acts of injustice or persecution."

I confidently rely upon your Lordship's sense of justice in leaving this case in your hands, nor will I act in any way until your wishes are made known to me.

There is yet another point upon which I would trouble your Lordship. From a private letter addressed to me by M. Netter, the Hebrew Director of an agricultural establishment near Jaffa, I gather that the Jews of Damascus are paid by their co-religionists in Europe to abstain from acts (as drawing crosses in mosques, etc.) which may arouse Moslem fanaticism. It would be much to the point to know this statement be a fact.

I have, &c.,
(Signed) RICHARD F. BURTON.

The Earl Granville, K.G.,
    Her Majesty's Secretary of State
        for Foreign Affairs.

[CONSULAR No. 18.]

DAMASCUS,
December 15, 1870.

MY LORD,

I have the honour to report to you the following occurrence:—

I was yesterday informed, through one of the most influential Hebrew merchants of Damascus, that on or about the 6th instant a meeting took place at the house of one of the three Israelities whom I have reported as heading a cabal against me.

It was then and there arranged to send to London a telegram reporting that I refused to recognise Jews as British protected subjects. Being signed by "all the Jews in Damascus," the telegram was sent back to Beyrout as informal; and, lastly, it was here signed by a Hebrew who is not a British subject, but who seeks protection alternately from the French, the Austrian, and the Greek Consulates.

I have the honour emphatically to deny that I have told any one, Jew or Gentile, that protection is to be taken from Jewish protected subjects, and to inform your Lordship that they come every day for business to this Consulate.

I have the honour to enclose a copy of a despatch (No. 1, July 26, 1862) signed by his Excellency Sir Henry Bulwer, and showing how long ago complaints against usurious creditors were made by the peasantry in this Consulate. As yet, however, I cannot find that anything has been done to discourage dealings which greatly injure the Province; I am not, therefore, astonished that in the attempt to reform abuses which are locally looked upon as vested interests, my conduct and my proceedings have been subject to all manner of misrepresentation.

I have the honour, &c.,
(Signed) RICHARD F. BURTON.

Her Majesty's Secretary of State
    for Foreign Affairs.

[TRADUCTION.]

Nous demandons à M. le Chef de Police de la ville de Damas de nous dire ce qu'il a pu constater à propos de l'affaire des croix tracées sur le mur de la Mosquée Elahmadié, et qui était l'auteur qui a été pris sur le fait, et quel âge pouvait-il avoir, et qui sont ceux qui l'ont arrêté, et à quelle époque et dans quelle circonstance le fait est arrivé.

Je suis, &c., &c,

Damas, ce 5 Décembre, 1870.

(Signed) RICHD. F. BURTON,
Consul de S.M.B. à Damas.

[RÉPONSE.]

Le 23 Août, 1870, quand le Gouvernement impérial était en train de ramasser les Redifs, (la réserve) à Damas et ses environs, les Chrétiens commencérent à s'effrayer, croyant à un (soulèvement contr'eux. Dans cet interval des signes de croix se virent dans le lieu commun de la Mosquée Elahmadié. Ce signe a été tracé en 1860 sur les portes et dans quelques quartiers Chrétiens.

A la vue du renouvellement de ces signes, une panique générale s'empara des Chrétiens, et l'autorité locale se mit à la recherche de l'auteur. Le lendemain deux agents de police se cachèrent dans la mosquée; un garçon israélite, de onze ans environ, se présenta au lieu commun de la mosquée; il commença à tracer sur le mur de l'édifice le signe de la croix, se servant pour cette opération d'un clou qu'il avait à la main.

Les deux zaptié (agents de police), Ahmed Kalagi et Mohamed Zamboua, saisirent l'enfant et le conduisirent auprès l'autoritée.

En l'interrogeant, le garçon a déclaré que c'est un autre garçon israélite, plus âgé que lui, qui lui a enseigné à tracer les signes de croix sur le mur du lieu commun; que tous les deux sont en apprentissage chez le nommeé Salamon Donemberg, tailleur, et protégé anglais.

L'autorité, voyant le petit âge de l'enfant, le mit en liberté, puis elle a informé verbalement le Consulat de ce fait.

J'ai l'honneur, Monsieur le Consul, de vous présenter mes respects.

Damas, le 5 Décembre, 1870.

(Signé) ISMAIL AGHA BIMBASHI (Colonel),
Chef de Police. (L.S.)

[COPY.]

DAMASCUS,
November 28, 1870.

DEAR MRS. BURTON,

We desire to express to you the great satisfaction which Captain Burton's presence as British Consul in Damascus has given us both in our individual capacities and n our character of missionaries to Syria.

Since his arrival here we have had every opportunity of judging of Captain Burton's official conduct, and we beg to express our approval of it.

The first public act that came under our notice was the removing of dishonest officials and the replacing them by honest ones. This proceeding gave unmixed pleasure to every one to whom the credit of the English name was a matter of concern. His subsequent conduct has restored the *prestige* of the English Consulate, and we no longer hear it said that English officials removed from the checks of English public opinion are as corrupt in Turkey as the Turks themselves. As missionaries we frankly admit that we had been led to view Captain Burton's appointment with alarm; but we now congratulate ourselves on having abstained either directly or indirectly endeavouring to oppose his coming.

Carefully following our own habitual policy of asking no consular interference between the Turkish Government and its subjects, we stand upon our right as Englishmen to preach and teach so long as we violate no law of the land, and we claim for our converts the liberty of conscience secured to them by treaty. In the maintenance of this one right we have been firmly upheld by Captain Burton.

A few months ago, when our schools were illegally and arbitrarily closed by the Turkish officials, he came to our aid, and the injustice was at once put a stop to. His visit to the several village schools under our charge proved to the native mind the Consul's interest in the moral education of the country, which it is the object of those schools to promote, and impressed upon the minds of local magistrates the propriety of letting them alone.

Within the last few days we had occasion to apply to Captain Burton regarding our cemetery, which had been broken open, and it was an agreeable surprise to us when after two days a police-officer came to assure us that the damage had been repaired by the Pasha's orders, and search was being made for the depredator.

Above all, in view of any possible massacre of Christians in this city—the all but inevitable consequence of a war between Turkey and any Christian power—we regard as an element of safety the presence among us of a firm, strong man like Captain Burton, as representing the English interests.

When, not long ago, a panic seized the city, and a massacre seemed imminent, Captain Burton immediately came down from his summer quarters, and by his presence largely contributed to restore tranquility. All the other important Consuls fled from Damascus, and thus increased the panic.

We earnestly hope that Captain Burton will not suffer himself to be annoyed by the enmity he is sure to provoke from all who wish to make the English name a cover for wrong and injustice, or think that a British subject or *protégé* should be supported, whatever be the nature of his case.

With kindest respects,

We are, dear Mrs. Burton,

Yours very truly,

JAMES ORR SCOTT, M.A., Irish Presbyterian Mission.

WM. WRIGHT, B.A., Missionary of the Irish Presbyterian Church.

P.S.—By-the-bye, on one occasion one of the most important Jews of Damascus, when conversing with me and the Rev. John Crawford, American missionary, said that Captain Burton was unfit for the British Consulate in Damascus, and the reason he gave was that being an upright man he transacted his business by fair means instead of by foul like the others.

DAMASCUS,
November 28th, 1870.

MY DEAR MRS. BURTON,

I was calling at a native house yesterday where I found assembled some leading people of Damascus. The conversation turned upon Captain Burton and the present British Consulate. One word led to another; and I heard, to my surprise and consternation, that Yaaskub Stambouly, Ishak Toby and David Harari, three men famed for their *various pecuniary* transactions, are boasting about everywhere "that, upon *their* representations, *the Consul is to be recalled;*" and all Damascus is grieved and indignant at them. For my part I cannot, will not, believe that Her Majesty's Government would set aside a man of Captain Burton's standing, and well-known justice and capacity in public affairs for the sake of these three Jews, who are desolating the villages and ruining those who have the misfortune to fall into their clutches. He is also so thoroughly adapted for this Babel of tongues, nations, and religions, and is so rapidly raising our English Consulate from the low estimation in which it had fallen in the eyes of all men, to the position it ought and would occupy under the rule of an incorruptible, firm, and impartial character like Captain Burton's.

At the risk of vexing you, I must tell you what I now hear commonly reported in the bazaar, for several merchants and others have asked me, " if it was true that Mr. Rogers wants to come back here?" You *must* have heard how the Jews treated him before, and how he allowed them to ruin the country villages, to the powerless annoyance of the Turkish Government, who could do nothing against the "*protected* Jews." Well, now they say he (Mr. Rogers) is putting them up to this; and although they complained of him at one time, they now wish to get him back, as our present Consul is too much a friend to the oppressed, and examines too much everything *himself* to suit their money transactions. The Consulate for an age has not been so respectable as now, what with the numerous intrigues publicly known; and should you really go, I should think any future Consul would shrink to do his duty for fear of his conduct being misrepresented at home by this Jewish triumvirate. You must write me a line to tell me the truth, if you may do so without indiscretion; and people are wanting to write to the F. O. and the "Times," so provoked are they at their lies and duplicity. The day I was with you and you refused to see Yackub and the other Jew, who seemed to dodge you about like a house cat, and looked so ill at ease and in a fright, did you then suspect or know anything about all this?

With regard to the Arab tribes, they, too, have an admiration for Captain Burton's dauntless character and straightforward dealing, so different from his predecessor. You know that Sheikh Mahomed el Dhouky and Farés el Méziad openly say in the Desert to those who ask them "that they owned having won the camel law-suit I had with them to the considerable sum they gave * * *," after he had told me himself that I had won it; and this affair, as you know, involved the loss of my British protection, which is such a serious misfortune in this country.

I had intended to scribble but two lines, and I have been led on till my note has become a long letter. So, good-bye; and I truly hope all these machinations will end in the discomfiture of their inventors.

Yours most affectionately,
(Signed)   J. E. DIGBY EL MEZRAB.

[TRADUCTION.]

DAMAS.

le 15 Décembre, 1870.

MONSIEUR LE CONSUL,

C'est avec le plus grand plaisir nous venons vous exprimer notre satisfaction et les sentiments de notre amour envers votre amiable personne, ayant toujours devant les yeux les belles qualités et les grands mérites dont vous êtes orné.

Il y a plus de d'un an que nous avons eu l'honneur de vous connaître, et nous sommes en même de pouvoir apprécier votre bonne disposition pour le soutien de la cause chrétienne sans distinction de religion; et, par conséquent, nous sommes extrêmement reconnaissants au bienfait philanthropique du Gouvernement de S. M. Britannique, qui a daigné nous envoyer à Damas un représentant si digne et si mérité comme vous l'êtes, Monsieur le Consul.

C'est avec regret que nous avons appris que des gens malicieux de Damas se sont plaints contre vous pour des causes qui vous sont très-honorables.

Nous venons vous exprimer notre indignation pour leur conduite inexplicable et méprisable en vous témoignant notre reconnaissance pour le grand zèle et l'activité incessante que vous déployez toujours pour le bien et pour le repos de tous les Chrétiens en général.

Nous espérons que vous continuerez pour l'avenir comme pour le passé à nous accorder les mêmes bienfaits.

C'est avec ce même espoir que nous vous prions, Monsieur le Consul, d'agréer nos sentiments de haute considération.

(Signé) EROTEOS,
Patriarche Grec d'Antioche.

A M. le Capitaine Burton,
Consul de S.M. Britannique à Damas.

[TRADUCTION.]

DAMAS,
le 13 Décembre, 1870.

MONSIEUR LE CONSUL,

Nous avons entendu avec beaucoup d'inquiet que certains gens malicieux à Damas se sont plaignés de vous pour des causes qui vous sont très-honorables.

Nous désirons vous exprimer combien leur conduite est méprisable et inexcusable à nos yeux.

Nous vous avons connu maintenant plus qu'un an; nous vous avons trouvé toujours prêt à assister la cause chrétienne, sans égard pour les différences de la religion et à nous appuyer quand nous aurions été peut-être traités durement.

Dans les circonstances actuelles de cette année nous aurions beaucoup d'inquiétude s'il y avait une chance même que vous nous quittiez. Nous espérons que vos bons offices seront continués pour nous dans l'avenir comme dans le passé. Nous vous prions de vous servir de notre regard pour vous comme Consul comme ami aussi publiquement que possible.

Daignez agréer, &c., &c.

(Signé) L'EVEQUE MACARIOS,
Le Vicaire du Patriarcat à Damas. (L.S.)
GREGOIR JACOB,
Archev. Syrien Catholique de Damas. (L.S.)
LE VICAIRE DU PATRIARCAT Maronite
à Damas. (L.S.)
LE VICAIRE DU PATRIARCAT Arménien Catholique
à Damas. (L.S.)

A Monsieur R. F. Burton, Consul de S.M. Britannique à Damas.

BEYROUT, January 14th, 1871.

SIR,

The enclosed statements from Messrs. Stambouli and Tobi, which contain complaint in regard to your official conduct towards them, only reached me as I am leaving Syria. I think it right to send them at once to you, and to request that you will be so good as to put in a memorandum any observations which you may have to offer on the matter therein referred to.

I also send the translations, which appear to be abstracts rather than full renderings of the originals. It is only from these papers that I have been able to examine the contents of the statements.

And I request that you will be so good as to return the four papers sent herewith with your memorandum to me through Mr. Eldridge, in order that he may also have the opportunity of making observations on the subject.

I have the honour to be, &c.,
(Signed) CHARLES M. KENNEDY.

Captain Burton.

A L'Illustre et Miséricordieux Monsieur Keindé.

Excellence,

Je me présente très-humblement à votre miséricorde, n'ayant pour but que le soulagement de mes malheurs. Vous vous souvenez, seigneur, de m'avoir promis, au Consulat de Beyreuth, de me secourir et d'entendre mes prières. Me voici prosterné à vos pieds pour implorer votre miséricorde et vous demander secours. Je ne puis rien faire sans me plaindre du Consul de Damas avec raison ; aucun moyen n'a pu lui fléchir le cœur. Il me regarde d'un œil agité ; je n'en connais point la raison. Je gémis quand je vois que la justice me compte pour étranger à elle ; puisque je suis Israélite. Pourquoi donc me persécute-t-on ? Pourquoi le Consul de Damas me traite-il comme son ennemi ? Ne suis-je pas de ses sujets anglais ? J'ai trop à parler de ce traitement tout à fait étrange, mais votre bon cœur peut savoir le reste. Comptant, Excellence, à votre promesse, j'ose plaider ma cause sans remords de conscience. Je n'ai jamais été difficile à l'égard de mes Consuls anglais pour l'être à l'égard de M. le Consul actuel. Je me glorifie même d'avoir été exacte à ce point-ci ; mais je ne sais pourquoi mon Consul actuel ne veut plus me rendre raison de ma cause. Le gouvernement local m'aide en voulant me rendre justice ; mon Consul l'empêche de le faire, en tirant les prisonniers condamnés à me payer les dettes qu'ils me doivent légitimement. Il me hait plus que je ne l'aime. Je veux rendre un bon témoignage de lui, mais ma conscience ne me le permet point. Je crois dire contre verité si je ne savais discerner le bien du mal. Puis je doute de son inclination pour moi en faisant mourir mes causes pour soulever les siennes. Pourquoi envoi-t-il son drogman, Jean Azar, me dire : "Ne demande pas ton propre droit ?" Pourquoi envoie-t-il chercher de la prison même, en mon absence, les endettés qui me doivent une somme considérable ? Est-ce de cette manière qu'un Consul anglais doit défendre ses sujets ? Je prends pour juge et les hommes pour témoins entre lui, son drogman et moi ? N'est-il pas obligé de me défendre comme un de ses sujets anglais dont j'ai l'honneur d'en être un ? Il m'est impossible de dire tout ce qui peut etre sous ce rapport, il me semble, dire un mot qui signifie tout dire ; il veut être la cause de la ruine de ma maison et la cause de mes malheurs. Je suis endetté, je souffre, je gémis, je pleure, et mon Consul anglais me regarde comme 'un étranger ou un ennemi. Son drogman, Jean Azar, va rendre témoignage de la part du gouvernement local qui ne se donne point la peine de le connaître comme flatteur ou plus fort, et qu'il trompe le Consul anglais qui doit être le modèle et le bon exemple de tous ses rivaux, soit en justice, soit en zèle, à l'égard de ses propres sujets. Il me serait impossible de citer en détail tous mes malheurs, car c'est inutile de choisir des preuves contre mon Consul que je désire qu'il soit le plus illustre du monde et le plus exacte des juges, et je n'ai pu que reveni à mon sujet ; je suis opprimé, je souffre pendant que votre justice reluit dans le monde. A Dieu et à vous je m'adresse ; daignez me secourir mes biens, en envoyant une recommendation au Gouverneur-général de la Syrie pour m'aider et me relever de mon état pitoyable, car je n'ai pour appui que vous. C'est à vous, à vos pieds, que je me prosterne ; ne rejettez pas les humbles prières d'un homme si malheureux, et je laisse à part les insultes que Mdme. la femme de mon Consul anglais a faites à la mienne. Je termine ma pétition en invoquant les cieux de prolonger vos jours sur cette terre, et vous préparer par le secours du Tout-puissant une couronne de gloire dans les cieux, et d'attendrir votre cœur envers votre très-humble serviteur,

(Signed) JACOB C. STAMBOULI.

Beyrout,
13th January, 1871.

Sir,

By your kind permission I now take the liberty of laying before you the following statements containing a few matters of complaint, and begin by stating that as regards the proceedings of Captain Burton, H.B.M.'s Consul at Damascus, towards the Israelitish community, you will, doubtlessly, have already been made acquainted with them on your visit to that place by our Chief Rabbi.

But as regards myself and affairs, I beg to state that ever since the appointment of the said Captain Burton to Damascus no attention whatever has been paid by him in that direction. All my affairs remain unattended to, as will appear by the petitions presented by me at that Consulate; by reason of which I have been obliged to dispose of some of my claims at a loss. Seeing matters such, I have been obliged to arrange the remainder of my affairs myself in the best way I could, but always at a loss, in order to prevent further trouble. I do not, however, know whether such disregard to my affairs has been caused through the said Consul or through his Dragoman, M. John Azar, as the former seldom goes to the Consulate, being most of the time absent, travelling.

The said Consul, however, sent for me a short time ago, and informed me that he would henceforth have nothing more to do with my affairs, nor with those of Messrs. Jacob Stambouli and David Harari, and that he had written home on the subject, and that in the mean time we were to remain under the arrangement of the Beyrout Consulate, but giving us no reason for the same.

What astonishes me most of all is that I have never given any cause for inconvenience or trouble to the said Consulate, as will plainly appear from its archives, and more especially so as no intimate intercourse has taken place between the Consul and myself as with his predecessors, to whom both I and the rest of the members of our community are under great obligations, on account of the great assistance they always rendered us, both collectively and individually.

I further beg to inform you that I have been told that the said Captain Burton has written home several letters against us on matters of which we are entirely innocent. I therefore most humbly beg, sir, that you will kindly cause enquiries to be made with regard to the correctness of those matters.

These, sir, are the statements I have taken the liberty of laying before you, and soliciting your early and kind attention to the facts represented herein, humbly demanding that justice be rendered to us.

(Signed)   ISHAK TOBI.
STAMBOULY.

C. Kennedy, Esq.,
    Beyrout.

DAMASCUS,
January 24, 1871.

SIR,

I have the honour to thank you for your courtesy in forwarding to me the complaints regarding my official conduct, made to you by the two Hebrew protected subjects, MM. Stambuly and Tobi. I need hardly say that in all such cases my sole wish is to have the opportunity of making a reply.

The first part of M. Stambuly, and nearly all of M. Tobi's charges, have been disposed of by me in my letters No. 16 and No. 17, of Nov. 28 and Dec. 6, 1870, to Her Majesty's Secretary of State.

I again distinctly deny having any enmity against these protected subjects, or that they have suffered from "persecution" in any form. I am ever ready to defend their lives, liberty, and property, but I cannot assist them in ruining villages and in imprisoning destitute debtors upon trumped-up charges which have been studiously concealed from me.

I cause the prison to be visited once a week by a janissary, in order to prevent such abuses as confining a man long past seventy years of age for the crime of owing one napoleon. I would willingly deserve the praise of every section of the Jewish community at Damascus, but that I fear is in certain cases incompatible with any conscience and sense of justice.

As regards M. Hanna Azar, I object to dismiss a Dragoman who has served nearly four years upon mere charges which cannot be substantiated, and of which some have proved untrue. On the other hand, I again distinctly deny that M. Hanna Azar has shown any animosity against the Jewish community generally, and that he in any way influences my proceedings.

The remark made by M. Tobi that I am seldom at the Consulate, and always travelling, is completely incorrect. My summer quarters at Bludán are those of all my predecessors. I ride there in four or five hours, and messengers keep me constantly informed of what is occurring at Damascus. My excursions to the villages of this Consulate are made solely on duty, and with the object of rectifying abuses. I did not "refuse to have anything to do with M. Tobi's affairs," nor did I tell him to "remain under the Beyrout Consulate," which would have been simply absurd. I declined to have anything to do with certain money transactions of one of my predecessors, whose agent he is.

Finally, I regret to have to inform you that on Tuesday, the 10th inst., M. Solomon Stambuly, the son of Yacub Stambuly, came to my office, and being left for a moment alone, stole and carried away a private note just written by Mr. Nasif Meshaka, Dragoman to this Consulate. The envelope of a Vizirial letter, addressed through me to his Excellency the Wali, also disappeared on the same occasion, and was presently picked up in the yard. No one was in the upper rooms of the Consulate when the note disappeared. M. Salomon Stambuly was found seated in the chair before it, and, unfortunately, the affair was not reported to me before he was permitted to leave the house.

I have the honour to return to you the originals and the translations of the documents which you kindly forwarded to me, and to be,

Sir, &c.,

(Signed)   RICHARD F. BURTON.

Charles M. Kennedy, Esq.

Copies of two certificates of character in favour of M. Hanna Azar, by H.M's Consuls, Damascus.

[No. 1.]

H.B.M. CONSULATE,
DAMASCUS,
January 2, 1859.

This is to certify that the bearer, Mr. Jean Azar, has been Dragoman to this Consulate during the last two years, and I have much pleasure in testifying that I have had every reason to be satisfied with his conduct.

(Signed)   E. C. ROGERS,
H.B.M. Consul.

[No. 2.]

H.B.M. CONSULATE,
DAMASCUS,
August 2, 1869.

I have much pleasure in testifying to the intelligence and activity which Mr. Jean Azar has displayed in the execution of his duties as Dragoman to this Consulate during the seven months he served under me.

(Signed)   CHARLES W. WOOD,
Acting Consul.

(True Copies.)
DAMASCUS, December 6. 1870.

DAMAS,

Le 7 Décembre, 1870.

MONSIEUR LE CONSUL,

J'ai l'honneur de vous exposer que j'ai eu connaissance de la lettre signée par M. Wieskopf, datée le 12 Septembre, 1870, adressée à Sir Francis Goldsmid, Baronet. Dans ce document, l'auteur dit de vous, Monsieur le Consul, que depuis votre arrivée à Damas vous prêtez l'oreille à vos drogmans, des Chrétiens indigènes, qui produisent à tout instant des calomnies contre les Israélites, dont plusieurs jouissent de la protection anglaise ; que l'un des plus acharnés adversaires est le premier drogman du Consulat anglais, Hanna Azar, damasquin qui vous inspire une attitude hostile vis-à-vis de vos protégés Israélites. On ajoute que dernièrement un zaptié turc prétendait avoir vu un garçon israélite faire des croix dans les lieux commun d'une école mahométane ; que ce garçon fut traduit devant vous et interrogé par moi ; qu'après avoir été intimidé, il aurait été frappé par moi et menacé d'être garrotté, et enfin à la vue de ces préparatifs, il aurait avoué son crime. Puis qu'on fit appeler un autre garçon israélite, qui, nonobstant les coups donnés, protesta contre tout ce qu'on voulu lui faire avouer par violence. Ensuite, que vous avez fait venir les patrons de ces jeunes gens israélites, et vous avez pris leur passeport anglais, et que la communauté israélite, consternée, députa alors son Grand Rabbin pour disculper les Israélites, et pour expliquer que les deux garçons n'avaient avoué que sous des coups. Enfin, qu'un pareil procédé était peu digne du Gouvernement anglais. Je viens donc défendre ma réputation attaquée. D'abord, je commence par exposer le fait tel qu'il est arrivé. Le 23 d'Août passé, quand le gouvernement local de Damas était occupé à ramasser le contingent du Redif (la réserve) parmi les Musulmans, et ceux-ci, croyant que les soldats étaient destinés à une guerre contre la Russie, avaient les esprits tellement surexcités contre les Chrétiens ; que ces derniers, consternés et pleins d'effroi, se préparaient à être massacrés comme en 1860. Dans cet interval on a vu des signes de croix tracées dans les lieux communs d'une mosquée mahométane, qui s'appelle *Yamé Elahmadié* (la croix était un signe précurseur des massacres du 1860). L'autorité locale, instruite de ce fait, se mit à la recherche de l'auteur, et deux agents de police, Ahmed Kalagi et Mohamed Zambouä, déguisés, se mirent en cachet dans la mosquée pour en découvrir le coupable. Sur ce fait un enfant israélite, de onze ans environ, se présenta ; il se mit à tracer sur le mur de l'édifice les signes des croix. Les agents de police mirent aussitôt la main sur lui en le conduisant à l'autorité, où étant interrogé, il n'a pas nié ; seulement il prétendait être poussé à cet acte par un autre enfant israélite plus âgé que lui, tous les deux étant apprentis chez le nommé Salomon Donenberg, tailleur israélite et protégé anglais. L'autorité a fait parvenir ce fait à la connaissance du Consulat britannique, et vous, Monsieur le Consul, avez sommé les deux garçons israélites pour les interroger par mon intermédiaire. Le plus jeune a avoué avoir tracé les signes des croix sur l'instigation de son camarade, et dit que tous les deux sont apprentis chez le dit Salomon Donenberg. Ensuite vous avez fait venir l'autre garçon, et l'ayant interrogé, il a nié ; alors vous avez fait venir leur patron, et vous l'avez interrogé par mon intermédiaire si le plus jeune enfant restait encore chez lui comme apprenti. Il a nié, en disant qu'il l'avait chassé depuis quelques jours ; mais l'ayant fait confronter avec l'enfant, celui-ci a affirmé en sa présence être toujours en son apprentissage.

Le lendemain est venu le Grand Rabbin, prétendant que les garçons israélites étaient innocents, et qu'ils n'avaient avoué que sous les coups, et que vous voulez faussement inculper les israélites (comme il est arrivé dans l'affaire du Père Thomas). Vous avez répondu au Grand Rabbin que le garçon avait déjà fait l'aveu devant l'autorité locale et devant vous, que les enfants n'ont pas été battus, que vous n'acceptez jamais une pareille calomnie, et que vous allez référer ce fait à Constantinople et à Londres. C'est ainsi que vous avez congédié le Grand Rabbin avec tous les honneurs nécessaires.

Les Israélites dans un de leurs écrits disent que les deux drogmans, Hanna Azar et Nasif Mechaka, appartiennent à ces familles qui, il y a trente ans, ont inventé des grandes calomnies contre les Israélites, et que votre prédécesseur, M. Rogers, voyant leur haîne contre les Juifs, les a chassé du Consulat ; que vous, Monsieur le Consul, par cause de conformité des sentiments, les avez fait rentrer au Consulat; enfin, que M. Rogers était ami avec les Juifs, et que vous ne l'étiez pas.

Pour montrer la fausseté des assertions des Israélites, et pour m'en justifier, je dirai, "Jamais de ma vie je n'ai pas inventé une seule calomnie contre les Israélites, ni contre qui que soit; du reste, il n'y a aucune ancienne animosité entre moi et eux. Et si les Juifs sont dans le vrai, pourquoi ne produisent-ils pas un seul fait, une seule preuve de leur assertion? Et vous, Monsieur le Consul, vous pouvez connaître mieux que personne si je vous pousse à leur haine. Je n'ai jamais touché au dit garçon israélite, ni intimidé, ni maltraité, ni garrotté, comme prétendent nos Israélites.

Les Israélites prétendent que les garçons n'ont pas tracé les signes de croix; peut-on avoir une preuve plus éclatante que le témoignage du chef de police de Damas?

Les Israélites n'ont pas hésité de déclarer que M. Rogers m'avait destitué du Consulat. Ce n'est pas vrai du tout; au contraire, c'est M. Rogers lui-même qui me nomma, et à votre arrivée à Damas j'étais drogman du Consulat, et je le suis toujours.

Il paraît que les Israélites ignorent l'impartialité du Gouvernement britannique, qui n'admet jamais une assertion non prouvée, comme ils s'imaginent.

Enfin, les témoignages dont la copie ci-incluse, donnés par M. Rogers et son prédécesseur, M. Charles Wood, parlent assez haut en ma faveur.

J'espère donc, Monsieur le Consul, que vous voudriez bien faire parvenir ma lettre au Ministère des Affaires Etrangères, et je ne doute nullement que le Gouvernement de Sa Majesté britannique me rendra justice en punissant d'une manière éclatante les personnes dont les calomnies sont ainsi prouvées.

J'ai l'honneur, Monsieur le Consul, de vous présenter mes très-humbles respects.

(Signed)   HANNA AZAR.

Damascus,
December 6th, 1870.

Sir,

Amongst the papers which you put into my hands for perusal, I find the following words (Letter of M. S. W. Weiskopf, Beyrout, le 12 Septembre, 1870.)

"Depuis l'arrivée du Capitaine Burton à Damas il prête l'oreille à ses drogmans, des Chrétiens indigènes qui produisent à tout instant des calomnies contre les Israélites, dont plusieurs jouissent de la protection anglaise." Also, "Toute une communauté est menacée par les machinations de ses drogmans, qui, s'abritant derrière leurs fonctions ne font que méditer la ruine des nôtres."

Again, in the letter signed by the Chief Rabbis, MM. Aaron Jacob and Jacob Perez (17 Elul 5630), I find the following words:—

"There are two interpreters connected with the British Consulate whose names are Hanna Azar and Nasif Meshaka, and belong to the families who thirty years ago brought horrible accusations against the Jews. Consul Rogers, seeing the hatred these constantly evinced towards the Jews, dismissed them from the Consulate. Consul Burton, however, doubtless on account of the similarity of their sentiments to his own, appointed them interpreters to the Consulate, and ever since it has been the endeavour of these men to wrong us, and to sow hatred between us and our neighbours of different creeds."

You, Sir, are well acquainted with the falsehood of these assertions, and with the calumnies which they contain.

The first passages I have quoted are so general that I can only declare them absolutely untrue as far as I am concerned, and I challenge their author to substantiate his charges by a single fact.

The letter of the Rabbis being more definite, its utter falsehood admits of demonstration.

The Rabbis state that Mr. Consul Rogers dismissed M. Hanna Azar and myself from the Consulate on account of our hatred to the Jews.

This statement would never have been made by the Rabbis had they supposed that it would have been made public, for every Jew in Damascus knows that M. Hanna Azar never was dismissed from the Consulate, and I resigned of my own free will and for reasons known to me to be honourable. These statements are confirmed by the consular books, and what refers to me by Mr. Rogers' certificate, No. 4, enclosed herewith.

It is very easy to disprove these foul charges. I have the honour to enclose copies of the different certificates of character which I have received from those whom I served. They are—

    No. 1 From Mr. Consul Brant .. .. Oct. 16th, 1860
    ,, 2 ,, ,, Acting-Consul Wrench .. May 30th, 1861
    ,, 3 ,, ,, Acting-Consul Sandwith .. April 17th, 1862
    ,, 4 ,, ,, Consul Rogers .. .. Oct. 28th, 1867

It appears then, that so far from dismissed by Mr. Consul Rogers, that gentleman testifies to my zeal and integrity after a personal knowledge of me for seven or eight years, and that I left the service at my own request, on private grounds.

As regards the allegation that I belong to "a family who, thirty years ago, brought horrible accusations against the Jews," it is notorious that the charges were brought by the Latin Community at the Consulat de France, Damascus. I was then one year old, my brothers were not born, and my father was the only member of the family alluded to who settled here a few years before that event; he was not even present when the investigations took place. The only part which my father took was as a chief of the Christian physicians to make an official examination, by order of the Government, in conjunction with the local hospital doctors, the chief of the Jewish and Moslem physicians, and the chief surgeon of Damascus—of certain bones taken from a sewer in the Jewish quarter, and to report whether or not they were human bones. Thus the part taken by my father in the affair of the Jews was purely official, and by order of the local Government. I may also add that my father succeeded in setting at liberty one of the principal Jewish prisoners, together with his son, and that when the rest of them were released, my father was the doctor who attended in his sickness the Jew in whose house the murder was said to have been committed. So far from being an enemy to the Jews, I have even looked after their interests to the best of my power. We belong to the Protestant community, and public and private individuals of the various religious bodies are well acquainted with, and are ready to testify to the uprightness of my father's character. My father, the well-known Doctor Meshaka, though now in years, and retired from public life, never hesitates, despite his being a confirmed invalid, to attend to the sick persons of the Jews, and to supply them medicine gratis when a certificate from the Chief Rabbi, M. Jacob Perez, assures him that they cannot afford to pay.

Had any one of these charges been proved against me, I should have been justly punished by the loss of my reputation and of my place.

I should now ask you, sir, what punishment must be dealt to these false libellers who have accused me to Her Majesty's Government of such serious offences?

                          I have the honor to be, &c.,

                              (Signed) NASIF MESHEKA.

To Captain Burton,
    H.B. M's. Consul, Damascus.

Copies of four certificates of character in favour of Mr. Nasif Meshaka by H.M.'s Consuls, Damascus.

No. 1.

Her Britannic Majesty's Consulate in Damascus.

I hereby certify that Nasif Meshaka has served in this British Consular Office for nearly three years in quality of clerk, translator, and Arabic scribe, and his conduct has been such as to have secured my good opinion and esteem. He speaks English and French well, and has by his intelligence acquired a very competent knowledge of written English and of his duties in a Consul's office, and has become a most efficient and useful assistant.

(Signed) JAMES BRANT,
H.B.M.'s Consul.

Damascus,
October 16th, 1860.

No. 2.

Having during the whole of the above time served as Cancellier to this Consulate, I hereby confirm the above character of Mr. Nasif Meshaka, who has also served under me during the time I was Acting Consul—viz., from October, 17th, 1860, to 24th May, 1861—and has given very great satisfaction by the efficient manner in which he discharged his duties.

(Signed) WILLIAM H. WRENCH.

Damascus,
May 30th, 1861.

No. 3.

Mr. Nasif Meshaka was Head Dragoman at this Consulate during more than two months that I was Acting Consul here in the beginning of the year 1862, and I have great pleasure in stating that he was well versed in his duties, and conducted the consular business entrusted to him in a straightforward manner, which met with the approval of all connected with him. I regret that an indisposition, rendering his departure from Damascus advisable, deprives me of his services.

(Signed) THOMAS B. SANDWITH,
Acting Consul.

Damascus,
April 7th, 1862.

No. 4.

I hereby certify that Mr. Nasif Meshaka has served in this, Her Britannic Majesty's Consulate, as interpreter and secretary, for seven or eight years past, and that during the whole of that period he has, by his zeal and integrity, afforded entire satisfaction to those who have been in authority over him. He leaves the service at his own request, on private grounds.

(Signed) E. T. ROGERS,
H.B.M.'s Consul.

Damascus,
October 28th, 1867.

A Monsieur le Capitaine Burton, Consul de S.M. Britannique a Damas,

Le 14 Janvier, 1870.

Cher Monsieur le Consul,

Je regrette d'autant plus aujourd'hui de ne pas avoir donné il y a quelque mois (de Constantinople) suite à mon intention de vous écrire que j'ai aujourd'hui à le faire pour vous demander une faveur, disons mieux justice. J'ai reçu de Damas plusieurs lettres des coreligionnaires, dans lesquelles on me raconte certaine histoire de croix peu claire, je l'avoue. *Mais ce que je sais positivement c'est que les Israélites à Damas sont payés pour ne pas plaisanter avec ces choses*, et qu'ils se garderaient de l'ombre de tort. Je ne sais jusqu'à quel point un polisson a pu contrevenir à cette règle, mais dans l'immense préjudice que peut causer aux Israélites de toute la Syrie la simple recherche du soi-disant crime. Ceci est un pays d'exagération. Qu'un Israélite soit accusé d'avoir fait une croix, à un kilomètre de là on dit qu'il a cloué quelqu'un après, a deux kilomètres c'est une famille entière qui a été terrifiée. Je suis presque honteux de debiter ce lieu commun à un homme qui a fait de ce pays une étude qui est aux mains de chacun. Mettons le cas où, ce que l'on nie formellement, un ou deux polissons israélites auraient fait une croix avec n'importe quoi sur n'importe quel mur, qu'on leur donne quelques gifles, et je crois tout doit être dit. On me désigne votre drogman indigène comme l'instigateur de cette affaire. On me dit que ce n'est pas la première fois qu'il témoigne de sa malveillance à l'égard des miens. Quand les Consulats seront-ils débarrassés de ces fléaux de drogmans indigènes ? Dieu veuille que ce le soit bientôt. Je profite de cette désagréable occasion, cher Consul, pour vous dire qu'en quittant Damas je me puis rendu à Constantinople, où j'ai obtenu, après trois mois de rhume de cerveau, le Firman impérial concédant à l'alliance un terrain assez grand pour fonder l'Ecole d'Agriculture dont je suis en train d'élever les bâtiments. J'avais résolu d'aller de Constantinople à Londres, viâ France, où j'ai une grande partie de ma famille ; mais j'ai cru bien faire de tout terminer d'abord et de partir ensuite seulement. Peut-être me serais-je contenti déboucher les choses, si un beau jour, sinon un bien vilain jour, la guerre n'avait éclaté entre Napoléon III. et M. de Bismarck, guerre qui dure, encore dont le début a été bien malheureux pour la France, et dont l'issue rentre, je le crains, dans la théorie de Darwin. Ceci me rappelle que vous avez encore chez vous un livre, "The Land and the Book," que je vous serais obligé de m'expédier à l'adresse de M. D. Picciotto à Beyrouth ; vous l'aurez trouvé un peu Thompson, mais il est bon à consulter pour moi. Vous m'avez confié sur ma demande deux échantillons, l'un de Reglisse, dont il se fait un commerce régulier, même de Jaffa, où y en avons sur notre terrain ; l'autre, d'une pierre minérale que j'ai gardée pour mon arrivée en Europe, si longtemps différée, hélas ! Je ne dois pas oublier de vous dire que j'ai fait un bon voyage de Beyrouth à Smyrne avec Mme. de Persigny, qui j'ai su depuis est heureusement arrivée à Paris, où elle a fait fureur avec les objets acquis à Damas. Je crains de ne pas trouver M. de Persigny à son poste à mon retour à Paris. Je crois inutile de vous faire mes offres de service au cas où je pourrais vous être utile, quoi qu'il soit à Jaffa ou Jerusalem voire même à Alexandrie ou Londres, endroits avec lesquels je suis en communications régulières.

Dans l'espoir de recevoir de vos bonnes nouvelles, agréez, Monsieur le Consul, l'expression de haute estime.

(Signed) C. NETTER.

Damascus,
October 4, 1870.

My dear Sir,

I have received from you a long note on public matters. It is not usual with me to correspond privately upon such subjects; as, however, you seem to want information, I will this time make an exception.

A man of your age and experience should know better than to write a long tirade upon purely *ex parte* statements, without knowing a word of the other side of the case. Of course you have been written to by your "co-religionists," and you have at once accredited all their statements, as a Jew would do at Damascus. You are aware that I speak Arabic, that I have been a year at my post, and that probably I know something about my Dragomans. Yet you volunteer the information that the whole affair is a plot of theirs, and that I am hoodwinked, gulled, and led by the nose.

I examined the crosses *in situ*. I got the boy to the Consulate and questioned him. Your co-religionists reported the lie that he had been flogged and tortured. I spoke to his master, who falsely told me that he had been dismissed when he was still in the house. The Khakham (Rabbi) came to the Consulate and was insolent: had it not been for his age and his sacred office I would have had him turned out by the Kawwáses. He insisted that the boy had not drawn the crosses (the boy did not deny it), that being a Jew he ought to be let off (because a Jew), and that I was persecuting his compatriots, as in the case of Padre Tommaso. The report was then spread that I had ill-treated the Khakham, when he had behaved very badly to us. I have no doubt that letters have been written in all directions as to you. Meanwhile I omit circumstances. If they want me to tell all I know they will get, perhaps, more than they want. Hitherto I have only written officially that the masters of the two boys concerned have had their British protection suspended till the receipt of orders from head quarters.

You know as well as I do that at Damascus there are two classes of Jews. One (and I hope that it is the more numerous) deserves all praise for hard work, inoffensive conduct, and commercial integrity. The other—I have many proofs, and so forth—manufactures false seals, forges documents, inserts lines below receipts, charges twice and thrice, double and treble, grinds down the peasantry, and is a perfect curse to the land. It stops at no act of violence, no crime.

Your pipe has been entrusted to Mr. D. Picciotti, Beyrout. I will send the "Land and the Book" to him as soon as I can get it from Bludan. I hope that you are well, and that the agricultural school is flourishing.

      Believe me, my dear Sir,
          Yours truly,
            RICHARD F. BURTON.

M. C. Netter.

CASE No. 4.

ASSAULT AT NAZARETH.

I had encamped at Nazareth on May 4th, 1871. On the 5th a Copt negro tried to enter our tents before sunrise, and was prevented by my servants. He became abusive and violent, and fought with my servants; some 150 Greeks (orthodox) coming out of Church service joined their co-religionist, the negro, and stoned my servants, wounding three of them dangerously, and myself slightly—when I say dangerously, one spat blood for two months, and another hung between life and death till August—when I say slightly, they disabled my sword arm, and I am still unable to use it properly. The Bishop of Nazareth and the Wali Rashid Pasha drew up a tissue of misrepresentations, signed and sealed them, and telegraphed them to Constantinople three days before I had reached Damascus, and of course before I had time to offer a word of explanation. The despatches will give an account of all the sham trials and false verdicts that have gone on for nine months, until Mr. Consul Moore, of Jerusalem, was sent to examine into the affair. At last all the respectable authorities who were anxious to prove the truth obtained a hearing, and the culprits were sentenced to three and four months' imprisonment and to a fine of 5,000 piastres.

DESPATCHES:—

A telegram from Rashid Pasha to Constantinople.
   Ditto   Sir H. Elliot to Captain Burton, and the latter's reply.
Captain Burton to Sir H. Elliot, June 7th, 1871.
Captain Burton to Rashid Pasha, May 20th, 1871.
Mr. Tyrwhitt Drake's evidence.
The evidence of four Englishmen encamped near us.
Dr. Vartan's Medical Report.
Mr. Tyrwhitt Drake to Sir H. Elliot, June 8th, 1871.
Letter from the Greek Patriarch of Jerusalem to Captain Burton on the occasion, 26th July, 1871.
Captain Burton to Sir H. Elliot, June 18th, 1871.
Extracts from various letters, showing general feeling upon the case.
A letter from the Rev. John Zeller, Protestant Clergyman at Nazareth, June 28th, 1871.

Captain Burton to Sir H. Elliot, July 7th, 1871.

Captain Burton to Sir H. Elliot, July 16th, 1871.

Captain Burton to Lord Granville, July 10th, 1871.

Captain Burton to Lord Granville, July 26th, 1871.

Letters from Captain Burton's agents at Nazareth,—Messrs. Finzy and Barbúr, August 1st, 1871.

Rev. John Zeller to Captain Burton, August 2nd, 1871.

Mr. Drake's appeal to the new Wali, Soubhi Pasha, and letter to Lord Granville, November 11th, 1871.

Letter from the Rev. John Zeller, February 23rd, 1872.

Letter from a Greek Orthodox, showing the feelings of the respectable people, November 14th, 1871.

[COPY.—TRADUCTION DU TURC.]

Télégramme envoyé par le Gouverneur-général du Vilayet de Syrie à S.A. le Grand Vizer, en date du 4—16 Mai, 1871.

Le Consul britannique à Damas, M. Burton, qui aime à se livrer à de continuelles pérégrinations, s'était rendu, il y a quelques jours, à Nassara, et s'était installé sous une tente dans le voisinage d'une église grecque. C'était le jour de la Fête de St.-Georges, et un rassemblement d'enfants encombrait les abords de l'église. Une querelle s'éleva entre ces enfants et les domestiques du Consul. Ce dernier s'était armé pour prendre part à la querelle, et s'étant servi de ses armes contre les Grecs, ceux qui se trouvaient dans l'intérieur de l'église en sortirent et se mêlèrent à la rixe, qui acquit des proportions considérables, et dans laquelle quelques-uns des domestiques furent légèrement blessés. Le Consul lui-même fut atteint au bras par une pierre, mais personne ne l'avait attaqué avec des armes, ce qui atténue de beaucoup le caractère de l'attaque dirigée contre sa personne.

Néanmoins, le Consul exigea qu'on fît conduire à Damas plusieurs personnes, les mains liées; mais les Chrétiens protestaient de leur innocence, en soutenant que le Consul les avait provoqués, dans un jour de fête, en tirant à balles sur eux.

J'ai commencé l'instruction de cette affaire, et je ferai parvenir à V.A. le résultat détaillé de mes informations dès que je l'aurai obtenu.

Telegram of Sir Henry Elliot, Constantinople, to Captain Burton, at Damascus, June 5th, 1871 (Kept by the Turkish authorities here till June 7th):—

"Report to me immediately, both by telegram and by post, the particulars of the affray at Nazareth."

Captain's Burton's reply to Sir H. Elliot, June 7th:—

"Your telegram of June 5th received only June 7th.

"My servants unprovokedly attacked by Greek orthodox at Nazareth, on account of a slight quarrel with an insolent negro. Three of mine severely hurt. Have applied to local authorities for redress. Great opposition at first from Greek clergy, who now own themselves mistaken, and wish for amicable settlement. Details by post."

[COPY.]

DAMASCUS,
June 7th, 1871.

SIR,
I have the honour to acknowledge your Excellency's telegram of June 5th, which arrived only to-day (June 7th). I had heard privately of it from one of the officials of the Serai some hours before it reached me.

As regard the affair at Nazareth, the best explanation which I can send is contained in the enclosures. The first is the despatch addressed by me to His Excellency the Governor-General of Syria. The second is the account of the assault forwarded to me by my fellow-traveller, M. O. F. Trywhitt Drake, who here represents the Palestine Exploration Fund. The third is the evidence given before the Majlis by an English clergyman (Rev. Mr. Taylor), and by three other gentlemen who were in Nazareth at the time.

I may also report that the Greek Bishop of Nazareth has confessed that he was compelled by his co-religionists to act as he did, that he was ordered not to return to his See without settling the affair in their favour, that he is ready to declare that those who committed the outrage were guilty, and that he wishes the affair to be settled amicably.

I have the honour to translate the telegram sent by the Right Rev. Serafim, Bishop of Damascus to Monsignor Garathaos, Patriarch of Antioch, now at Tripoli, and likewise to the Greek Patriarch at Jerusalem :—

"We have received from H.B.M.'s Consul at Damascus the details concerning the Nazareth affair; we are satisfied with this account, and we will send details by post."

Finally, as regard the claim of 300 napoleons to be distributed amongst my wounded servants and muleteers, I have, at this instance of Right Rev. the Greek Bishop of Damascus rendered it to 50 napoleons which will be claimed after three months only in the case of bad conduct being repeated.

I have, &c.,
(Signed) RICHARD F. BURTON.

His Excellency,
Sir Henry Elliot, &c., &c.,
Constantinople.

[COPIE.]

DAMAS,
Le 20 Mai, 1871.

EXCELLENCE,
J'ai l'honneur de porter à votre connaissance les faits suivants :

Le Vendredi, 5 Mai, 1871 (Fête de St. George); j'étais campé à Nazareth, endroit célèbre depuis bien d'années pour l'inhospitalité et le mauvais traitement des voyageurs. Il paraît que le public peu respectable était prévenu contre moi parce que j'empêchai l'évêque grec, Monseigneur Niffon, de saisir un terrain à Tiberias, contenant une synagogue juif. Un Copte attaché au couvent grecque de l'Annonciation se présenta devant nos tentes, et se moqua de nos gens. On commença à l'éloigner, et il se vengea en nous menaçant avec une pierre, et se servant d'un langage qui paraît propre à Nazareth. Peu à peu une rixe s'engagea. Enfin, entendant des cris derrière le mur du couvent, M. Tyrwhitt Drake, mon compagnon de voyage, et moi, nous courrûmes pour calmer l'affaire. Nous y fûmes sans armes, et nous trouvâmes une foule de Grecques, enfin, toute la congrégation de l'église qui assomaient nos gens à coups de pierre qui tombaient comme la pluie. Le nommé Simaan el Asfour attaqua à l'instant M. Tyrwhitt Drake, et sans un coup de revolver tiré dans l'air par un de nos domestiques, une fatalité aurait pu résulter. Le nommé Yusuf Mouammar se rua sur moi. Je pris le revolver, et tirant un coup dans l'air, je le fis retirer avec ses acolytes, mais pas avant avoir reçu trois coups de pierre. Le total de nos blessés se porte à sept personnes, dont deux étaient très-gravement atteints ; un de nos domestiques eut une hémorragie qui mit sa vie en danger.

Après les sus-nommés, les criminels les plus coupables sont les suivants :—

1. Daoud Soleyman, qui encouragea les assaillants en disant, "Izbahúm ! ana bati Diyathum,"—tuez-les, je paierai le prix de leur sang.
2. Yusuf el Maragbi, barbe blanche, qui cria quand on lui dit "C'est le Consul anglais de Damas que vous assomez," "Wa in kan,"—assomez-le quand même.

A ces quatre j'ajouterai les neuf suivants :—

1. Georges Dib.
2. Elias Varvar et son frère,
3. Georges Varvar.
4. Ishac Sakron.
5. Halil Jarjura.
6. George Azzam.
7. Halil Chamoche.
8. Georges Soleyman, et
9. Yusuf eben Schallufe, qui parvint à s'évader.

Votre Excellence aura lu le procès verbal qui se fit à Nazareth. Je la prie de sommer à Damas les 13 personnes dont les noms ont été cités, et de les confronter avec mes témoins.

J'ai aussi l'honneur de vous représenter les bons offices que je reçus de la part de Kurchid Effendi, Kaimakám de Nazareth ; du Bimbaschi de la police ; Kuwwatayn Agha ; et du Moufettiche de St. Jean d'Acre, M. Elias Dibban.

Je ne saurai terminer mon rapport sans démontrer à votre Excellence l'état actuel de Nazareth et de son voisinage. La police est si faible que les coupables ne peuvent se punir. Un Juif ne saurait traverser le bazar sans être outragé, et les sujets du Sultan ne peuvent habiter Nazareth.

Il y a un an on assoma le maître d'école protestant de Jaffa, et le missionnaire protestant, M. Zeller, a subi des injures sans nombre. On vola pendant l'année dernière un voyageur anglais, le Révérend Shafto Douglas. Deux personnes nous ont cherché querelle à Ayn Dor ; à Tahun Tabyett on me menaça d'un coup de feu ("Kavv as hum") parce que je traversai le coin d'un champ qui n'avait ni haie ni mur. A Tibérias on a frappé Madame Zelmina Füchs et le protégé anglais Yahuda Sampton. Peut-être votre Excellence jugera bien de faire venir à Damas les procès verbaux de Tibérias et de Safet.

La raison de ces outrages est simplement la faiblesse de la police. Avec une addition de 150 hommes distribués entre Nazareth, Saffureh, Ayn Dor, Yenicis et Ayn, les Kaimakáms seraient respectés, et on n'assomera plus les voyageurs. Sans ce moyen les circonstances les plus regrettables peuvent arriver à chaque instant, surtout dans l'état d'excitation anormale actuellement existante partout en Syrie parmi les nations latines et grecques.

Enfin, Excellence, j'ai l'honneur de vous soumettre ma demande d'une amende pour les blessés, que je fixerai à trois cents (300) napoléons, et qui sera payé par la congrégation grecque de Nazareth. Un des notables de l'endroit m'a envoyé l'offre d'une somme plus considérable pour abandon de justice et pour la gratification de mes gens. J'ai jugé convenable de laisser l'affaire dans les mains de votre Excellence.

Veuillez agréer, Excellence, l'assurance de ma très-haute considération.

(Signé) RICHARD BURTON,

Consul de S.M. Britannique.

A Son Excellence Mohammed Rachid Pacha, Gouverneur-Général de Syrie, Damas.

[COPY. MR. DRAKE'S TESTIMONY.]

On May 5th, 1871, Captain Burton and I were encamped at Nazareth (which is within his jurisdiction), near the Greek Church of the Annunciation. Early in the morning I happened to be at a short distance from the tents, and hearing an angry voice, I went to see whose it was. I found an Abyssinian boy using violent language to Habib, who was telling him to leave the neighbourhood of the tents. The Abyssinian continuing his abusive language, and picking up a stone to throw at Habib, Mohammed, the Kawass, went down and began to beat him.

Four or five Greek Christians now set upon Habib and Mohammed, and then the other two servants, Antún and Sába, ran down to help. A *melée* ensued, which assumed no serious aspect till the Greek Christians ran round to the south side of the church, where they were out of sight of the tents, and where they were reinforced by the congregation from the church.

The servants (four in number) and two Makaris followed them, and very shortly Captain Burton and I heard such a noise that we judged it advisable to go down and see what was taking place, as from the tents nothing could be seen. We accordingly ran down with only riding whips in our hands; but on sharply turning the corner found ourselves face to face with some seventy to a hundred Greek Christians, who were throwing stones with all their force at the Consul's servants and, immediately that Captain Burton and I appeared, at us.

The first stone thrown at me was a very large one, from the hands of *Simáan el Asfúr*, at a distance of only four or five metres, which narrowly missed my head. At this moment Habib fired a shot from a revolver into the air. This checked the ruffians for an instant, and we were able to retreat to the south-east corner of the Church. Here Captain Burton took the revolver and fired a shot, as before, into the air. This daunted the mob, and we were able to retire slowly to the tents, though followed by a shower of stones. Then as the mob seemed menacing we prepared our arms, and requested some English and American travellers, who were camped close by, to do the same.

Seeing these preparations, the mob melted away, many returning to the church where they had been at service (it being the Feast of St. George) at the commencement of the disturbance. Two of the servants—namely, Habib and Saba, were so much injured that they were unable to move for several days, and the former has continued to spit blood.

Mohammed the Kawass was severely injured in the ribs, head, and groin. Autún the Sáis and two of the Makaris were also injured.

When Simáan el Asfúr had the impertinence to accompany a deputation of Greek Christians to the tents for the purpose of begging Captain Burton to set justice aside and forego punishing the culprits, I immediately recognised him as the man who had thrown the stone at me, and who was always in the front of the mob, and busiest in throwing stones.

When *Yusaf Moámmur* was brought to the tents, I distinctly recognized him as one foremost and busiest of the mob.

This mob was by no means made up of only lads and young men, as some of the Greeks wished to make out, but many old men were there, and those the richest and most influential members of the Greek community—men whose duty should have been to restrain their juniors, and not, as they did, to excite them to acts of extreme violence.

CHARLES F. TYRWHITT DRAKE.

Damascus,
May 22nd, 1871.

Evidence of Englishmen encamped close by.

Ces messieurs soussignés étaient dans la tente à Nazareth le matin le 5 Mai 1871. Mme. Burton les a prié de prendre leurs armes et de venir, parce que le Capitaine Burton et M. Drake et les domestiques étaient attaqués par les Grecs orthodoxes; quand ces messieurs sortaient de leurs tentes ils rencontrèrent le Capitaine Burton et M. Drake allant chercher un domestique qui était encore entre les mains des Grecs. Le rapport que le Capitaine Burton et M. Drake ont entré à l'église avec des armes pour la profaner, c'est un mensonge ; ils ont seulement entré la cour pour chercher ces domestiques cités. Ces messieurs ont aussi vu les domestiques très-sérieusement blessés, et le nommé Sabba était évanoui. Ces messieurs témoignent que le Capitaine Burton, M. Drake et les domestiques ont agi avec la très-grande modération, considérant qu'ils étaient blessés, et que la foule des Grecs était très-menaçante et vingt fois plus nombreux qu'eux. Ces messieurs croient que les douze Zabtiés qui sont sous le Kaimmakam ne peuvent rien faire avec leur population turbulente de 7000 personnes, et que c'est une obligation pour le Gouvernement turc de rendre cet endroit sûr pour les voyageurs, parce que ce n'est pas la première fois que les voyageurs européens ont été insultés à Nazareth. Ils croient aussi que si les criminels ne seront pas sévèrement punis les conséquences seront graves, non-seulement pour les voyageurs, mais encore pour la sûreté et la paix de la Syrie.

(Signature)   J. W. W. TAYLOR, Clergyman,
                                  29, Fitzwilliam Street.
                    F. W. PARSONS,
                                 Huddersfield, England.
                    FRANK BARNUM.
                    E. A. NEVILL,
                                 45, Charles Street, Berkeley Square.

The Doctor's Evidence.

I beg to state that I have found Habib Jemayl and Saiba Waket both in one tent, the former being wounded in the left cheek and leg, and bruised on his right side over the ribs, all apparently being inflicted with stones or sticks. He was suffering from much pain, especially when touched in his side ; the latter being wounded in his right cheek and leg, and bruised in some six or seven places on his right side and shoulder. His cheek was already swollen. He also was under great pain, his bruises being apparently inflicted by similar means of violence,

Witnessed by me on the morning of May 5, 1871, at Nazareth.
(Signed)   P. K. VARTAN, L.R.C.P.S.E.

P.S.—Since I have drawn the above Habib Jemayl spat clots of blood daily, apparently from the rupture of small bronchial blood vessels. The Kawass also had sustained dislocation of about three middle ribs of the left side from their cartilages. Two or three of the other servants besides showed marks of violence perpetrated on them in various places.

(Signed)   P. K. V.
May 9, 1871.
                             True Copy.
Richard F. Burton,
H.B.M.'s Consul, Damascus.

To Sir Henry Elliot.   DAMASCUS,
                                                                  June 8th, 1871.
YOUR EXCELLENCY,

On my return yesterday from the Eastern desert, I found that most gross and exaggerated misrepresentations had been made to Constantinople with reference to the disturbance at Nazareth, in which Captain Burton's servants were so maltreated. As I was present, travelling with Captain Burton, and saw as much of this riot as anyone, I consider it my duty to lay before you a correct statement of the whole affair. You are quite at liberty to make any use of this letter that you please. I shall first observe that the notice generally in the Hadikat el Akbar (of May 13-25, 1871), especially the statement that " La foule était si considerable qu'il fut impossible de reconnaître les auteurs de la rixe, ainsi que celui qui avait lancé la pierre au Consul" is a deliberate and intentional lie, as will be seen below. The injuries to the servants were by no means slight; two of them were unable to move for three days, and one has continued to spit blood for some time.

The affair commenced early in the morning of May the 5th by a Copt lad attempting to enter one of the tents and refusing to leave when requested to do so by the servants. He then proceeded to use most abusive language, and picked up a stone to throw at one of Captain Burton's men, who then naturally enough beat him. During this little "fracas," which would by itself have finished here, the Greeks were in the Church of the Annunciation, which was close to the tents, but three or four who were outside chose to take the part of the Copt, and attack the Consul's servants (four in number). Two of the Makaris then joined in, the alarm was given, and the Greeks rushed out of church, and managed to get the servants to the east side of the church enclosure, where they were not in view of the tents. Captain Burton and I, hearing a considerable noise, ran down half dressed, and on turning the corner of the wall, suddenly found ourselves in a perfect hailstorm of stones. One man (Siman el Asfúr) threw a large stone at me from a distance of only three or four yards, which narrowly missed my head. Of course I took especial care to remark his face, and when he had the extreme impudence to accompany a deputation of Greeks who came to Captain Burton to request him not to punish the offenders, I recognized him at a distance of fifty or sixty yards, as he was approaching the tents. Captain Burton also immediately recognized, as we both did, Yusuf Moámmur. These two were foremost in the stone throwing. Several of these, now prisoners, I distinctly saw in the riot: all of them were recognized by the servants, but a few whose identification was rather doubtful were of course immediately set free. Luckily, one of the servants had a revolver in his belt and fired a shot in the air, which checked the mob for a moment. Captain Burton then took the pistol and fired again in the air, and we were able to retreat to the tents, assailed by showers of stones. Had it not been for Captain Burton's coolness we should probably not have escaped with our lives, as the mob was very excited. We then gave the alarm to some English and American travellers, who were camped near. They armed themselves and came out, and the crowd dispersed. Captain Burton and I then went with pistols in our hands to the walled-in court which surrounds the church in search of the cook, who was missing: he was found fainting, and very severely knocked about. This probably gave rise to the ridiculous stories of our having entered the church, and done some damage there, which we did not do. The turbulence of the people at Nazareth is well known, and the Greek influence there was so strong that the Kaimakam, who has only twelve Zaptiéhs under him, four or five of whom are only lads, with a population of 7,000 (2,500 Greeks) was almost helpless. Everything is now being done to get the culprits off. The Bishop of Nazareth has been sent by his flock to do his utmost, but I hear from the priest Kyrillos, deacon to the patriarch here, that he deeply regrets the part he has already taken. The policy of the Governor-General of Syria, His Excellency Rashid Pasha, has always been to oppose European influence as much as possible—so much so that it is a common saying in Damascus, "The Consuls used to unmake the Wali, now the Wali unmakes the Consuls;" and consequently he sides with the Greeks. A firm, independant man, with a thorough knowledge of the country and ways of dealing, like Captain Burton, is of course peculiarly obnoxious to him, and I have no doubt he would be very well pleased to see him removed, in hopes of his successor being easier to use as a tool. This policy of antagonism to European influence must prove very detrimental to Syria, as the reaction which must necessarily ensue will naturally turn too much to the other side. Syria is now in a peculiarly feverish state, and sect feeling runs very strong, especially between the Greek and Latin Churches, as the former gains so much ground by the growing influence of Russia as the latter have lost by the defeat of France and the occupation of Rome. If this affair is allowed to pass unnoticed, the arrogance of the Greeks will undoubtedly cause a quarrel with the Latins at Nazareth, and should the fire once be lighted it would, with the present state of feeling, spread over the whole country. At Nazareth Captain Burton took all possible precautions, by making the Greeks, Latins, and Moslems sign a guarantee for the preservation of peace.

Apologizing for the length of my letter,

I remain your Excellency's
Obedient humble Servant,
CHARLES T. TYRWHITT DRAKE.

[TRADUCTION.]
From the Patriarch of the Orthodox Greek Church in the East.

MONASTÈRE BALAMEND,
Le 26 Juillet,

MONSIEUR LE CONSUL,

Avec grand plaisir nous avons reçu votre chère missive du 27 Juillet, par laquelle nous apprenons que Votre Seigneurie nous a adressé une précédente lettre nous parlant de l'affaire de Nazareth, laquelle lettre ne nous est pas malheureusement parvenue jusqu'à l'heure qu'il est, et nous ne savons pas où elle peut être perdue.

Nous nous empressons maintenant de répondre à votre estimée lettre que nous avons devant les yeux. Nous vous remercions de tout notre cœur pour les sentiments de sincérité et de véritable affection que vous nous tenez, vous priant de vous assurez que ces sentiments mêmes nous les avons pour votre honorable personne ; conséquemment nous ne doutons pas qu'ils ne se changent point par les affaires de Nazareth quelle que soit leur fin. Tout au contraire, nous nous assurons bien que Votre Seigneurie, doué de principes de vérité et de la sublime justice, qui sont des qualités des anglais, nous tende la main d'aide si précieuse, lors que nos besoins la demandent de quoi nous vous adressons nos remerciements en implorant au Seigneur ardemment pour la santé et la prospérité de Votre Seigneurie en toute chose.

Vous priant d'agréer l'expression de notre considération distingué, avec laquelle nous prions ardemment le Seigneur pour vous, Monsieur le Consul.

(Signé)   IROTHE, Patriarche d'Antioche.

A Monsieur le Capitaine R. Burton,
Consul de S.M. de la Grande Bretagne, &c., &c.,
Damas.

Captain Burton to Sir Henry Elliot.

DAMASCUS,
June 18th, 1871.

SIR,

I have the honour to acknowledge the receipt this day of your Excellency's despatch (No. 4 of June 6th, 1871), and to reply to it paragraph by paragraph.

I deeply regret that my report of the assault at Nazareth was not sent to you before; the delay, as has been explained, arose from the dangers of the local Turkish post, and from a desire to forward the case in a complete form.

Until the last few days I have been expecting a personal visit, with a written apology, from the Bishop of Nazareth. He began with an attempt to suborn four Moslem witnessses —unhappily not one of them was in Nazareth at the time when he proposed that they should perjure themselves. A copy of his letter from St. Jean d'Acre was duly forwarded to me. At Damascus he has openly admitted the untruth of his statements, declaring that he was compelled to make them by his flock, who forbade him to return unless he would carry them through the affair harmless. He has hinted his danger from personal violence, and his fear that his followers would "turn Protestants."

Since the date of my last despatch, however, the Bishop of Nazareth has been encouraged at the Serai to withdraw all offers of conciliation, and I have been compelled to urge a trial upon the local authorities. Your Excellency may be pleased to hear that my proceedings have been thoroughly approved by his Eminence the Greek Patriarch of Damascus; and I have reason to think that the same is the case with his Eminence the Greek Patriarch of Jerusalem. The latter is said to have written me a friendly letter, but the document has not been suffered to reach me.

The youth Habib Jemayl (aged twenty-two), seeing Mr. Tyrwhitt-Drake likely to be severely injured by a stone, fired a shot high over the assailant's head, and did good service by preventing that gentleman from receiving a dangerous wound. I then took the revolver from him, and as three stones had struck me, though partially sheltered by a tree, I fired also in the air. Many men, it may be asserted, when exposed to be brained by a Syrian fellah would have shot the foremost agressor.

Not one of our assailants, however, was wounded even by a stone; and had not the pistol been at hand one or both of us might have been killed, so reckless and infuriated was the mob urged on by their priests and elders. The same lad, Habib Jemayl, on October 20th, 1870, seeing Mrs. Burton threatened by a similar mob at the Zebdani village, and in dread of their violence, was drawing a pistol, when five or six men seized his arms, and the weapon went off in the struggle without injury to anyone. The ringleaders of the riot were severely punished by the authorities, and no one complained against the youth. I pay more than usual attention in this part of the world to the bearing of my followers, and lately I dismissed one of them for speaking roughly to a priest. It may be mentioned that one of the men most severely beaten at Nazareth was my cook, a Greek Rayyah, and that since my return to Damascus he has been tampered with and begged to give false witness.

When the rioters were arrested, confronted with my people, recognized, and duly committed for trial, I despatched a special messenger to Rushdi Effendi, Governor of St. John d'Acre, requesting that at least two of the ringleaders might be sent in irons to Damascus. I offered to telegram to His Excellency the Governor-General, but Rushdi Effendi did so himself, and the men were forwarded accordingly. At that time two of my men were lying severely wounded, one of them spitting blood, as can be proved by the medical certificate of Dr. Vartan, Nazareth Mission. A third, the Kawass Mohammad, an Affghan, and an English subject, who served in India and in the Crimea, sustained a severe injury, and since that time his life has been despaired of. The other ten prisoners were marched down in cords to St. John d'Acre, when I am informed the richest of them were at once allowed to go almost free. Two of those identified as having joined in the affray have not yet appeared. Jiryus Azzam, a wealthy man, remains at St. John d'Acre, whilst Yusuf Shalluf escaped from Nazareth. This was reported by me (20th of May) to His Excellency the Governor-General of Syria, but no reply has hitherto been received. The fact is His Excellency has skilfully converted a village riot into a question of religion and politics. The success of his projects can hardly be brought about except by siding with the so-called "Greek" Rayahs, whom he hates, and he would the more willingly place me in a false position, as the field would thus be cleared of one obstacle. This assertion, I believe, embodies the general opinion throughout Syria.

Your Excellency will have received the depositions of Englishmen who all testify to the fact of my having shown, under somewhat trying circumstances, coolness and moderation.

During the four years which I passed in the Brazil, the Argentine Republic, Chili, Peru and Paraguay, after travelling through the wildest parts of somewhat lawless regions, I cannot call to mind having had a single dispute. In Syria, however, party feeling carries everything before it. The mere fact of my having prevented Monseigneur Niffon, Bishop of Nazareth from seizing ground which belongs to the Jews of Tiberias, under the protection of Great Britain, was enough to place me in complete antagonism with him, and through him with his turbulent and fanatical "flock."

I may conclude with asserting that during my twenty-one months' residence at Damascus I have laboured incessantly to promote justice and conciliation, with a due regard to our national dignity. An English colonist long settled in the country writes to me, "We are very proud of the affair at Nazareth; the English in Syria are looking up at last." Travellers who have lately passed through Nazareth (Miss Fullerton and Mr. Cunningham Graham) can answer for the respect with which they are now treated. I hold documents from nearly every race or creed in Syria, and amongst others from the Greek and Latin Patriarchs of Damascus, showing that they consider me their friend, and look forward to my assistance in case of disturbances. The Jewish *protégés* of Damascus who last year forwarded complaints against me to Her Majesty's Foreign Office are proposing to draw up an apology in writing, and to own that they were wholly in the wrong. The Jews of Tiberias and Safet have applied, I am told, to the Home authorities, with a view of being placed under this Consulate. I am equally on good terms with the Druzes, the Metaweli, the Nusayri, and all other sections of the Moslem community. Those only wish me ill who are jealous of or are restrained by my knowledge of the country and of Eastern character, and by my insight into their plans, from carrying out the objects of their ambition, and from the unjust and corrupt measures which are now, and especially under the present administration, the curse of the country.

     I have the honour to be, Sir,
      Your Excellency's obedient humble Servant
        RICHARD F. BURTON.

His Excellency,
  The Right Honourable
    Sir Henry Elliot,
      Constantinople.

SPECIMENS OF LETTERS RECEIVED EVERY DAY SHOWING THE FEELING IN SYRIA RESPECTING THE GREEKS AND THE AFFRAY AT NAZARETH

An English colonist in our own district writes:—

"We are all very proud of the affair at Nazareth. The English in Syria are looking up at last after playing second fiddle to the French Consulate for so long."

Another English settler in Mr. Eldridge's jurisdiction writes:—

"I have heard various accounts of all that befel you at Nazareth. I think that we may all, even Mrs. Mott, send in a vote of thanks to Captain Burton for his firm dealing with such a mob. The fact is, I believe, now that poor France is down, Prussia is lifting up her head, and the Greeks are becoming a little impertinent, and need a lesson or two. I only wish that we were in Captain Burton's district, or that we had a Consul like him to take an interest in our behalf here."

From a Maronite at Beyrout who is learning French:—

"Ce qui m'a peiné c'est la contrariété que vous avez eu durant votre voyage dans la terre sainte. Dieu l'a voulu ainsi pour donner à ces sauvages barbares par votre moyen une leçon qui les mettra à la raison, et de savoir respecter à qui on doit le respect. Oh oui! ils ont reçu ce qu'ils ont mérité—une leçon qui ne sera jamais effacée de leur mémoire."

From an English Consul:—

"I was glad to hear of your safety. The affair at Nazareth must have been very unpleasant, and I hope the stone throwing caitiffs will get a lesson."

From the Latins at Nazareth:—

"Doppo della loro partenza da Nazaret, non solo Latini ma anche altri di altre nazione rne rimasero stupefatti, pensando al insulto che riceettero S.S. E.E. in Nazaret dai Greci e lo accontano in questo modo, che il giorno di festa per i Greci dedicato a S. Giorgio, nel mentre che era per finire la loro funzione si presento un Copto alla tenta della signora mà indecentemente ed i servitori nel vederlo lo invitarono a partire, ma lui insisteva e per la dua resistenza, si viddero i poveri servi a mandarlo via per focsa, cosicche dopo di una piccola zuffa fini tutto, ma il Copto si miro verso la lora Chiesa e non appena che fu giunto era finita la nazione ed usciano in grace numero. Il Copto allora si pose a gridare e raccondare il fatto a suo modo ed i Greci senza riflessione tutti di un animo (come se fosse gia concertato) alzarono le pietre e senza altro feciro piovare una quantita de sassi sulle tente del Console e sopra ai servi, ed il Console senza sapere cosa era usci dalla tenta unito al suo campagno e nel videre di che si trattava gridava per mettere pace ma tanto il Console che il compagno recévettero dei colpi di sassi che per salvarsi fu costretto anascondersi dietro di un albero; e cosi in questa zuffa rimasero tre servi gravamente feriti ed uno di questi sputava sangue; è vi era uno dei Greci che diceva " Tirate ammazzatelo che io paghero il loro sangue," che nel en tendere questo, el Capo Muchero del Console disse " Cosa dite, attenti, che voi dovete sapere che questo e il Console Inglese di Damasco," e il Greco rispondeva "Che Console! che Damasco! tirate! tirate!" E qui bisogna riflettere la gran prudenza e carita che uso il Signor Console che non voleva far male a nessuno in tempo della zuffa ma pero quanto fini subbito spedi delle persone a domandare soldati e di far prendere i principali della zuffa e fargli condurre in Damasco e cosi fece non ostante i vacciri che si facevano il Console forte quanto li vidde partire da Nazaret per Acri allora parti anche lui da Nazaret ed ecco la cosa come viene più referita e nul altro.

From the Protestant Clergyman at Nazareth.

June 28, 1871.

Dear Sir,

On my return from Jerusalem the 26th inst., I found your letters of May the 23rd and June the 9th, with this order from H.E. the Wali regarding Mich. Kawar. I beg to thank you in the name of the Protestant community for your kind assistance, and I hope this order, demanding that no case of a Protestant should be tried except in the presence of their representative, may be the means of protecting them in future from injustice.

I am very sorry to see that the tone of the Greeks is still of a defiant character, and that they not only at Damascus, but also at Jerusalem, spread exaggerated and false reports in the hope to escape the punishment which their brutal attack upon yourself and servants so well deserves. I deeply regret this occurrence, and I am well aware that the savage conduct of the Greek Christians may lead you to form an exaggerated idea of their turbulent character. Yet since Protestant missionaries came to Nazareth in 1850, the behaviour of the Greeks formed a favourable contrast to the intolerance and violence of the Latin Christians, who repeatedly attacked the missionaries and their premises. The conduct of the Greeks on the 5th of May was probably not prompted by any ill feeling against European travellers, none of whom during the last years were molested by a Greek Christian; however, it shows the highly excitable and impulsive character of the people, who, needless of the consequences, are delighted to fight any one, relying on the superior number of their community.

The defiant spirit exhibited by the Greeks after this occurrence is principally due to the influence of their leaders, who often use their power to prevent the punishment of an offender, if he belongs to their party, and thus vitiate the moral ideas of the people, whilst Turkish officials are too weak to offer any opposition. All measures taken by you for the arrest and subsequent punishment of the ringleaders were therefore absolutely necessary; for if an outrage like this should escape punishment, no Englishman would in future visit Nazareth without a feeling of shame, or without experiencing considerable inconvenience.

This riot strikingly shows the necessity of an improvement in the police arrangements of this place. Nazareth is every year visited by a large number of English travellers, and they, as well as the English residents here, have neither the assistance of a British consular agent, nor is there a Consulate with easy reach. It is therefore necessary that a *superior* and perfectly trustworthy individual should be appointed Kaimacam of Nazareth, who might be independent from the above-mentioned local influences, and afford a guarantee for the security of foreigners.

In case my opinion about some farther particulars should be welcome to you, I shall, as far as my knowledge goes, be happy to give it.

With kind regards,

I remain, dear Sir, yours very faithfully,

(Signed). JOHN ZELLER.

Captain Burton,
   H.B.M.'s Consul, Damascus.

DAMASCUS,
July 7th, 1871.

SIR,
I have the honour to lay before Your Excellency an account of what has taken place in Damascus touching the assault committed on myself and others at Nazareth.

On May 29th, 1871, ten of the twelve accused reached this city, having been summoned by a telegram from the Governor-General. Their names are—

    Daud Sulayman,
    Elias Warwar,
    Yusuf Warwar,
    Khalil Jarjura,
    Jiriyus Dib,
    Bashárah Sikran,
    Jiriyus el Habashi,
    Yusuf Muammar,
    Jiriyus El Sulayman,
    Simán El Usfur.

Of these ten the three first mentioned, being persons of property, were at once allowed to purchase sick certificates. Daud Sulayman lived in the house of a Greek, M. Mikhail Banná, while E. Warwar and Y. Nuwaysir were lodged at the Greek Patriarchate. The two wanting were Jiryus Azzam, also a man of property, who acquired a medical certificate, and remained at St. John d'Acre, and Yusuf Shalluf: this person had fled from Nazareth, and presently returned; a letter from the Latin Convent informed me that he was hidden in a Greek house. I reported (No. 38, June 29th, 1871) the fact to the Governor-General, but he did not think proper to notice my report.

The ten accused were detained under arrest until, beginning to fear being charged with maliciously prolonging their confinement, I informed the Governor-General (June 14th, 1871) that the delay did not come from me. At length, on June 24th, the Great Court of Appeal (Majlis Tamiz el Hukuk el Vilayet) met. The President was the Mufettish (inspector) Sayyid Mohammad Izzat, an official wholly under the influence of the Governor-General. The seven members were Jibran Effendi Shamiyeh and Mikhail Effendi Námi, both Greeks, and Asad Effendi Hamzah and Mohammed Effendi Minini, Moslems, as was also the head writer, Mohammed Effendi Habib. The three latter are completely under the influence of the Serai. I named as my agent M. Hanna Azar, Dragoman of this Consulate, and he was accompanied by M. Awadys, another dragoman, to witness proceedings.

The tribunal began with debating whether the *procès verbaux* (*fornálát*) drawn up at Nazareth and at St. John d'Acre were or were not admissible. At the second *séance* (Monday, June 26th), I requested my fellow traveller, Mr. C. F. Tyrwhitt Drake, to be present, and he can testify to the one-sided views, the delays, and the chicanery which as usual formed the favourite tactic. In vain my agent pleaded that the tribunal of Acre had displayed such partiality by examining only Greek witnesses, and by refusing to hear all others, that MM. Finzi and Barbour, who represented me, had telegramed to me at Damascus; that I had sent on the message to the Governor-General, and that the latter had himself ordered the prisoners to be brought to head-quarters, and to be tried by the Grand Court of Appeal; that His Excellency could not have been ignorant of the law, and that it was for him to have refused the request till sentence had been passed at St. John d'Acre. The tribunal, however, declared both documents informal.

I may here mention that a few days after this decision the same Tribunal of Appeal heard a cause (Finzi versus Bannay) arising out of the main suit, instead of transferring it to the Tribunal of First Instance (Majlis Tamyiz el Hukuk el Liwa.) The fact is, that this course suited them best for the purpose of withholding justice, and thus the law is openly set at nought in Damascus.

On July 3, the Governor-General informed me that a Vizirial letter and the decision of the tribunal directed that bail be taken from the accused, who were once more to be examined at Nazareth. I protested against this proceeding, and formally placed the responsibility of all delay and evasion of justice upon the authorities of this province.

The accused have spent, it is said, several hundred napoleons to procure this temporary release, and they will spend hundreds more. Their object is simply to gain time; as usual, they trust to the chapter of accidents, and to the carefully spread report of my recall. This affair, like my visit to Hauran, has been used here and at head quarters to rid the Vilayet, or rather the Vali, of a Consular Officer who is determined to see justice done—the head and point of my offence will be found in the six millions piastres which I claim for British *protégés* and in my reports to your Excellency.

On July, I officially named Messrs. Finzi and Barbour as my *procureurs* at Nazareth, requesting the Governor-General to make especial arrangements for their personal safety. I also proposed that Rushdi Effendi, Governor of St. John d'Acre, preside over the tribunal at Nazareth, for reasons which hardly need to be explained. On July 8, the Governor-General informed me that he had acceded to the latter proposal.

I have the honour, &c.,

(Signed) RICHARD F. BURTON.

His Excellency the Right Hon. Sir Henry Elliot, K.C.B.

[CONSULAR No. 8.—COPY SENT TO EMBASSY.]

DAMASCUS,
July 10, 1871.

MY LORD,

I have the honour to acknowledge the receipt of Mr. Odo Russell's despatch (No. 17) of June 14, 1871, and to supply full details concerning the telegram from the Governor-General of Syria to Aali Pasha.

The telegram I will observe is dated May 16, or three days before my return to Damascus; therefore it is a purely *ex parte* statement.

The Governor-General says truly that I am often on the move. Nothing can be more disagreeable to him. This course of action makes me master of the serious maladministration which of late years has characterized the Government of Syria. I am aware, he knows, of his appointing his own creatures to all important posts; of his intrigues with the Greek Church, and through it with Russia; of his wasting the revenues of the Porte and, of numerous other malpractices which will presently see the light. When leaving Damascus to inspect my district, I place the Consulate under the charge of Mr. Nasif Meshaka, whose name commands the highest respect, and with him are three other Drogomans, so that work at the capital is never intermitted. I cannot ascertain the truth of a single report unless I visit in person the place when it originated. I therefore hope that your Lordship will be pleased to leave my movements within the range of this extensive Consulate free and at my own discretion.

It was not an assembly of children only that collected round the Greek convent on May 5, 1871. Most of them, including the Copt who began the disturbance, were adults. He has been here in Damascus, and my fellow-traveller, Mr. C. F. Tyrwhitt Drake can bear witness to the correctness of this and all the following statements.

I did not arm myself in order to take part in the quarrel. My fellow-traveller and I, though we had arms in plenty, went out without weapons to see what the disturbance was, and we ran the risk of losing our lives.

I did not use my arms against the Greeks, nor did I fire bullets upon them, I took a pistol from one of my servants and fired once in the air. Most men when three times struck at a distance of 6 or 7 feet, and attacked by a furious mob, would not have been so merciful. The moderation of my conduct is testified by the Rev. Mr. Taylor and his three companions.

My servants were not slightly wounded; three were severely hurt, and of these one has lately been upon the point of death. Another spat blood for a fortnight. Even the muleteers were not suffered to escape. I can, if necessary, forward the medical certificates given by Dr. Vartan, of the Nazareth Mission, and by Dr. Nicora, the surgeon established by the French Government at Damascus.

I did not exact that several persons should be sent with hands tied to Damascus. I laid my complaint in due form before the Governor and the tribunal of Nazareth; both were powerless to assist me. I then sent a special messenger to St. Jean d'Acre, the *chef lieu* of the department, requesting that a telegram be addressed to the Governor-General to the effect that twelve men had been identified as being most active in the affray by myself and my fellow-traveller, by the servants, and by the muleteers. Two of the ringleaders were first sent in confinement to Damascus by the orders of the Governor-General, the rest were marched down, also by his orders, to St. Jean d'Acre, and thence, also by his orders, to Damascus. At that time two of my servants were dangerously hurt, and I did not expect that one of them would live.

Your Lordship will not be a little surprised to see the utter want of truth and malicious perversion of facts which characterise the Governor-General's telegram. It is now my duty to show the cause of its animus.

Rashid Pasha has ever sold his favour, his personal friendship, and his good word to the Consular Corps at Damascus at the price of their not pushing the claims of their *protégés*, especially by reporting to Constantinople; of their not opposing his policy, and of their ignoring as far as was possible his ambitious projects, his rapacity, his corruptness, and his openly encouraging the malpractices of his dependents. When Mr. Consul Rogers remonstrated against certain new taxes levied upon British protected subjects (No. 31, Damascus, October 3, 1866), Rashid Pasha threatened to complain at Constantinople of his wishing to obstruct the free action of the local Government.

During the later months of 1869, and almost through 1870, I patiently listened to the succession of promises by word of mouth, by telegram, and by letter, with which Rashid Pasha systematically and, as is his wont, put off my just requisitions. In early 1871, I found it my duty to declare that I could no longer countenance delays in settling the claims of British subjects, which amount to six millions of piastres, and to delays which were ruining sundry houses.

Hence the personal hostility of Rashid Pasha: he has left nothing untried to injure a Consular officer who has dared to do his duty.

Meanwhile, I am urging the claims of British subjects through Her Majesty's Embassy, and I venture to hope that I may be permitted to superintend the settlement of these claims, with whose every item the study of twenty months had made me familiar.

I may conclude with informing your Lordship that during the last month Rashid Pasha has been attempting an attack on the Druzes, which a timely visit on my part happily frustrated. He has openly sold to the Bishop of Nazareth a graveyard and a synagogue at Tiberias which have belonged to the Jews for the last four hundred years. I am energetically protesting against the injustice; and he has, contrary to the treaty which secures life and liberty to all converts in the Ottoman dominions, lately imprisoned and maltreated a certain Haj Hasan who became a Christian at Beyrout. A great movement, and one of the utmost gravity, is about to take place; and I shall not fail to make your Lordship acquainted with it as soon as the details are in my hands.

I am too well acquainted with the justice of Her Majesty's Government to fear that it will be influenced against one of its servants by the succession of petty complaints, which is the favourite tactic of Rashid Pasha. His telegram proves how utterly unfit he is for the high and honourable position which he occupies. It is the misfortune of Syria that this Governor-General, a *protégé* of Aali Pasha, should have been allowed to rule it for five years, and to cause in it an amount of misery, of starvation, that the country cannot ever remember. One of the richest provinces of the Empire shows the sad scene of human beings living on grass and wild roots. I venture to hope that even the large sums of money which he is known to remit to Constantinople will not save him from the disgrace which he merits.

I have the, &c.,
(Signed) RICHARD F. BURTON.

Her Majesty's Principal Secretary of State
for Foreign Affairs.

[No. 25.]

Copy sent to Foreign Office.

DAMASCUS,
July 16th, 1871.

SIR,

I have the honour to inform Your Excellency that on the 5th instant a letter from the heads of the Jewish community of Tiberias was put into my hands. This document renewed a complaint previously—namely, that the Governor-General of Syria had sold to Monseigneur Niffon, Greek Bishop of Nazareth, a synagogue and a cemetery belonging to the Jews of Tiberias. Many of these persons are protected British subjects, and they have procured the testimony of eight Moslem witnesses to prove that the ground containing the Synagogue has been in their hands during the last 400 years.

When at Tiberias in March and May, 1871, I protested strongly against this sale to the native authorities. Receiving the letter from the Jews I at once (July 6th) brought the affair to the notice of the Governor-General Rashid Pasha, and a private note (July 13) informed me in reply that the "authorities are occupying themselves with this question." I need hardly add that the authorities are himself.

It will now become evident to Your Excellency why the Greeks of Nazareth are so hostile to me; why the Greek Bishop so strictly opposed justice, even writing to suborn and to pay four Moslem witnesses, and why he was energetically supported by the Governor-General. The ground has been taken from the Jews for the purpose of building a Greco-Russian hospice and convent, and thus this sect will add another and a valuable item to its actual possessions, the "Oak of Abraham," near Hebron, Mount Tabor, and "Jacob's Well," near Nablus (Shechem).

I venture to hope that Your Excellency will support me in resisting this injustice.

I have the honour, &c.,
(Signed) RICHARD F. BURTON.

To His Excellency,
The Right Honourable
Sir Henry Elliot,
Constantinople.

(Separate.)

HER BRITANNIC MAJESTY'S CONSULATE, DAMASCUS (CITY),
July 26th, 1871.

MY LORD,

I have the honour to acknowledge the receipt of Mr. Odo Russell's Despatch (No. 2) of June 23rd, 1871, calling upon me immediately to explain why I had not reported to your Lordship the assault made upon myself and my people at Nazareth.

Having already furnished the explanation in my Despatch (No. 28) of July 21st, I have now only to regret that any delay was suffered to occur, as such delay might be subject to misconstruction. Suffering from the hot and sickly season at Damascus, I was unable to give the office that supervision which which was desirable, and thus the copy of my Despatch (No. 10) of June 18, addressed to Her Majesty's Embassy, Constantinople, was not forwarded to your Lordship till July 25.

I have already explained to Her Majesty's Ambassador, Constantinople, the cause of the delay in reporting the assault to him, and I have the honour once more to assure your Lordship that the affair would have presented no grave aspect had not the bad will of the Governor-General, Rashid Pasha, converted a village riot into a political and racial dispute. Such things have happened to almost every traveller who has seen much of Syria, from the Reverend Mr. Porter to the Rev. Dr. Tristram, and will be found duly recorded in their books. Usually the authorities have no difficulty in punishing the rioters.

It has reached me through a private source that the Governor-General has found fault with my conduct generally, for encroaching upon the domain of the local authorities and for assuming a position inimical to their interests by making myself their rival. This I emphatically deny, Such a proceeding would be on my part an error of judgment of which I am incapable.

The Governor-General is bound to show categorically where, when, and how I have in any way exceeded the bounds of legitimate Consular interference in Turkey. This he cannot do. I have, it is true, opposed his unceasing efforts to annihilate the due influence of this Consulate, as he has done that of all others at Damascus. I have advocated the rights which he has withheld from British protected subjects, and have extended this usual semi-official aid to the Druzes whom he wishes to ruin, and I have taken, in the cause of religious toleration and missionary schools, a stand which has hitherto been productive of the best results against the Governor-General's open infraction of Treaties. That such a line of conduct should be offensive to His Excellency Rashid Pasha I have no reason to doubt. But, convinced that I have in no way exceeded my powers as Her Majesty's Consul for Damascus, I look forward without fear to the support of my Chiefs.

I have the honour to be, My Lord,
Your most obedient and humble Servant,
RICHARD F. BURTON.
H.M.'s Consul, Damascus.

Her Majesty's Secretary of State
for Foreign Affairs.

NAZARETH,
August 1st, 1871.

SIR,
By last post we had the honour of transmitting to you a letter dated February the 26th, in which we explained how the Commissioner, Othman Bey, commenced the investigation regarding the attack made by the Greek community on your party at Nazareth.

When we saw the open partiality of the Commissioner for the accused persons, we presented our objections against his proceedings; however, without any effect, We therefore wrote two formal protests, and presented them to the Pasha of Acca, in the hope that the Commissioner would be induced to take up the case with more regard to truth and justice. But it proved otherwise, for the said Commissioner continued assisting the accused party even more openly than before by his way of putting his questions and hinting at the same time what answers they might give for their excuse and defence, and by correcting their statements whilst they were written down. Whenever we wished to make our remarks and protests against this, and have them stated in the protocol, the Commissioner objected, would only hear us verbally, and then register our protest in the manner it pleased him.

On this account we presented yesterday a protest through the Superior of the Franciscan Convent, objecting against this manner of conducting the trial, giving at the same time our reasons for protesting. When the Commissioner heard this he got angry, denied that he had ever refused to accept our remarks, and obtained from the Medjlis a document in corroboration of this assertion. This is the custom of Medjlisses here.

On the 31st of July the Pasha acknowledged our letter, but objected to the protest, informing us that the protocol had been sealed and made over to the Commissioner, who would bring it to the Wali. He returned in the night to Acca, and Ottoman Bey left for Nablous without having given us a copy of the protocol, or even shown it to us.

If it had been the intention of the authorities to do justice to your case, they would not have broken off the investigation in this manner, and prevented us from seeing the protocal. *The accused Greeks have been given freedom.* We enclose a copy of our protest, and also a copy of the Pasha's answer.

We have only to add that the Commissioner, in questioning the Greeks, suggested the idea that the wounds and bruises of your servants might have been caused by a quarrel among themselves, and that the stone-mark on your arm had perhaps been inflicted by a fall on the journey previously. The Greeks naturally took up this bold way of defence, and the Commissioner recorded their answers accordingly.

We have the honour to remain, Sir,
Your humble and obedient Servants,
(Signed) FINZI & BARBOUR.

Captain Burton,
    H.B.M.'s Consul, &c., &c., &c.,
        Damascus.

NAZARETH,
August 2nd, 1871,

DEAR SIR,

The investigation against the people who made the attack upon your party was suddenly broken off, and all the prisoners were set at liberty. The Commissioner and the Pasha of Acre left on Monday evening. The whole trial was from the beginning a wretched farce, and with this conclusion must necessarily produce the impression upon the population of Nazareth that any outrage committed upon an Englishman, resident or traveller, can be committed without fear of punishment, as the Government will do its utmost to screen the offenders.

On Monday the workmen at our church were hindered and attacked by some Moslems, and in spite of repeated complaints, verbally and by writing, the local authorities have done absolutely nothing in the matter. It is now the third day.

Our church is on the south side, bordering on the property of some Mohammedans, and I am, under the present circumstances, obliged to discontinue the work there.

It is urgent to send strong orders to the local authorities. Kaimacam and Kadi are at present absent.

I sent a similar letter to the Consul-General, Mr. Eldridge, in Beyrout.

Will you kindly excuse the great haste in writing this, and

Believe me,
Yours very truly,
JOHN ZELLER.

Captain Burton,
    H.B.M.'s Consul,
        Damascus.

[COPY.]

DAMASCUS,
Nov. 11th, 1871.

YOUR EXCELLENCY,

It is with regret that I feel myself obliged to make this protest (copies of which have been sent to H.B.M.'s Government in London, and also to H.B.M.'s Ambassador at Constantinople) against the mazbatah (sentence), dated Akka, 18 Jemad el Awwel (August 6th, 1871), with reference to the affray in May last between the Greek Christians of Nazareth and the servants of Captain Burton, then H.B.M.'s Consul for Damascus, in which both the Consul and his servants were injured.

As an agent for Captain Burton in the matter, I should not be fulfilling my duty were I to omit urging upon your Excellency to examine into the case, and cause a just decision to be made. I hope to make clear to your Excellency that neither Captain Burton nor his servants have been justly dealt with, to say nothing of the fact that the evidence I gave in writing—having seen the whole affair from the beginning to the end—is completely ignored. The evidence of the Rev. Mr. Taylor and his three companions, which they signed in presence of the Mejlis Tamyiz el Hukuk el Vilayet, is equally ignored. The evidence of the Rev. Mr. Zeller, of Nazareth; of Dr. Vartan, M.R.C.S.E., of the same place; of Dr. Nicora, médecin sanitaire de France à Damas, has undergone the same treatment.

Your Excellency will perceive the *animus* which has instigated the unwarrantable imputation against Captain Burton and the biassed manner in which the *ex parte* statements of the Greeks have been received, Your Excellency is of course aware Ottoman Bey Mardum Bey, the agent of the late Wali Rashid Pasha, is one of the men who, by virtue of a mazbatah drawn up by the notables of Damascus and the Mejlis, and deposited in the Jamia El Amawi (Great Mosque), is debarred from ever being employed as a Government functionary; and it is not perhaps impossible that this man's presence, backed by Rashid Pasha, whose inveterate hatred to Captain Burton is well known, may have caused this decision to be arrived at by the Courts of Akka and Nazareth.

I now beg your Excellency to grant a fair and impartial trial, where both sides can be heard; and from what I have heard of your Excellency's even handed justice, I venture to hope that my appeal will not be in vain.

I will now touch as briefly as possible upon some points in the above-mentioned maybatah, which are very incorrect, and upon others which cast wholly unwarrantable imputations upon the character and conduct of Captain Burton, the representative of H.B. Majesty at Damacus.

To His Excellency (Signed) C. F. TYRWHITT DRAKE.
   Soubhi Pasha,
      Vali of Damascus and the
         Vilayet of Syria,
           &c., &c.

---

1. The mazbatah says that Captain Burton's servants, Habib el Jemayel, Mahomed Kawass, Autun el Says and Saba Waked, by their "present and past" avowal and declaration, were found to have been in the affray.

These men were none of them at the "present" examination (*i.e.*, at Akka).

2. It is stated that the wound received by Captain Burton has never been proved, and that it is simply asserted.

The Greek doctor sent by the Government from Akka two or three days after the affray saw the severe bruise on Captain Bruton's shoulder, as did Dr. Vartan, of Nazareth; and I myself saw the stone strike him.

3. It says that the acts and misconduct of the Consul depend for their punishment upon the will of H.I.M. the Sultan.

It is impossible to prove—except by false witnesses—that H.B.M.'s Consul in any way misconducted himself throughout the affair.

4. The complaint of Captain Burton is then inserted without comment, and the *resumé* of the depositions of the Greeks is given at considerable length. These depositions state that—*a*, Jerius el Habashi was unjustly beaten; *b*, that when Jerius Sulayman went to his assistance firearms were discharged by the travellers; *c*, that these travellers entered the church with firearms and profaned it; *d*, that after these events the Greeks learned that it was the English Consul who had so acted with an "*arrière pensée!*"

- *a*. Jerius el Habashi was on the point of entering a lady's tent early in the morning, and was only beaten after he had refused to go away on being asked to do so. after he had used vile language and picked up a stone to throw at one of the servants. The tribunal, however, seems to consider that this Jerius el Habashi was to blame for the way in which he acted; as they have condemned him to " peine majeur."
- *b*. Firearms were not discharged—except twice *in the air*—till not only the lives of the servant, but also of Captain Burton and myself, were in great danger from the violence of the mob.
- *c*. This assertion is false, as Captain Burton and myself did not penetrate more than two or three metres into the outer courtyard which surrounded the church, and did not remain there more than a quarter of a minute, and neither said or did anything in the least disrespectful to God or man.
- *d*. When Captain Burton and myself turned the corner of the churchyard wall and found ourselves in the thick of the affray, I myself heard a man call out, " It is the English Consul from Damascus ;" and immediately numbers of stones were thrown at us.

I leave it to your Excellency's justice to deal with those who have dared to say that H.B.M.'s representative acted in an unworthy manner with an "*arrière pensée*."

5. Certain Bedouins, named Adwán el Músa and Rasim el Hamargos, of the Jaatin diversion, and Zabteych from Runayterah (distant in a direct line forty English miles), were called to give evidence; but had none to give. How is it possible that men like these, and at such a distance, could know anything except by vaguest hearsay.

6. It is not true that the Abyssinian was driven away for playing with children in front of the tents, but for the reasons above mentioned (4—*a*).

7. It is stated that Captain Burton and I went "armed" to the place where the quarrel was taking place.

My only weapon was a light riding-whip, and Captain Burton had none at all.

8. On our arrival the three Greeks are said to have taken flight, and shots were fired off behind them. This would imply that there were no more than three Geeeks present, whereas on our turning the corner of the churchyard-wall we found ourselves face to face with the whole mob; and then two pistol shots were there fired in the air to check them for a moment and allow us to retreat.

9. The untruth of Captain Burton having entered the church armed is repeated.

10. The unworthy and childish argument that the wound received by Habib el Jemayel were perhaps caused by stones thrown by Captain Burton's other three servants is too feeble to require an answer; but as these three men were wounded—one, viz. Mahommed Kawas, most dangerously, being laid up for three and a half months—is it supposed they wounded themselves? I myself, as did Captain Burton, saw them struck by several stones thrown by the Greeks.

11. The six men—Daud Sulayman, Jerius Dib, Jerius Azzam, Besharah Sakran, Yusuf Moammir, and Seman el Asfúr—deny that they were present; and the mazbatah states that there is no proof against them to show their presence there, and that nothing can be said against them.

When a deputation of Greeks waited on Captain Burton the day following the riot, and asked him not to go with the affair, Siman d'Assur accompanied them, and at a distance of some 50 metres from the tent, I recognized him as a man who had thrown a large stone deliberately at me, which had it hit, would in all probability have killed me. He was also recognized before the Kaimakam and Zabtiyeh by Captain Burton and by some of the servants as having taken an active part in the affray.

12. Elias Warwar deposes that he was struck down by one of the travellers with a club, but during the whole of Captain Burton's stay at Nazareth no Greek complained of being in the slightest degree injured. His brother, Jerius Warwar, states that his "kumbaz" (gown) was pierced by a small bullet fired by the travellers; this statement is a deliberate lie.

13. The Mazbatah finds fault with Captain Burton on these grounds:—

a. For complicating the affair by firing shots.

b. For entering armed and disrespectfully into the Church.

c. For dismissing the Onbashi (serjeant) and three Zabtiyeh, given as a guard on Thursday by the Government, and not keeping them later on the Friday than half an hour before the affray. This he did on purpose to be without Government guards at the moment of the riot.

a. The two pistol shots were, as I have before stated, (4—*b.*) not fired till the lives of Captain Burton, his servants, and myself, were in great danger, and then they were only fired in the air.

b. This I have already disproved (4—*c.*)

c. The Onbashi and three Zabtiyeh who had been on guard at Captain Burton's tents during the night, left, as I believe is customary, half an hour after sunrise, without either asking permission of or being dismissed by Captain Burton.

The base assertion that Captain Burton dismissed them for the purpose of being without Government guards at the time of the affray, insinuates that this was a pre-arranged riot got up by Captain Burton. If the tribunal really believed this, why did they condemn any of the Greeks to even the slightest punishment.

14. The Mazbatah considers that these altogether prove Captain Burton's extreme hatred and disdain for the Greeks, and say that he acted so to help the protestants "recently—that is for some years" established at Nazareth. The idea of this course of action, were the allegations true, being undertaken to "help the protestants," is too imbecile and spiteful to need any comments.

15. The Mazbatah states that Captain Burton called the Kaimakam several times into his presence, "as one calls a sergeant chowwish" (*sic.*).

This is untrue, as the Kaimakam (formerly pipe-bearer to Rashid Pasha) treated Captain Burton with civility, and he, as an English officer and gentleman, returned it.

16. The (Ottoman) Government is stated to have "condescended to comply for a time" with the request of Captain Burton that ten of the prisoners should be sent to Akka, and two to Damascus.

The late Wali Rashid Pasha gave orders to this effect. If it were illegal why did he do so? Was it that he intended to deny having given his sanction, and thus throw blame on the shoulders of his adversary, Captain Burton?

I do not now trouble your Excellency with the extent of the injuries sustained by Captain Burton's servants, and the still greater injustice offered to himself, but I feel sure that the perusal of the above will have shown your Excellency that the trial was conducted in a one-sided and partial manner.

Trusting to your Excellency's justice,

I am, your most obedient humble Servant,

CHARLES F. TYRWHITT DRAKE.

DAMASCUS,
November 11th, 1871.

My Lord,

I beg to enclose a copy of the protest which I have been obliged to send to the new Wali of Damascus with reference to the attack upon Captain Burton and his servants at Nazareth.

Your Lordship will perceive in what an insulting manner the sentence is worded, doubtless by order of the late infamous Wali, Raschid Pasha.

I shall not, though remaining in Palestine, be living much longer at Damascus, so I hope your Lordship will instruct H.M.'s representative here—who at present seems unwilling to do so—to prosecute the case to the utmost. If it be allowed to drop, English influence must be annihilated in this country, and serious, if not dangerous annoyances experienced by English travellers.

I remain, your Lordship's
Most obedient humble Servant,
CHAS. F. TYRWHITT DRAKE.

To the Right Hon. Earl Granville, K.G.,
&c., &c., &c,

NAZARETH,
February 23rd, 1871.

Dear Captain,

Since you left Syria I have not had the pleasure of hearing from you. No doubt your engagements made it impossible for you to write, yet I should be thankful to know whether my letters, with the enclosures from the Latin Convent, reached you.

Many important changes have taken place in Syria in consequeece of Ali Pasha's death. The misrule of the late Wali of Damascus has been exposed probably mainly through your energetic representations. The Foreign Office had opportunity to discover how false the impressions were under which they acted. It is inconceivable to me how the argument of the animosity of the Moslem population in Damascus could be used against you in England, for this is the old threadbare plea used in the Orient, in Turkey, as well as in China, whenever a foreigner is determined to expose the misrule of a powerful satrap.

On the 23rd of December I heard from Messrs. Finzi and Barbour, that the investigation against the Greeks was to be renewed. Soon afterwards, six of the offenders were imprisoned here, and Rauf Pasha, from Beyrout, set out to meet Mr. N. Moore from Jerusalem. But he received counter-orders, and I hear now that Mr. Moore has gone to Damascus, to which place Bishop Nifon from here was summoned about a week ago.

The six Greeks are still imprisoned here. Simaan Asfoor died in November.

The arrangement that the British Consulate of Damascus is to be only a Vice-Consulate is so contrary to British interests, and has elicited already such strong feelings on the part of English residents in Syria, that I can only regard it as *temporary.*

If the English Government wishes to make the recently announced reforms in Tarkey anything better than a sham, it must send you back to Syria, and, if it were possible, send a number of similar men with you. Nobody here believes in reforms, for every new Governor *begins* his office with ostentatious zeal for reform, and for strict justice and honesty, and *ends* his short career worse than his predecessor, leaving the country in a more hopeless condition than before.

I still trust that the sale of the twenty villages in the plain of Esdraëlon to Mr. Sursuk, of Beyrout, by the late Wali, will be looked into. The worst of this sale is this—that Sursuk and his agent, Tannoos Kawar, of Nazareth, extend the limits of the land bought by them as if they were india-rubber, and thus take the land of the neighbouring villages, and utterly ruin them. Yafa and Monjedel have already suffered so much that many houses are deserted.

The Greek Bishop Nifon began a crusade against the Protestants, and succeeded in preventing several Protestants from Keneh from cultivating their land, the possession of which was guaranteed to them by the local authorities, and by several orders from the Pasha of Acca.

I see from the papers that you are very busy in England, and I hope that you and Mrs. Burton enjoy perfect health. We had a good deal of illness in our family, else I should have written earlier. In October I was in Salt and Amman.

With mine and Mrs. Zeller's kind regards to Mrs. Burton,

I remain,

Dear Captain,

Yours very truly,

(Signed) JOHN ZELLER.

Captain R. Burton,
care of the Ottoman Bank,
Beyrout.

From a Greek (Orthodox) of position, showing the feelings of that large and influential body of Christians towards us.

A DAMAS,
Le 14 Novembre, 1871.

MADAME,

Ma lettre à Monsieur le capitaine vous apprendra les détails de mon séjour après votre départ. Il y a déjà cinq mois que nous nous sommes quittés, et je me reproche fortement de n'avoir pas encore pu vous écrire une lettre. L'orsque mon cousin m'avertit de Damas que vous êtes descendu à Beyrouth, je fis tout mon possible pour y aller vous voir. Veuillez, Madame, croire que pour moi et tous les hommes sensibles, la Syrie est comme un cadavre mort sans vous; vos amis ne vivent plus, tous vos amis sont persécutés, même Rashid Pasha m'a mis en prison puisque j'osai dire une fois que je suis protégé du Consul anglais, et à l'arrivée du nouveau Vali, je me suis rendu à lui, et il ordonna qu'on me livra vite. Le gérant anglais, Monsieur Jago, n'est à Damas que comme un homme sans signification, la Syrie ne respirera que lorsque le Capitaine Burton y présidera. Si le Gouvernement anglais désire que tous les Grecs et les autres Chrétiens de Syrie vivent en paix, il faut qu'il envoie le Capitaine Burton; il n'y a que lui qui sait se battre avec les ennemis du christianisme et rester ami avec les Moslems en même temps. Il est vraiment Capitaine; il ne demande que la justice, il ne recherche que la vérité; c'est un pasteur fidèle du troupeau de Jésus-Christ, il est un gardien vigilant de la vigne du Seigneur; il n'y a que lui, et lui seul, qui protège les droits des sujets anglais. Les juifs même se souviennent des bienfaits du capitaine, et ne font que dire, "Plût à Dieu qu'il retourne chez nous." Mais vous, Madame, vous étiez auprès de lui ce que la Sainte Vierge fut auprès de Jésus-Christ, vous ne faisiez qu'ajouter vos prières aux miennes, et vous priiez afin qu'il pardonne les prisonniers nazaréens; nous nous sommes donnés tant de peine pour leur faire du bien, et ces méchants me médisent toujours, et surtout ce Monsieur l'évêque, dont le visage me paraît semblable à celui d'un brigand, et pas d'un ministre du Seigneur. Madame, souvenez-vous que je vous appelais toujours ma protectrice et ma sœur, cependant vous m'avez laissé pauvre et orphelin, sans secours, sans aide. Je ne veux plus rester à Damas sans vous et le Capitaine; tâcher donc de revenir, ou bien cherchez-moi une place en Angleterre pour que je puisse venir vivre parmi les gens instruits et civilisés; c'est ma plus grande punition de me trouver au milieu d'un ignorant peuple: ils ne différent point des animaux. Mais à qui me plaindre? Que faut-il que je fasse pour vous faire revenir? A qui faut-il écrire? Je ne connais que M. Kennedy. Je ne fais que réciter tous le soirs mon chapelet priant la Sainte-Vierge pour votre retour; tout ce que dépend de moi je le ferais avec le plus grand plaisir. Madame, ici tout le monde vous regrette; tout le monde se souvient et raconte tout ce que votre conscience chrétienne faisait aux malheureux. Vos pauvres Kawass toutes les fois qu'ils me rencontrent me demandent, le cœur ému : Est-elle partie ? Quand reviendra-t-elle ? Il n'y a pas comme elle. Petits et grands espèrent vous voir un jour comme un soleil éclairer le ciel obscur de Damas et de Syrie ! Pourquoi les ministres anglais paraissent-ils maintenant tellement indifférents pour nos intérêts ? M. Drake a eu la bonté de m'inviter dimanche à dîner ensemble ; croyez, Madame, que j'allais pleurer, car la maison me paraissent toute à fait froide et tranquille, et se taisait elle-même pour montrer sa tristesse à cause de l'absence de sa maîtresse.

Veuillez, Madame, agréer l'expression de mes sentiments distingués, et l'hommage de mes respectueuses civilités.

Votre très-obéissant serviteur,
(Signed)   L'ABBÉ * * * * * * *

FOREIGN OFFICE,
March 27, 1872.

SIR,

I am directed by Earl Granville to transmit to you herewith a copy of a Minute which his lordship has received from Mr. Consul Moore relative to the result of the inquiry made by himself and Soubhi Pasha into the facts connected with the affray at Nazareth.

I am to add that it has been arranged that the indemnity money should, on its receipt from Nazareth, be paid over to Mr. Vice-Consul Green for distribution amongst those of your servants who were injured in the affray.

I am, Sir,
Your most obedient, humble servant,
(Signed)   ENFIELD.

Captain R. Burton.

H.M. CONSULATE, JERUSALEM,
February 15th, 1872.

SIR,

Referring to my despatch of the 18th ult., I have the honour to report the termination of the inquiry, held at Damascus by H.E. the Governor-General and myself, into facts connected with the affray at Nazareth, resulting in the condemnation of the principal offenders to three months' imprisonment, the secondary to two months, exclusively of the thirty-five to forty days' incarceration they had already undergone at Damascus and here, and the payment of a fine of five thousand piastres, as compensation to Captain Burton's injured servants.

On the 30th January I telegraphed to you from Damascus the redress I had obtained, adding that it was subject to your approval, and inquiring whether I might return to my post, after making arrangements for the due execution of the sentence. Having waited ten days for a reply, I feared that some error might, as sometimes happens, have altered the meaning of my telegram. Venturing to think the reparation obtained quite satisfactory, I returned to Jerusalem.

Soubhi Pasha was very sore about the discharge of firearms by Captain Burton, and because certain of the Greeks charged with being amongst the assailants were bound together and taken to Acre on foot, which, so far as I could ascertain, appears to have been the case. Moreover, the Greeks had been already subjected to the expense of journeying between Nazareth, Acre, and Damascus, and to detention of about forty days at the latter places.

I felt bound to take these various circumstances into consideration in discussing with Soubhi Pasha the degree of punishment to be inflicted, and agreed to some diminution of that which I had originally demanded.

Soubhi Pasha referred to the accusation directed against Captain Burton, of having entered and profaned the Greek church. To this I replied that I must absolutely reject the charge until it be proved, and that if it be insisted upon I must have clear evidence; and should proceed to Nazareth to investigate the matter on the spot. At our next meeting Soubhi Pasha agreed with me in considering the accusation as false.

It was arranged that the indemnity money should, on its receipt from Nazareth, be paid over to Mr. Vice-Consul Green for distribution amongst the injured servants.

On my arrival here I communicated with Mr. C. Tyrwhitt Drake, the companion of Captain Burton on the occasion in question, and requested him to inform me who and how many the attendants were, and in what proportion he considered the money should be paid to each, with reference to the greater or less severity of the hurt he sustained. I have received Mr. Drake's answer, and will communicate it to Mr. Green for his information and guidance in effecting the distribution.

I have also requested the Rev. Mr. Zeller, of Nazareth, to see that the sentence of imprisonment is duly carried out.

I beg leave to enclose a translation of the Minute signed by the Governor-General and myself, recording the result of the inquiry.

It only remains for me to record my high sense of the frankness, courtesy, and friendliness with which his Excellency Soubhi Pasha met me, and which greatly contributed to the speedy and satisfactory solution arrived at.

           I have &c., &c.,
            (Signed) NOEL TEMPLE MOORE.

H. Rumbold, Esq.,
  H.M. Chargé d'Affaires,
    Constantinople.

CASE No. 5.

THE WALI (GOVERNOR GENERAL) RASHID PASHA.

The Druzes having paid me several friendly visits, and frequently begged me to call upon them in the Hauran, I was anxious to keep up neighbourly relations, I also wished to copy Greek inscriptions and to explore volcanos which the road would show. I was not aware that the Wali Governor-General had a political move in the Hauran which he did not wish me to see, or that, seeing, it was to be the signal for him to try and obtain my recall. On the contrary, I thought it was both the wish of himself and Mr. Consul-General Eldridge that I should go. Some time previously H.M.'s Secretary of State for Foreign Affairs had kindly telegraphed sick leave to me, but I was unable to use it till the end of March, 1871, for reasons which can be satisfactorily explained, if required. I took advantage of that leave by passing the Holy Week at Jerusalem, and I ended by visiting the Hauran, which is within the jurisdiction of Damascus, simply as an act of courtesy to the Druzes. Anxious not to offend anybody by omitting them, nor to lose time, I tried to make a general rendezvous at the house of the principal religious Shaykh, which should be considered common ground, and I addressed them a note, which has been strangely altered.

I called upon Rashid Pasha before my departure, and spoke freely of my projected visit. He expressed his gladness, saying, "Go soon, or there will be no water." I then wrote to Mr. Eldridge, who had often proposed to make the excursion with me, but he did not answer me. On the 24th of May, 1871, accompanied by Mr. Charles F. Tyrwhitt Drake, who was fortunately a witness of all my words and actions, I set out, little suspecting what was prepared for me upon the strength of my few days' trip.

The despatches attached to this case are:—

A letter the Wali addressed to Mrs. Burton, 31st May, 1871.
A despatch the Wali addressed to Captain Burton, 7th June, 1871.
Captain Burton's reply, 8th June, 1871.
Captain Burton to Sir H. Elliot, 9th June, 1871.
Captain Burton to Sir H. Elliot, 11th June, 1871.
Copy of the true letter addressed by Captain Burton to the Druzes, and the one altered by the Wali to suit the case.

The only two letters that passed between Captain and Mrs. Burton whilst the former was in the Hauran and the latter at Damascus are put in, because Captain Burton was said to have written the success of his political schemes to Mrs. Burton, and to have sent them into Damascus by Shaykh Hamzeh, an old Druze. The Wali pretended to have captured that correspondence, as proof against Captain Burton.

C. F. Tyrwhitt Drake to Earl Granville, July 8th, 1871.
Captain Burton to Earl Granville, July 21st, 1871.

DAMAS,
Le 31 Mai, 1871.

MADAME,

J'ai l'honneur de vous annoncer d'une manière tout à fait privée et confidentielle que M. Burton en se rendant dans le Hauran a fait une grande réunion des Druzes et de leurs chefs religieux. Vous n'êtes pas sans ignorer que pour faire rentrer les troupeaux de moutons que ces derniers avaient enlevés des environs de Djebel-Calemoun nous avons éprouvés beaucoup de difficultés, et nous avons même dû avoir recours à la menace pour arriver à un résultat satisfaisant. La dite réunion opérée par M. Burton nous a fait beaucoup de tort, et je ne serai nullement surpris de voir les Druzes changer de tactique à la suite de cette réunion. Vous savez que les gens de ce pays-ci sont d'une crédulité extrême et attachent facilement de l'importance à une chose bien simple. J'apprends en outre qu'à la suite de cette réunion M. Burton aurait proposé aux Druzes de lui présenter une pétition dans le but de demander la protection de la Grande Bretagne. Si avant son départ pour le Hauran M. Burton m'avait entretenu de son projet, je l'aurais certainement dissuadé d'éviter cette réunion, qui pour nous peut avoir des conséquences fâcheuses. De plus, M. Burton a demandé au Mutessarif du Hauran l'emprisonnement de deux individus qui, sans avoir obtenu la permission de M. le Consul d'Angleterre, se sont assis dans la même chambre que lui. Je pense qu'une simple réprimande suffisait pour des gens qui, en entrant dans une maison de paysan, ne savaient pas rencontrer le Consul d'Angleterre, et qui n'ont aucune notion des manières des salons et du grand monde.

Veuillez agréer, Madame, l'assurance de mes sentiments les plus distingués.

(Signed) RASHID.

[COPY.]

GOUVERNEMENT GENERAL DU VILAYET DE SYRIE,

DAMAS,
Le 7 Juin, 1871:

MONSIEUR LE CONSUL,

Lors de mon arrivée en Syrie, la tranquillité était loin de régner, comme aujourd'hui, dans le Hauran. Le pillage, le vol, les déprédations, étaient à l'ordre du jour. Les auteurs de ces méfaits—ai-je besoin de les nommer?—étaient les Bédouins et les Druzes. Leurs chefs ne connaissaient l'autorité du Vali; ne venaient jamais à Damas qu'avec des Rai-aman et d'autres précautions, qui indiquaient combien leur méfiance était grande. Rendre au pays le calme et la sécurité dont il était privé; convaincre les Druzes des intentions bienveillantes du Gouvernement Impérial, les forcer au besoin à reconnaître l'autorité, les habituer au paiement des impôts, prendre aux Bédouins les garanties pour assurer la non-violation de leurs promesses, tel est le but vers lequel ont tendu tous mes efforts; ce n'est pas à moi à dire si j'ai réussi, mais Damas vit un jour avec surprise Ismael Attrache accepter l'hospitalité que je lui avais offerte. Depuis, tous les chefs Druzes ont marché sur les traces de leur vieux chef, et sans aucune formalité et à notre premier appel, ils se sont toujours empressés de se rendre à Damas. Nos rapports avec eux n'ont pas cessé d'être sur un pied convenable.

Le moyen auquel j'ai eu recours pour obtenir cet heureux résultat, ce fut d'empêcher les Druzes d'entretenir toute espèce de rapports avec les agents étrangers, et notamment avec le Consulat d'Angleterre. Lors des événements de 1860, la responsabilité qui pesait sur les Druzes excita probablement la pitié et l'indulgence du Commissaire anglais. Les Druzes interpretèrent tout autrement les sentiments de M. le Commissaire; ils s'imaginèrent dans leur simplicité que l'Angleterre les couvrait d'une protection toute spéciale. De là, ils ont constamment étudié les faits et gestes des Consuls anglais de Damas, et leur ont attribué une signification qu'ils n'avaient certes pas. C'est ce que je fis comprendre à M. Rogers qui, abondant dans mon sens et dans mes idées, fut très-circonspect à l'avenir; il cessa toute espèce de rapports avec les Druzes, tandis que vos relations avec eux devenaient de jour en jour plus aisées.

Dans un pareil état de choses, je ne vous dissimulerai pas que j'ai été vivement peiné de voir que vous avez entrepris un voyage dans le Djebel Druse, et que vous vous y êtes fait annoncer par une lettre officielle.

J'ignore le but que vous vous êtes proposé dans cette excursion, mais certes les Druzes et le Hauran y ont aperçu un tout autre que celui que vous aviez en vue. J'ai déjà dit quelle opinion erronée ont les Druzes vis-à-vis des dispositions de l'Angleterre à leur égard. Bien différent eut été votre voyage, Monsieur le Consul, si vous aviez bien voulu me le faire connaître d'avance, et si les Druzes et le Hauran vous avaient vue accompagné d'un officier du Gouvernement.

Tout recemment les Druzes, témoins impuissants de la violation de leur " Lejáa," qu'ils croyaient impénétrable, ont vu s'évanouir jusqu'à la dernière trace de leur prestige. Il eût été politique de les laisser dans cette impression de découragement. Et c'est dans une circonstance pareille que vous faites un voyage au milieu d'eux.

On me rapporte que vous avez été chez les Druzes pour les reconcilier; si le fait est vrai c'est une démarche très-grave, et il aurait fallu pressentir à ce sujet les dispositions du Vilayet.

Ainsi, M. le Consul, quelque soit le but d'un voyage entrepris à l'insu de l'autorité, et accompli au milieu d'une peuplade demi-soumise, et dans les circonstances que je viens de rappeler, je ne puis que ne le point approuver, et je crois devoir même vous exprimer les regrets que j'en ai éprouvés.

Veuillez agréer, M. le Consul, l'assurance de ma considération distinguée.

(Signed)   RASHID.

A M. Burton, Consul de S.M. Britannique à Damas.

[COPY.]

H.B.M. CONSULATE, DAMASCUS,
8 Juin, 1871.

EXCELLENCE,

J'ai l'honneur d'accuser reception de votre pièce officielle du 7 Juin, dont le contente m'a surpris au plus haut degré.

Personne ne connaît mieux que moi la tranquillité que les sages mesures du Gouvernement impérial ont fait régner dans le Hauran. Mais j'ignorais, et j'ignore encore, qu'un simple voyage avec but de faire un retour de visites, de copier quelques inscriptions, et de passer par un pays inhabité (Le Diret el Tulul) aurait pu troubler cette sécurité.

Depuis vingt mois M. Eldridge, auquel d'ailleurs j'annonçai mon intention, m'avait proposé de faire ce voyage avec moi; le Consul-Général ne fit rien comprendre à l'égard de M. Rogers. M. Wetzstein, ancien Cousul de Prusse, voyagea comme moi dans le Lejáa et dans le

Safa, et bien sûr il ne fut pas accompagné par un officier du Gouvernement. Kanawát et les autres ruines sont annuellement visitées par des touristes européens. La dite lettre qui me précéda n'avait autre intention que de réunir les Shaykhs afin de leur rendre visite sans perte de temps. Je ne pense pas que les Druzes ont besoin d'être reconciliés, et, certes, je n'aurais entrepris une démarche si grave sans les instructions de mon Gouvernement.

Enfin, Excellence, je n'ai qu'à regretter votre résolution évidente d'attribuer à un simple voyage sans conséquences, des vues et des intentions qui n'ont jamais existé.

Veuillez agréer, Excellence, l'assurance de ma considération la plus distinguée.

(Signed)   R. F. BURTON,
H.B.M.'s Consul, Damascus.

A son Excellence, Rashid Pasha,
Gouverneur-Général du Vilayet de Syrie, &c., &c.,
Damas.

[COPY.]

From Captain Burton to Sir Henry Elliot.

H.B.M. Consulate, Damascus,
June 9th, 1871.

SIR,

I think it my duty to bring to your Excellency's notice the state of affairs actually existing in Northern Syria.

As I have already reported (No. 5. May 20th, 1871) the administration of the police and the protection of the city and its environs are left wholly in the hands of the Mir Alai Mustafa Bey, a man of noted incapacity and unusual fanaticism. His second in command is one Abdullah Agha, a negro who, under the direction of his chief, encourages the conversion of Christians to Mahommedanism, and the feelings of the former, Greeks as well as Latins, are very strong upon this point. At the same time Bedouin raids are becoming the order of the day, and one has just been announced to me as having penetrated to within a few miles of Damascus.

During the last few months various reports about complications between the Sublime Porte and Egypt have caused the people of Syria to believe that the Khedive awaits only an opportunity to declare himself independent; and it is the general idea that Syria will take part with Egypt. The conduct of the Wali Governor-General of Syria, His Excellency Rashid Pasha, who belongs to the family of Mohammed Ali, has contributed not a little to increase popular excitement. He has now held office for six years (since 1866), during which time he has amassed an immense fortune, and has allowed his partizans to follow his example. He has systematically dismissed all those who will not be the mere instruments of his will—for instance, Abd-el-Hadi Pasha, late of Beyrout and of Hamah. He has filled up all the most important posts with his own creatures: for instance, the Governor of Nazareth (Khurshid Agha) was his pipe-bearer. In order to make himself master of the situation he placed the Post-office in the hands of the Turkish authorities, and the privacy of letters has ever since been openly violated. A copy of every telegram is forwarded at once to head-quarters. It is the prevalent idea that the policy of Rashid Pasha is suspected by the Porte, and that Ali Bey Bala was sent to Jerusalem in an independent position in order to counteract the dangerous influence of the Governor-General. But the latter contrives to make interest at Constantinople by means of many friends, notably of Saib Effendi, whose son married his daughter, and the result is he retains his appointment.

To Europeans and European subjects His Excellency Rashid Pasha has shown himself invariably hostile. He declares openly that he has removed the Italian Consul (M. Pilastri), the Russian Consul (M. Ionine), and the Spanish Vice-consul (M. Rivadeneyra), because they would not become his tools. He is now intriguing with all his strength against this Consulate, and he adopts the plan of affecting to believe all the false reports which he has himself originated. The Druzes of the Hauran, having paid me many visits, and wishing to return them I left Damascus on the 25th ultimo, after writing to the Shaykhs that I desired to meet them all. We met, and I found them in great excitement, expecting to be attacked by His Excellency the Wali. I calmed them by assuring them incidentally that they had nothing to fear, and openly exhorted them to act like peaceful and loyal subjects of the Porte. His Excellency affects to believe that my visit had for object some political intrigue. It is reported that he is preparing to attack the Druzes in their fastnesses, the Leja and in the Jebel Druze Hauran, and he would willingly charge me with having rendered this expedition necessary. I may briefly show the animus of Rashid Pasha against all European *protégés* by quoting an order lately issued in this Vilayet : " None but Rayyahs are henceforth allowed to buy the ushr or Dime of the villagers, and all villagers who enter into such transactions with foreigners are to be accountable for disobeying this order." A French *protégé* has thus been compelled to renounce his foreign nationality. I need not point out the retrograde and anti-progressive nature of such a step, especially in these days when Turkey affects to encourage immigration.

No English subject or *protégé* can expect justice in Damascus. The Protestant cemetery has again been violated; the violaters were detected, and have been allowed to escape unpunished.

Two English subjects, the Affghans Mohammed and Ahmed were condemned without the presence of a Consular Dragoman, and though I have had a lengthy correspondence upon this subject I cannot obtain a revision of the sentence thus pronounced contrary to the capitulations. Upon the subject of the large debt owed to M. Zelmina Fuchs, and the village taken from M. Hanna Misk, I shall be compelled again to address your Excellency The Bagdad postman was robbed by the Ruwalla Bedouins during the last winter, and Colonel Herbert, H.M. Consul-General for Bagdad, has applied for compensation to the extent of sixty-six ghazi and a half. This sum I have been for months attempting to recover, but in vain. An English caravan led by Mr. Gaze was plundered when passing through Kunaytirah of goods estimated at thirty-one pounds stirling (£31); I have applied for the amount, but no answer has been returned. For many months I have been writing to his Excellency about the claims of a British protected subject, Khawajah Yakub Smouha, who demands seven thousand piastres (T. p. 7000), the value of his merchandise plundered about a year ago from a Bagdad caravan by the Bedouin in this neighbourhood. I cannot even obtain a reply. A Maltese surgeon, Dr. Dupont, having been compelled to send in his resignation, applied through this Consulate for his arrears of pay, I sent a Consular Dragoman to request liquidation, and the enclosed report will show how he was received.

In conclusion, I would warn your Excellency that this part of Syria is at present in a state of abnormal excitement. The Latins and Greeks are upon the worst of terms, and the Mahommedans are equally hostile to both; whilst the policy of the Governor-General is evidently to discourage all manner of bad feeling and to thwart those who would allay it. My best exertions have been devoted to the task of keeping peace and order, nor shall they cease so long as my services are required. This is the only Consulate at Damascus which at present maintains a shadow of independence; and I venture to hope that your Excellency will understand the reason should vexatious reports be circulated about it.

I have the honour to remain,

Your Excellency's

Obedient, humble Servant,

(Signed)   R. F. BURTON.

[COPY.]

From Captain Burton to Sir Henry Elliot.
H.B.M. Consulate, Damascus,
June 11th, 1871.

Sir,

I have honour to draw your Excellency's attention to the following circumstances :—

The whole of northern Syria has been, and is still, discussing the probability of an attack upon the Jebel Druze Hauran. The Druzes are of course well acquainted with these rumours. They have spies in all directions, who inform them that a Firman, whose contents are kept secret, has lately arrived from the Serai. They know that the local press, especially the Hadikat el Akbar, which is salaried by Government, has in many late issues advised strong measures against them. They remember that in 1869 his Excellency Rashid Pasha successfully attacked the Bedouins about Salt, and that in 1870 he led an overwhelming force into the Nusayri Mountains. They are aware of troops, now 6000, being massed on the Dimas Plain, within eleven kilometres of this city; and when told that it is merely a summer camp for exercise, they ask why men are collected from Beyrout, Tripoli, and other places. They have a report that biscuit is being baked in secret, and that tents are about to be sent from Damascus at night. They know that the Mutissarif of the Hauran, Mohammed Bey el Yusuf, has been sent to their stronghold, the Leja, and that the Mutissarif of Damascus, Ibrahim Pasha, has been carrying out certain high-handed measures amongst the Druzes in and about Hasbeyya. And finally, there is a report that H.E. the Wali proposed to visit in person the Jebel Druze Hauran.

As far back as October, 1869, H.E. Rashid Pasha had prepared to carry out by force his favourite project of reducing the Druzes of the Eastern Mountains. He has since that time often complained to me that the Druzes do not pay their taxes regularly, and has openly declared his determination to put their country upon the same footing as the rest of Syria. This means simply the levying of recruits—a measure which will be resisted by the whole Druze people, *forcibly* if necessary.

Should a campaign take place in Jebel Druze Hauran, the inhabitants will be joined by the fighting men of the Libanus, the Anti-Libanus, and the Hermon. The country is eminently fitted for defence, and the Druzes, though badly armed, are brave, and animated by the memory of past victories. Should the Governor-General be defeated, the results will be serious disturbances throughout this province, where his rule is hated except by the few whom he allows to make large fortunes out of the public revenues, and the danger to the Christian population generally, especially to the European *protégés*, will be imminent. I will not dwell upon the fact that for centuries—indeed, almost since the days of the Crusades—Great Britain has ever extended a kind of unofficial protection to the Druze people, and that they still hold us to be, " under Allah, their only friends." They are, indeed, the sole source of influence left to us in Syria, where our interests have, since 1840, been so persistently neglected. H.E. the Governor-General is perfectly aware of this, and his firm resolution to crush all European *prestige*, especially that of England, since he has ceased to fear France, is another stimulus to attack the Druses of the Hauran.

In the enclosed copy of his Despatch (7th June, 1871) His Excellency has completely shown his game, and from my reply (Enclosure No. 2) he will probably see that I have understood it. He knows that I am narrowly watching his proceedings, and he would silence me by any means possible. The " official letter " of which he complains was a note publicly written in the Chancellerie to the Druze Shaykhs, who were complaining that I had not returned their repeated visits. It requested them to meet me at Kanawat, a central point, annually visited by travellers and tourists, as I could not afford time to visit them severally. In order to avoid any semblance of political action, I lodged only with the principal Akkáls (religious men), Hosayn Ibrahim, and Ali el Hinawi, both of whom I have long known intimately. I could have no idea of reconciliating the Druzes, because I ignored that any reconciliation was required! I was careful to be accompanied everywhere by Mr. Charles F. Tyrwhitt Drake, and when called upon as customary to address the Shaykhs, I recommended them in a few words to be peaceful and loyal subjects.

It is incredible that my predecessor, Mr. Rogers, should, as stated in the Governor-General's Despatch, have abandoned all manner of intercourse with the Druzes, nor can I see the reason why, at a time when profound peace is supposed to reign, I should be escorted by a Government official to watch my proceedings. His Excellency also forgets that I verbally announced to him my intention of visiting the Druze country, and of returning by the desert road. He was probably not aware that Mr. Consul-General Eldridge, during the last twenty months, had proposed that I should accompany him on a tour to the mountain, and that before leaving Damascus I wrote to him at Beyrout, whence a telegram would at once have recalled me.

The fact is, His Excellency Rashid Pasha, as the enclosed Despatch shows, was irritated by the knowledge that I had foreseen his projects, and would certainly report them to your Excellency. He therefore adopts the transparent plan of turning my visit to the mountain into a political step, which, duly misunderstood by the Druzes, may necessitate a course of action to which he has long been looking forward. His feelings towards me, because I have preserved my independence, are well known to Her Majesty's Foreign Office, and he hopes by collecting trivial complaints with as little delay as possible, to injure me in the estimation of your Excellency. He would then find the field clear for his career of ambition, a career which due regard for the integrity of the Turkish Empire requires to be arrested.

I have the honour to be, Sir,
Your Excellency's obedient, humble servant,
(Signed) R. F. BURTON.

Real Copy Translated.	False Copy translated by the Wali.
To the Shaykhs of the renowned Druze Mountain.	Traduction d'une lettre adressée par le Consul Britannique, en date du 22 Mai, 1871 (3 Juin), aux Cheikhs Druzes du Hauran.
After the usual compliments, we want to inform you that this time the wish to visit you has moved us, and to take the direction of your country.	Après les compliments d'usage, *je m'empresse* de vous informer que, animé *du désir de m'entretenir* avec vous, je quitterai Damas mercredi *pour vous rejoindre*, et que j'arriverai *ce jour même* à Hedjan, et le lendemain à *Lahita*, et le troisième à Finvate. Je nourris l'espoir que vous ne manquerez pas *tous* de venir me rencontrer au dit village de *Finvate, afin de prendre part à cette entrevue.*
For which reason we will leave Damascus on the Wednesday, and sleep at Hejaneh; the second day at Lahtah, and the third at Kanawát.	
We therefore hope that you will meet us in the above-mentioned place that we may see you.	
This one is a simple general *return visit* to the visits of the Druzes, not to waste time in going to each man's house, nor to make jealousies by singling out some and neglecting others.	This one *adds in* all the words that are dashed, to give it a semblance of a secret political meaning.

The only two letters that passed between Captain and Mrs. Burton whilst the former was in the Hauran and Mrs. Burton in Damascus.

SHAHKA,
Friday, June 2nd, 1871.

These notes will probably both be opened. This one is taken by old Shaykh Hamzeh, the Druze. Be civil to the old boy; also give him some medicine.

1. A little quinine in very small doses for a sucking child, in packets half a grain each.

2. A little eye salve for the old man.

3. A strong purge and four big doses of quinine for a grown-up man. Also ample directions how to use it. Make Khamoor write them in Arabic.

Drake sends his watch and wants it at once repaired. The best man is a Jew whom Nasif Meshaka knows. Order it to be done directly.

I hope you keep a look-out on the Greeks.

&c., &c., &c.,

R. F. B.

SHAHKA,
Same day, Friday, June 2nd.

Old Amin Agha brings this. He rides the Rahwán whose tail wants doctoring; two bran mashes and cooling treatment, very little grain (two Tumniyyehs) a day, one in morning, other in afternoon.

Send letters to house of Rashid the postman, at Dumayr. We shall be there probably on the 7th. Drake quite well. We have suffered a little from the cold. Enquire about Mrs. Wright for me.

The old boy has behaved very well, but I can't take him to a place of very hard work; and we are going to do the volcanoes.

Ever, &c.,

R. F. B.

Copy of a Letter to LORD GRANVILLE from C. F. TYRWHITT DRAKE.

DAMASCUS,
July 8th, 1871.

MY LORD,

I consider it my duty as an eye witness to address you on the subject of the attack made on Captain Burton's servants by the Greek Catholics at Nazareth, as I find that H. E. the Wali has misrepresented the matter in a gross way, shewing the animus which has prompted him to use this and Captain Burton's excursion to the Hauran for his own political ends.

Having obtained some insight into eastern ways of thought and action during several years travel, I have less diffidence in vouching for these facts to your Lordship than one unacquainted with the language and people would have, and my present work on behalf of the Palestine Exploration Fund induces me to mix much with the people.

As I was travelling at the time with Captain Burton, and saw the whole of the affair at Nazareth, and am thoroughly acquainted with the proceedings which have taken place since I can shew that the telegram sent to Constantinople by H. E. the Wali two days befor, Captain Burton's return to Damascus, is a malicious perversion of the truth. His Excellency of couse, only heard the Greek side, and was too glad to be able to report to Captain Burton's detriment such a (seemingly) grave matter. I forwarded an account of the *émeute* to Sir H. Elliot, H.B.M.'s Ambassador Extraordinary at Constantinople (on June 8th, 1871), as I knew that absurdly false reports had been sent with the Wali's knowledge and sanction. Had I known that an official in his high position would have personally attacked Captain Burton behind his back in such a dastardly and ungentlemanly way, I should have taken the liberty of writing to your Lordship as well.

I also accompanied Captain Burton for the few days that he was in the Hauran, and was present at *every* interview, long or short, that he held with the Druzes: on one occasion his advice was asked respecting the course of action they ought to follow. He shortly replied that they must submit to the Turkish Government, and that it would be madness to oppose it. To this they agreed. Except in these few minutes politics were never touched upon.

Our trip to the Hauran was simply devoted to geographical and antiquarian researches, but at the same time we naturally desired to see something of the people, and Captain Burton, not wishing to be away from Damascus more than a few days, invited some of the shaykhs to meet us at Kanawát as we could not spare time to visit them separately. This they were very glad to do.

As regards the telegram sent by His Excellency Rashid Pasha to the Vizier at Constantinople on May 4-16, 1871, I beg leave to observe to your Lordship that the passage, "*Un rassemblement d'enfants encombrait les abords de l'Eglise. Une querelle s'éleva entre ces enfants et les domestiques du Consul,*" gives an utterly false impression. We camped about 80 yards from the outer wall surrounding the church, and at least 160 from the entrance to the church. The children never meddled or were meddled with. The Copt who came up to the tents and wished to enter Mrs. Burton's before she was up, and refused to go away till compelled by the servants, and thus began the disturbance, was at least eighteen or nineteen years old. The continuation, "*Ce dernier (i.e., le Consul) s'étant armé pour prendre part à la querelle et s'étant servi de ces armes contre les Grecs,*" can only be designated as a lie. Captain Burton and I, hearing the disturbance, which was behind the church wall—as the Greeks had decoyed the servants thither—ran down half dressed in our slippers, and unarmed. I can only admire and praise Captain Burton's coolness in firing one shot only over the heads of the mob with a pistol which one of the servants had, and which was the only one amongst the whole party in the riot. Again, the sentence, "*Quelques uns des domestiques furent légèrement blessés,*" can also only be stigmatized as a lie, which the Wali has since tried to prove true by the testimony of two (self-entitled) doctors, whose testimony is so absurd as to prove its own falsehood. Two of the servants lay for several days unable to move, and one continued to spit blood till after his return to Damascus. The Kawas, an Afghan, complained to me (as I mentioned in my letter to Sir H. Elliot) of being severely struck in the groin, but was too brave to lay up for it. Since the date of that letter he has been near death's door, with a very bad gangrened rupture (I speak as an eye witness), but is happily now recovering.

The telegram goes on to state that extenuating circumstances are found in the fact that the attack upon the Consul's person was not made with arms. Large stones, however, when thrown by a mob of 100 to 150 men, at the distance of a few feet, are weapons of offence not to be despised. The only wonder I can feel is that none of our party were killed.

As regards the *exaction* made by the Consul for the prisoners to be taken to Damascus, I beg deferentially to suggest that it was in the power of the Turkish authorities to refuse to accede to Captain Burton's request if it were not *en régle*, and I think it cannot but suggest itself as a snare set by H. E. Rashid Pasha. Again, the Christians are said to have protested their innocence, declaring that they were provoked on a fête day by the Consul shooting at them with bullets. The latter part is a double lie, as they were neither shot at nor did they say so at Nazareth. Of course they protested their innocence—as criminals usually do—but the accused were thoroughly identified; several whose identification was doubtful were instantly dismissed.

There was a certain amount of feeling against Captain Burton on the part of the Greeks for his having opposed their lawless appropriation of the site of an old synagogue at Tiberias, which clearly was Jewish property. The Wali, too, favours the Greeks in every way, and aids them in trampling upon the Latins, who have suffered severely by the downfall of France. Captain Burton is naturally hated by His Excellency the Wali, as being the only man in the country—I speak advisedly and the same will be found to be the opinions of all educated natives who have the true interests of Syria at heart, and do not look on the country with the eyes of a Turkish official burning with lust of peculation—the only man who has the wit to foresee and the courage to oppose acts of the Wali, which, if carried out, would bring ruin or a massacre on Syria. From personal experience I can state that the country is in such an abnormal excited state that any injudicious act of the Wali might light a fire which he would be quite unable to quench.

In conclusion, I may say that wherever I have been, as I have through the length and breadth of the country, I never heard a good word spoken for H.E. Rashid Pasha, or a bad one against H.M.'s Consul for Damascus. The general prayer—often confidently addressed to me—throughout the whole Vilayet of Syria is that Captain Burton's influence might be extended by making Damascus a Consulate-General, and that the present Governor-General, Rashid Pasha, may be removed; for, say the people, "we cannot in any way lose, and we probably shall gain by the change; for it is hardly likely that another man can be found who will so systematically plunder our country and depopulate our villages to fill his own pockets." The enormous amount of bribes taken by His Excellency is so notorious and undeniable, that it is quite superfluous for me to draw your Lordship's attention to it; but it renders his hatred and opposition to H.M.'s Consul quite intelligible as directed against a man who will neither accept bribes, nor, when he has it in his power, suffer others to do so, and who energetically demands that commodity so distasteful to Turkish officials—viz., simple justice.

Hoping that your Lordship will consider this letter of sufficient importance to excuse its length,

Your Lordship's obedient, humble Servant,
(Signed) CHARLES F. TYRWHITT DRAKE.

No. 28. (Copy sent to both Foreign Office and Embassy.)

H.B.M.'s Consulate, Damascus,
July 21st, 1871.

My Lord,

I have been informed that great exception has been taken to my not having reported at once to your Lordship the assaults upon my servants at Nazareth, and that this omission has been looked upon as an omission of duty. I have therefore the honour to lay this statement before you.

Nazareth is not connected by telegraph with the rest of the province; and even if it had been, the state of the telegraph office is such that my telegram must have come before the Governor-General, who would probably have tampered with it. The post-office is in the same condition, except that letters are not tampered with, but destroyed. I was not at the time aware of the extent of Rashid Pasha's animus against me; and looking upon the assault as a village disturbance, I thought that it would easily be settled by the punishment of the offenders at Damascus. All around me were of the same opinion: no one imagined that the affair would be used as a manœuvre to satisfy private revenge. Arrived at the capital of Syria, I was again delayed by wishing to obtain the evidence of the Rev. Mr. Taylor and his fellow travellers before submitting the case to Sir Henry Elliot. I have reported the unjust action taken by the local Government in the defence of the Nazareth people; and unless your Lordship allows me to see justice done to myself by remaining at Damascus till the case be determined in my favour, or by appealing to Constantinople if justice be withheld, I shall not only sustain the greatest possible injury, but also the unworthy intrigues of Rashid Pasha, such as sending, two days before my arrival, a telegram to Constantinople endorsing every Greek fiction as fact, will completely triumph. I need hardly say that the English name will suffer throughout Syria worse than I shall myself.

I am also informed that my expedition to the Hauran was not desired to take place. I again venture to solicit your Lordship's attention to the fact that this journey had been purposed at least a year and a half ago by Mr. Consul-General Eldridge and myself. Moreover, that before setting out I spoke of it when visiting Rashid Pasha, who did not offer the least objection. His report to Constantinople was the most transparent effort to rid himself of a man who has opposed his unjust and rapacious measures; and the secret of his hostility will be found, in the six millions of piastres which I claim from him in liquidation of British creditors.

I have the honour to be,
My Lord,
Your most obedient, humble Servant,
(Signed) RICHARD F. BURTON,
H.B.M.'s Consul, Damascus.

CASE No. 6.

MISCELLANEOUS.

I have every reason to believe that my chief fault in the eyes of Rashid Pasha was pushing the just claims of British subjects, amounting to six millions of piastres, an explanation of which follows.

Then follows the case of Haj Hasan, who was a Moslem, and became a Christian, and some account of the religious persecution in Syria.

The case of Mr. Hanna Azar comes next. He was a Consular Dragoman who, having convicted the Wali in the Divan of an untruth, incurred his hatred. His Excellency denied his signature to a certain document, whereupon Mr. Azar held it up. As he had long served as unpaid Dragoman in H.B.M.'s Consulate, Damascus, and had good testimonials from all my predecessors for ability and fidelity, I refused to abandon him to the tender mercies of the Governor-General.

On June 29th, 1871, I received a despatch, which virtually placed me under arrest. The heat at that time in Damascus was 105 degrees in the shade: even the natives could not endure it, and we were all suffering from fever. I battled with it until July 16th, when I found myself obliged to consult with my medical attendant, Dr. Nicora, who ordered me to the mountains directly, and offered to forward a certificate to H.M.'s Government. Here I held myself in readiness (at $4\frac{1}{2}$ hours' distance, with messengers plying between) for any order I might receive. I telegraphed, also, for permission to do this to Constantinople, and obtained it.

The next despatch shows the corruption of Syrian officials, and another contains a plan for Syria regarding our own *employés*—how many we want, of what kind, and in what places, which I submitted to H.M.'s Secretary of State for Foreign Affairs.

The despatches concerning the claims are:—
Captain Burton to Earl Granville, June 3rd, 1871.
A list of the Claims, consisting of eleven cases.
Captain Burton to Sir H. Elliot, July 4th, 1871.

Despatches relating to Haj Hassan and religious persecution.
Captain Burton to Sir H. Elliot, July 1st, 1871.
Testimonial from the Missionary Body.
Captain Burton's reply to the missionaries.
Six letters asking Captain Burton to interfere in Haj Hasan's behalf.
Captain Burton to the Foreign Office and Embassy, July 14th, 1871.
The case of Mr. Hanna Azar, Consular Dragoman.
Captain Burton to Sir H. Elliot, July 17th, 1871.
Mr. Consul-General Eldridge to Captain Burton, August 11th, 1871.
The Wali to Mr. Consul-General Eldridge, August 9th, 1871.
Earl Granville to Captain Burton, June 14th, 1871.
Captain Burton's reply, July 21st, 1871.
A despatch showing the corruption of Syrian officials, from Captain Burton, sent both to Earl Granville and Sir H. Elliot, July 19th, 1871.
A despatch showing our requirements in Syria, and a plan for our *employés*, sent by Captain Burton both to Earl Granville and Sir H. Elliot, July 24th, 1871.

[Circular No. 7.]

DAMASCUS,
June 3rd, 1871.

MY LORD,
 I have the honour to enclose the copy of a despatch addressed by me to Her Majesty's Ambassador at Constantinople, and to solicit for it your Lordship's attention.

The existence of these large claims is a continual source of irritation to the local authorities; it is my duty to press them—it is their interest to reject them. Since correspondence upon this point has commenced I find the transaction of business somewhat facilitated. My letters, which before were laid aside for months, are now answered after the shortest possible interval. As regards the apparent resolution at head-quarters to take my proceedings in ill part, and to regard my movements with suspicion, I expect to see the effects cease as soon as the cause shall be removed.

 I have the honour to be,
  My Lord,
   Your Lordship's most obedient, humble Servant,
    (Signed) RICHARD F. BURTON.

Her Majesty's Principal
 Secretary of State
  for Foreign Affairs,
   London.

List of Long-pending British Claims Presented at Different Times to H.E. Rashid Pasha, Governor-General.

1. M. Yakub Stambouli, Jewish protected subject. The case of this claimant was settled in 1863, and again in 1867 and 1868, by the local Government, which has repeatedly refused to fulfil its solemn engagements. It has often been reported and commented upon, especially by Mr. Consul Rogers (No. 1 of Jan. 2, 1869), and by Mr. Acting Consul Wood

(No. 10, July 16, 1869). The amount presented to this Consulate, as far back as Dec. 6, 1869, amounted to 3,973,375 piastres, to which interest and compound interest are now added.

2. Mr. Honorary Dragoman Hanna Misk, whose claim to the village of Rayyah was forwarded in my official letters, No. 10 of Oct. 6, 1870, and No. 8 of June 9, 1871. I have repeatedly referred to the local Government, and on one occasion Mr. Consul-General Eldridge and I waited upon H.E. the Governor General in order to plead the cause. But nothing has been done, and, after promise upon promise, the case is simply ignored.

3. M. Zelmina Fuchs, Jewish protected subject. His claim has been more than once reported by me, especially in my despatches No. 13 of Nov. 16, 1870, and No. 11 of June 21, 1871. The amount in June, 1871, was 624,439 piastres. This case was supposed to have been settled by the Vizirial letter of 26 Ramadan, 1287, but the document merely directed that the claim be raised from Bedawin plunderers, who have already been stripped in the claimant's name of all their property.

4. Messrs. Finzi, Barbour, and Co., an Anglo-Belgian house established at St. Jean d'Acre. Their case was undertaken by me in Nov., 1869, pursued by Mr. Consul-General Eldridge, and reported by me in No. 13 of June 27, 1871. On January 4, 1870, the amount was 225,000 piastres, to which must be added interest at the rate of 18 per cent. per annum. This case was also supposed to have been settled by the Vizirial letter, dated Shubat 13 A.H. 1286 (Feb. 25, 1871). But instead of ordering the ex-Governor of Akka, Mohammed Bey el Yusuf, who authorized the heads of villages to ignore their debts, and who thus ruined the firm, to pay the sums with whose recouping he had maliciously interfered, this document confuses the demands from the villagers with the demands from the ex-Governor. Moreover, it does not mention the sum due, nor does it order any inquiry to be made into the case of Messrs. Finzi and Barbour's servant, the Druze Yusuf Hamdan, who was beaten and tortured in the ex-Governor's private house. M. Finzi, jun., on June 6, 1871, visited Damascus in order to push his claim; the case has been ignored by the Governor-General, and there is at present no prospect of the house being able to save itself from ruin.

5. M. Yusuf Smuhah, Jewish protected subject. His claim upon certain Bedawin who had plundered his camels close to Damascus was reported by me to the local Government in November, 1869, and lastly in May 23, 1871. The amount is now a total of 15,300 piastres.

Amongst minor claims are the following:—

1. That of Suleyman el Haddad, the English courier from Bagdad, plundered by the Ruwalla Bedawin of goods valued at 66½ ghazis (16½ napoleons), and reported by me to the local Government on Jan. 10, 1870, and lastly on May 23, 1871.

2. That of Mr. Excursionist Gaze, whose party was plundered at Kunayterah of £31. I reported the theft to the local Government on May 21, 1871, and again on June 24, 1871.

3. M. Hanna Azar, dragoman to this Consulate. On June, 22, 1871, the Ghiyas Bedawin and others attacked his village, Suwaydah, and plundered from it 700 mudds of barley, valued at 7700 piastres. After I had made repeated representations, H.E. the Wali sent certain inspectors to estimate the damage, and those persons, by threatening the Shaykhs of the neighbouring villages with the vengeance of the Bedawin, secured testimony to the effect that the loss was only 120 mudds, and that the plunder was the work of wild boars.

Amongst cases which cannot be called claims, but which call for settlement, are the following:—

1. The violation of the Protestant cemetery by the people of the Shaghur quarter of Damascus. This outrage has occurred thrice within twenty months, and where justice is so studiously withheld I can hardly hope that it will not be renewed. The last act of plunder was reported by me to Constantinople on May 20, 1871 (No. 5). I would suggest that a fine of 20 napoleons be levied from the Moslems of the Shaghur quarter, and be applied to repairing the tombs and to building a second or outer wall, which would render the place inaccessible. Such a mulct is not contrary to law at Damascus, and is the only measure capable of arresting similar misdeeds.

2. The British Syrian schools have long been applying for the grant of a village in the Bukáa (Cœle Syria), and I am informed that a deputation has waited or will wait upon H.M.'s Secretary of State for Foreign Affairs with a view of supporting the application. I need hardly say that where the claims of justice are so little considered, all my endeavours during upwards of a year have failed to obtain an act of generosity.

3. Asad Zalzal Bey, of Beyrout, agent to Messrs. Asad Zalzal & Co., of Manchester, has been for months endeavouring, but in vain, to have an order carried out by the local Government that issued it. At last he has addressed a complaint to H.M.'s Secretary of State for Foreign Affairs. It was the custom at Damascus (for instance, in the case of M. Fureij, No. 15, March 13th, 1858), temporarily to confer British protection upon agents for English firms or for firms settled in England, and I venture to recommend that such a step be taken in this instance. Asad Zelzal Bey has a son born in England, and the family is exposed to be ruined by the personal animosity of H. E. the Governor-General.

I have the honour to be, Sir,
Your most obedient, humble servant,
(Signed) RICHARD F. BURTON.

[COPY.]

No. 17.—To Sir H. Elliot, G.C.B., Constantinople.

H.B.M. CONSULATE, DAMASCUS,
July 4, 1871.

SIR,

At the risk of importuning your Excellency, I am compelled once more to represent the wrongs done to British subjects and *protégés* residing in this Vilayet, and to forward a list of their claims, some of which date from upwards of four years. Such a reference to superior authority has not been found necessary at Damascus since Aug. 2, 1863, when Mr. Consul Rogers was obliged to appeal against his Excellency to Governor-General Rushdi Pasha.

The present state of affairs is causing profound dissatisfaction amongst British subjects and *protégés*, and is seriously injuring English interests in this part of the East. The local authorities are deaf to all the calls of justice, and they are supported by His Excellency the Wali Mohammed Rashid Pasha. The object is evidently to ignore all foreign protection, and more especially to lower as much as possible the influence of European Consulates.

The three claims first mentioned date from the days before my taking charge of this Consulate. I have exercised all possible patience in the matter, and have freely given to it my time and labour. Hardly a week has passed without my making an effort to procure justice. At last, it has become evident to me that the repeated promises by word of mouth, by letter, and by telegram, were made only to be broken, and that the rights of British subjects and *protégés* will be withheld until your Excellency thinks proper to press for their being granted. I need hardly point out that my determination to procure from the local government payment of its lawful debts is most distasteful to His Excellency the Governor-General and to all his subordinates. They cannot view with pleasure so large a sum diverted into the pockets of foreign *protégés*, and they oppose me by all means, direct and indirect. The latter is of course the favourite tactic.

With respect to the claims Nos. 3 and 4, Vizierial letters were forwarded by your Excellency, and in several of my despatches (for instance, No. 17, Jan. 24, 1871; No. 2, of March 13, 1871; and No. 13, of June 13, 1871) I have explained what has been their fate. Both instruments purporting to be "orders for the settlement of those claims," and thus represented to your Excellency were ambiguous, and were evidently written under the usual influences at Constantinople. I need hardly say that even had they been satisfactory, the usual secret sign would have made them of no avail. The Vizierial letters having failed to produce any effect, I have the honour of submitting to your Excellency the following plan for obtaining an equitable settlement of the claims in question, and to suggest that the amount, which may reach six million piastres, justifies an exceptional measure.

The only way to secure justice would be by a Commission of two or three members ordered in Constantinople to sit at Beyrout, where they would be less liable to be influenced than at Damascus. The Commercial Tribunal of Beyrout would, I doubt not, depute, if requested to do so, three European members to associate themselves upon equal terms with the commissioners. This Consulate could name a dragoman who would look to the interests of the claimants, and claim repayment of his expenses from the local government. Finally, disputed points might be referred either to Her Majesty's Consul-General for Syria or to myself. Should the Sublime Porte object to the expense of such a Commission, the Commissioners might be reduced from two or three to one on each side.

Such a commission, especially if the Ottoman members are carefully chosen at Constantinople, would not only remedy past evils, it would prove that the Government of His Imperial Majesty the Sultan does not countenance the wrongs inflicted upon the subjects of a power which has ever been his most faithful ally, and it would have the happy effect of securing their rights and privileges in the time to come.

But such a measure will, I fear, be strongly resisted as constituting a precedent. My expectation is that a *bond fide* order will be sent from Constantinople directing His Excellency the Governor-General to settle the claims, but at the least possible outlay of capital. However strongly this order be worded, all my work will begin again, every item will be disputed, and the inquiry will be prolonged, perhaps for years, in fact, until His Excellency Mohammed Rashid Pasha finds it no longer worth his while to govern Syria.

I have the honour, &c.,

(Signed) R. F. BURTON.

[COPY, No, 15.]

H.B.M.'s CONSULATE, DAMASCUS,
July 1st, 1871.

SIR.

I have the honour to bring the following circumstance to your Excellency's notice :—

About noon on Thursday, June 29, 1871, I received a letter from Miss James, superintendent of the British Syrian schools at Damascus, and covering a note from Mrs. Mentor Mott, of Beyrout. The object was to suggest active measures in the case of a Moslem convert to Christianity. Haj Hassan el Arbajee, after having been waylaid and beaten (according to Dr. John Wortabet), had been ordered up from Beyrout to Damascus in the custody of a policeman by His Excellency the Governor-General.

I at once wrote to His Excellency, representing that such action was an infraction of the treaty of 1856, which secured life and liberty to the so-called "Renegades." On the evening of the same day His Excellency replied to me, apparently ignoring the treaty, and denying my right to interfere in a matter concerning the subject of H.I.M. the Sultan. At the same time he courteously forwarded for my perusal a despatch which he had addressed to the Doyen of the Consular Corps, Beyrout, complaining of the conduct of Protestant missionaries in secret proselitizing, though he admitted that the convert Haj Hassan had openly attended a Christian church for some time, and justifying the arrest of the convert upon the plea of his requiring to be "counselled." Haj Hassan arrived at Damascus on the evening of Thursday, the 29th ult.; and on the morning of Friday, the 30th ult., I requested M. Selim Meshaka, Dragoman in this Consulate, to wait upon His Excellency, and to beg that the convert might be visited by the resident missionaries—Messrs. Wright and Crawford. The answer was a refusal. I was upon the point of sending a telegram to your Excellency when it was announced to me that the prisoner had been set free. On the following morning I addressed a letter of thanks to Rashid Pacha, and had the honour to assure him that such an act of justice and toleration would win for him the esteem and goodwill of the Christian community in Syria. Haj Hassan, after being placed in safety at H.M.'s Consulate, will leave Damascus this evening in charge of the Rev. Mr. Waldmeier, of the British Syrian schools.

It is reported that an association of young Moslems at Beyrout purposes to murder the convert after his return home. His Excellency Raouf Pasha, Mutaserrif of that city, is strong enough to prevent such an outrage, and a telegram from Constantinople to the effect that justice is expected from him would doubtless determine the authorities energetically to protect the convert.

On the morning of Friday, the 30th ult., it was reported to me that a certain Arif Effendi Ibn Abdel Ghani el Nablusi (a well-known family at Nablus), who had sacriligiously stolen fourteen lamps and a silver padlock, had been found hanging in the prison of the Great Amawi mosque at Damascus. Knowing the locality well, I cannot understand how the man could have hanged himself without attracting the attention of the numerous night guardians, not to speak of the Indian and Affghan pilgrims who swarm in the cloisters; nor do I see why an inquest was not held upon the body. It is certain that some years ago the man in question became a Christian at Athens, and that a strong feeling against him existed at Damascus.

The convert Haj Hassan, when making his deposition at the Consulate, declared that a Moslem acquaintance of his named Hammúdeh Ibn el Bekk, a native of Latikia, and domiciled at Bayrout, had disappeared about twelve days before the date of the *Proces Verbal* (July 1). I will not vouch for the truth of this report. The treaty of Feb. 12, 1856 (Hertslet, vol. x.) absolutely confirms life and liberty to all converts and so-called renegades. But this concession was made in direct opposition to the spirit of the Moslem world, which denounces the apostate as being unworthy to live, and which holds his private assassination lawful and right. As early as December, 1857, one of my predecessors—Mr. Consul Brant, C.B.,—was compelled to invoke the aid of H.M.'s Ambassador, Constantinople, in order to guarantee the immunity of a certain Khalil, and the affair was not settled without a long and exciting correspondence.

Almost as soon as I took charge of this Consulate (Oct., 1869) certain Moslems belonging to the Shazili order of Dervishes became Catholics, and fell under the displeasure of the local Government. As they took refuge in the Spanish Terra Santa, as Catholic questions were then chiefly in the hands of France, and as the converts dealt in strange stories about visions and the supernatural falling off of their fetters, I did not think it proper to move in the matter. Still, it attracted the attention of travellers, especially of Mr. George Lane Fox. It appears then that the Moslem authorities in Syria do not consider themselves bound to treat the person of the convert as inviolable. In his letter of June 29, 1871, His Excellency the Governor-General suggests that I should have pointed out the article which forbade him to bring up the Haj Hassan under charge of a policeman to Damascus, and to place him in the house occupied by the Chief of Police.

In conclusion, without wishing in any way to impede freedom of action in cases of conversion, I venture to suggest that missionaries—especially Protestant missionaries in Syria—be invited carefully and conscientiously to consider whether they are justified in exposing a Moslem convert to the imminent risk of losing his life; and by irritating a fanatical people to risk causing for themselves and their co-religionists such outbreaks of fury as characterised the last decade at Aleppo, Jeddah, and Damascus.

I have the honour, &c.,

(Signed) RICHARD F. BURTON.

To Sir H. Elliot, G.C.B.,
    Constantinople.

[COPY.]

DAMASCUS,
July 12th, 1871.

SIR,

We beg to tender to you our heartiest thanks for your prompt, decisive action in the case of Hassan, the converted Moslem, and also to congratulate you on the result of your determination and firmness.

For some time we had heard that a Moslem, converted to Protestantism at Beyrout, had become subjected to considerable persecution. A convert, more obscure than himself, had been put out of the way, and has not since been heard of, and Hassan had been subjected to a series of arrests and imprisonments, and had several times narrowly escaped assassination. The chief Consulates, however, had become publicly interested in him, so that his safety from legal execution seemed ensured; and as he was always accompanied by some one to protect him from assassins he seemed for the time to be safe. But on the 29th of June we were surprised to find that he was being transported to Damascus, having been arrested and bound in chains. The English colony in Beyrout became alarmed, as they declared that none so transported to Damascus ever returned again. Two agents of the missions were despatched from Beyrout, one preceding the prisoner to give us information as to what had taken place, and the other accompanying the prisoner to watch what became of him. On receiving intelligence of the convert's transportation to this city, the missionaries of the three missions at Damascus resolved to lay the case before you, but on doing so found that you had with your usual energy already taken up the case, and categorically demanded the release of the prisoner. And though the authorities ignored the Firman granting civil and religious liberty to the people of this empire, and denied your right to interfere on behalf of the prisoner, the unflinching stand you took by the concessions of the Hatti Sheriff, secured the release of the prisoner.

You have thus vindicated the cause of humanity, for on the day on which the prisoner escaped through your intervention, the Moslem authorities strangled, in the great mosque in Damascus, a Moslem convert to Christianity. The man had made application to the Irish-American Mission for protection, and declared that he lived in daily fear of strangulation. He was imprisoned in the great mosque, and strangled, as they say, by St. John the Baptist, and then carried away by one man, and thrown into a hole like a dog. This accident proves that pure, uncompromising firmness with the authorities was an act of pure mercy, and that the worst apprehensions of the Beyrout missionaries were not unfounded.

But more important still, you have asserted the binding character of the spiritual privileges of the Christian subjects of the Porte contained in the firman of 1866, and which, according to Fuad Pasha's letters to Lord Stratford de Redcliffe, "comprises absolutely all proselytes."

We are sure, Sir, that your conduct in this affair will receive the unqualified approbation of the best public opinion in Christendom, and we have no doubt it will receive, as it merits, the warm approval of your own Government.

We, who were near and anxious spectators of the proceedings in this affair, cannot too warmly express our sense of the satisfaction with which we witnessed the fearless, firm, and efficient manner in which you conducted this important case until the convert was permitted to leave the city.

(Signed) E. B. FRANKEL, Missionary of the London Jews Society.
JAMES ORR SCOTT, M.A., Missionary of the Irish Presbyterian Church.
FANNY JAMES, Lady Superintendent of the British Syrian Schools, Damascus.
WILLIAM WRIGHT, A.B., Missionary of the Irish Presbyterian Church, Damascus.
JOHN CRAWFORD, Missionary of the United Presbyterian Church of North America at Damascus.

To Captain Burton,
H.B.M.'s Consul
Damascus.

BLUDAN,
July 19th, 1871.

To The Rev. E. B. Frankel,
,, The Rev. J. Orr Scott,
,, Miss James,
,, The Rev. William Wright, and
,, The Rev. John Crawford,

      I have the pleasure to return my warmest thanks for your letter, this day received, in which you have expressed so flattering an estimate of my twenty-two months' services as Her Majesty's Consul for Damascus. Nor must I forget, at the same time, to record my gratitude to you for the cordial support and the approval of my proceedings connected with your several missions which, during that period, you have always extended to me. This friendly feeling has helped, in no small degree, to lighten the difficulties of the task which lay before me in 1869. You all know, and none can know better, what was to be done when I first assumed charge of this Consulate. You are familiar with the several measures taken by me, and you are well acquainted with the obstacles thrown in my way, and with the manner in which they were met. My path is still beset with difficulties, yet the prospect is full of hope. I shall continue to maintain the honest independence of Her Majesty's Consulate, to defend our rights as foreigners in the dominions of the Porte, and to claim all our privileges to the letter of the law. Should I meet, and there is no fear of its being otherwise, with the approval of my Chiefs, who know that an official life of twenty-nine years in the four quarters of the world is a title to some confidence, I feel assured that we may look forward to happier days at Damascus, when peace and security shall take the place of anxiety and depression. Meanwhile, I take the liberty of recommending to your prudent consideration the present critical state of affairs in Syria. A movement which cannot but be characterized as a revival of Christianity in the land of its birth, seems to have resulted from the measures adopted by the authorities, and from the spirit of inquiry which your missions have awakened in the breasts of the people. The new converts are now numbered by thousands: men of rank are enrolling themselves on the lists, and proselytizing has extended even to the Turkish soldiery.

    I need hardly observe that it is our duty, one and all, to assist, with all our strength, in advancing the sacred cause of religious toleration, and to be ever watchful lest local and personal interpretations be permitted to misrepresent the absolute right of every convert to liberty of conscience and to the security of his life and liberty. And I trust that you will find me at the end as in the beginning, always ready to serve your interests, to protect your missions and schools, and to lend my most energetic aid to your converts.

        Believe me ever most sincerely yours,
          (Signed)   RICHARD F. BURTON,
                      H.B.M.'s Consul, Damascus.

From Mrs. Mentor Mott, Superintendent of British Syrian Schools.

EMMBYEHAN, BEYROUT,
June 27th, 1871.

Dear Captain Burton,

    I write you these lines in favour of a Moslem named Hassan, who has become a Christian. Contrary to the Hattahamyaum, he has been seized this morning, thrown into prison, and is now, by order, to be sent to Damascus. The Pasha of Beyrout says he cannot interfere. One of the man's children is in one of our schools.

    The various Consulates and the Missionaries are interesting themselves in his behalf, but I venture to write to you *direct*, to entreat your good offices with the Wali for him.

    He was coachman to a respectable native here.—M. Wahim Najjár.

        Yours faithfully,
          (Signed)   AUGUSTA MENTOR MOTT,

Captain Burton,
    H.B.M.'s Consul, Damascus.

[From Dr. WORTABET.]

BEYROUT,
29th June, 1871.

MY DEAR CAPTAIN BURTON,

I write these few lines with the hope of interesting you in the case of a poor man who is in danger of losing his life for his religious opinions.

Hassan, a Moslem some thirty years of age, by profession a coachman, in the service of Mr. Joachim Najjár, took it into his head a few months ago to become a Christian. He has attended the Protestant service, but has not been baptized. The Government, hearing of the case, took it up lately, and the man has been called a number of times before the authorities, where pressure was put on him as to his change of religion, his name not appearing on the conscription roll, &c., &c. Being a simple-minded and apparently sincere man, he gave direct answers to the questions put to him. Besides, he was waylaid and beaten once, and his life often threatened. During all this trying time he has stood firmer in his profession of Christianity.

This morning he was sent by the omnibus to Damascus, with a zaptieh, by order of the Governor-General, to appear there on account of having changed his religion.

The British, Prussian, and American Consuls-General here took up the matter with the Government warmly, as you may have read some official account to that effect. You will doubtless hear more fully of the case from others in Damascus.

I believe the man to be really sincere, though simple and ignorant, and the principle involved in his case—that of religious toleration—is of great importance. It is on these two grounds that I hope you will be interested in the poor fellow, and do all that you can for him—shield him from a power and measures with which you are well acquainted. Believing that if the real circumstances were known to you, you will take a kind interest in the case, I have taken the liberty to drop you this line.

Everybody has either left or is on the point of leaving for the mountains, and Beyrout will soon be enveloped in heat and dust. Hoping you and Mrs. B. are in good health,

I remain,
My Dear Captain Burton,
Yours, very faithfully,
(Signed) JOHN WORTABET.

P.S.—I sent you by the Sais the other day a copy of the Oratory, with a few lines, which I hope you have read. In writing to me about Persia, I hope you will also have the goodness to let me know what you think of the book.

BEIRÛT,
June 29th, 1871.

MY DEAR SIR,

Our community is greatly interested in the fate of one Hassan, a convert from Islam to Christianity, an humble, simple, but determined man, who has been arrested on no other charge than that of his change of religion, and was sent this morning to Damascus. What will be his fate it is hard to say. Under the proclamation of toleration he is entitled to his life and liberty. I think I can safely say that Mr. Weber and Mr. Eldridge, besides the English and American residents, feel the greatest sympathy with him, and desire to vindicate the principle. If you should find it within the range of your inclination and duty to look a little into this case, you would secure the thanks of the community here, who feel much anxiety as to the result. I presume Mr. Wright and the other missionaries know all the facts.

Yours sincerely,
(Signed) L. M. JOHNSON,
Consul-General United States.

Captain Burton,
H.B.M.'s Consul, Damascus.

EMMBYEHAN, BEYROUT,
July 3rd, 1871.

DEAR CAPTAIN BURTON,

While acknowledging your favour of June 30th, permit me to return cordial thanks for your prompt and decisive action. You will doubtless hear from others what may be suggested for the man's future career.

Mr. Waldmeier handed the man over to the American missionaries, and delivered the documents with which he was was entrusted to Mr. Abkarius.

Again offering you sincere thanks, believe me to remain,

Yours, truly obliged,

(Signed)   AUGUSTA MENTOR MOTT.

Captain Burton,
   H.B.M. Consul,
      Damascus.

From the Consul-General of the United States.

BEYROUT,
July 8th, 1871.

MY DEAR SIR,

Your note and that of Mrs. Burton relative to Hassan were duly received, and read with much interest. The case remains here without any change. Of course all are anxious to know whether the Vali will attempt to execute his threat to excite. So far, there has been no further violence, and none is anticipated at present. Much appreciation is expressed of your kind interest and earnest efforts in behalf of the victim of intolerance. The remarkable letter of the Vali is still not fully comprehended in its object.

With much regard I remain,

Yours sincerely,

(Signed)   L. M. JOHNSON.

July 22nd, 1871.

MY DEAR MRS. BURTON,

It is more probable than not that Captain Burton has been informed of what I now write; if so, you will pardon the repetition—if not, I feel sure that, with his usual caution and promptitude, he will *act* as he knows best.

Hassan was to have left by the Austrian steamer on Friday morning for Alexandria. Ishak therefore went with him to the proper authorities for a *passport*. The party *refused* to give him one, saying he could not do so without an express order from the Wali. Ishak begged him to telegraph to the Wali for the permission, but up to last night no answer had been given to Hassan's inquirers. Of course he could not go without a pass, and yet he is condemned to leave Beyrout within twenty days of the sentence passed upon him. He is kept somewhere in concealment. But this cannot possibly last—the man's life is in jeopardy.

No one has been told of my communicating this to you; but, as I have said, it may be merely a repetition of what Captain B. may have already been informed of officially.

Yours most sincerely,

(Signed)   AUGUSTA MENTOR MOTT.

[No. 14.]

Copy sent to Foreign Office.

DAMASCUS,
July 14th, 1871.

SIR,

I have the honour to lay the following circumstances before your Excellency, hoping to be favoured with your orders as to the course of action which Her Majesty's Government would wish me to pursue in a matter which is evidently of the greatest gravity.

The maladministration of Syria during the last five years—especially the last two of Rashid Pasha's government—is causing a revival of Christianity. Hence the Moslem is the only subject of the Porte who has no defender, unless his purse be well lined.

The so-called "Greek" Christians are backed, especially at the present time, by Russian influence and gold. The Latins receive support from their ecclesiastics and from the Catholic Consulates; until the late war they were strenuously aided by France. The Protestants and the Druzes look to England for their help and sympathy, which her policy has wisely extended to them. The Jews either obtain the protection of foreign passports or they rely upon the influence of their co-religionists throughout the civilised world. But the Moslem Rayyah cannot look to any of these sources for aid. Plundered, crushed, starved, and driven to despair by taxes and imposts, and by the exactions of rapacious Government officials, who are ever being changed, and who are never satiated, he has at length learned to envy the privileges enjoyed by the various Christian sects—such as immunity from conscription and facilities of obtaining the justice which he cannot expect. El Islam will not help him: Christianity will. As long as the present maladministration keeps the people starving and discontented, so long will the movement, now that it has made a start, continue to gain influence; and if freedom be allowed to it, it is hard to foresee where it may end. I am at present unprepared to supply a full and exhaustive report upon the subject. Much of my information, though to all appearance reliable, must be verified by me in person before I can vouch for its truth. Yet I have thought it my duty to lay before your Excellency this outline of a revival which is working under the surface of society, and of the causes which have brought it about—in order that no time may be lost in preparing for its development.

The revival dates from 1869, when a private soldier—then named "Ahmed-es-Sahar," and now "Isaac"—became a Christian, and when, notwithstanding the proclamation of religious liberty to converts by the Hatt-i-Sheriff of Gul-Khanah and the confirmation by the Firman of February 12, 1856, he was imprisoned and loaded with chains. According to his own account he saw visions of the Saviour, and he was favoured with various revelations; his fetters fell off, and his jailors did not attempt to replace them. When released he was joined by twenty to thirty Moslems of the "Shadili" order of Dervishes. Of these men twelve were arrested and summarily departed without formal trial to Tripoli and Marzuk, whilst their wives and children—then numbering sixty-two, and now fifty-three—were left to starve in Damascus. As usual, persecution increased the number of converts, who though secretly baptised have succeeded in concealing their change of faith. Now, however, the disappearance of Said el Hamawi, the case of Hadj Hassan, the hanging of Asif Effendi (the Neophyte Enstathios), and the report that the son of a Kadi (judge), whose name I have not yet discovered, has been put to death at Damascus, would seem to show that the Government, which is here the Governor-General, has become aware of the movement and is trying to nip it in the bud.

It is too far advanced by this time for such treatment. I have spoken to some of the principal converts in the City of Damascus, and they declare that at the end of 1869 the total of males who had turned from El Islam was 500; that in 1870, the number had risen to 4000 souls, and that the present amount may be 5000. Moreover, that not only in the city, but even amongst the Bedawin of the Eastern country, and amongst the Fellahs of the Bukáa (Cœlesyria) the revival is progressing. Regarding the latter place, a case in point has just now fallen under my personal notice, although it was unknown to the Damascus converts.

The villagers of a hamlet on the eastern slope of Mount Lebanon, having through the non-interference, or rather the connivance of the Government, been despoiled of their houses, their lands, and in fact of all their property, came to this capital and sent me word that they were prepared to become Protestants. It is plain that the prescrit is no common matter of conversion. If steps be not taken by the Governments of Europe to prevent the treaty and the Firman becoming dead letters, religious persecution will become rampant, and this persecution, carried one step too far by the Turkish authorities, will undobtedly cause a repetition of the fearful scenes of 1860.

Regarding this revival of Christianity in the gravest light, I am the more anxious to be favoured with your Excellency's directions as to my future proceedings.

I have the honour, &c.,
(Signed) RICHARD F. BURTON.

To His Excellency
    The Right Honourable Sir Henry Elliot.

[No. 26.]

Copy sent to the Foreign Office.

DAMASCUS,
July 17th, 1871.

SIR,

I have the honour to bring the following circumstances to your Excellency's notice.

M. Hanna Azar, Dragoman of this Consulate, having reported to me (July 12th) that certain friendly villagers had warned him that his life was threatened by a tribe of Bedouin bandits known as the Ghiyas, I addressed, on the same day, a despatch to the Governor-General applying for the personal protection of M. Azar, who is proprietor of two villages in the Marj district near Damascus, and who is obliged periodically to visit them on business. Up to this date no answer has been received.

M. Azar's village "Suwaydah" was lately plundered by the Ghiyas, as I reported in the list of British claims appended to my despatch No. 17, of July 8th; and on this occasion, when speaking to the peasantry of Dhumeir, they threatened M. Azar's life.

The Governor-General has long regarded with dislike this *employé* of the British Consulate. In 1869, about seven months before I took up my appointment, M. Azar, in presence of Mr. Acting-Consul Charles Wood produced a document signed by Rashid Pasha, when the latter had denied having signed it.

Since that time Rashid Pasha has never lost the least opportunity of injuring M. Azar, and of applying indirectiy to me for his removal from the Consulate. I always replied that some offence must be brought home to a Consular Dragoman before he can be dismissed; and as the Governor-General only insisted the more, it presently became evident to me that he was trying, as his custom is, whether I was more likely to be pliant than others. Still, there was no reason to find fault with M. Azar, whose services became more valuable when Rashid Pasha began to intrigue for my recall.

At last I absolutely refused to entertain the idea any longer. It need hardly be remarked that had M. Azar been dismissed from this office he would at once have been ruined, and that this Consulate would have acquired that reputation for subserviency which Rashid Pasha desired to affix to it.

The Government of Damascus is answerable for any action of the Ghiyas plunderers. The latter have since many months given hostages, and are held to be submitted; no outrage like that to which I have above alluded can therefore be committed without the connivance of the authorities.

The last report at Damascus is that the Governor-General has ordered the purchase of 500 mules, and that 200 head are already collected.

This step shows a hostile movement is in contemplation, but I cannot yet determine whether the Druzes, or the Arab tribes of the Druze Mountain, whose raids have become insufferable, are the object proposed. The silence of his Excellency, and his delay in replying to my letter about M. Azar, perhaps suggest the latter. I shall not fail to supply your Excellency with all the information which I can gather.

I have the honour, &c.,

(Signed)   RICHARD F. BURTON.

To His Excellency
    The Right Honourable
        Sir Henry Elliot,
           Constantinople.

BEYROUT,
August 11th, 1871.

SIR,

I have to transmit to you for your information a copy of a note which I have received from the Governor-General, complaining of the conduct of Mr. Hanna Azar, one of your Dragomans.

I have informed his Excellency that the nomination and dismissal of Dragomans depend upon the Consuls to whom they are attached, but that seeing the gravity of the charges brought against Mr. Azar, I have considered it my duty to forward a copy of H.E.'s note to H.M.'s Ambassador at Constantinople, to whom you can forward such explanations as you may consider advisable, furnishing me with a copy thereof.

For the sake of preserving good relations with the local authorities, I would suggest to you the expediency of suspending Mr. Azar from his functions of Dragoman, at least until you have investigated the charges brought against him.

I have the honour to be, Sir,
    Your obedient Servant,
        (Signed)   G. JACKSON ELDRIDGE,
                             Consul-General.

Captain Burton,
    H.M.'s Consul, Damascus.

[COPY.]

Gouvernement Général du Vilayet de Syrie.—No. 558.

DAMAS,
Le 9 Août, 1871.

MONSIEUR LE CONSUL-GENERAL,

Une des causes principales de la mésintelligence qui a éclatée entre M. Burton et moi, c'est sans contredit M. Hanna Azar, un des drogmans indigènes au service du Consulat de S.M. Britannique à Damas. Vers la fin de son séjour à Damas, M. Rogers, convaincu de la duplicité de Hanna Azar, avait fini par lui retirer sa confiance, et ne le chargeait plus d'aucune affaire. M. Wood, dans son bon sens, comprit aussitôt que Hanna Azar était une pierre de scandale entre l'autorité et le Consulat, mais il ne voulut point servi contre cet employé infidèle, n'étant qu'intérimaire lui-même. M. Kennedy, informé lui-même d'un pareil état de choses aussi déplorable, promit de faire changer Hanna Azar, mais l'importance des occupations de M. l'Inspecteur a fait qu'il n'a pas songé à s'occuper d ecette affaire.

Enfin, j'ai eu plus d'une fois l'occasion de me plaindre à M. Burton de la conduite de Hanna Azar, lui faisant observer que cet employé ne croyait pouvoir mieux faire ses affaires que lorsque la discorde régnerait entre nous. J'ajouterais en outre que Hanna Azar de tout temps, par ses intrigues en ville, par les faux bruits qu'il répandait, il donnait à entendre que la sécurité et la tranquillité publique étaient menacées. Il faisait partout entrevoir le péril que les Chrétiens courraient, et le spectre de nouveaux malheurs. Rien ne fit. M. Burton garda quand même M. Azar; il lui défendit seulement de se présenter devant moi, et voici à quelle occasion.

L'année dernière lorsqu'une rixe éclata sur le passage de M. Burton allant à l'église de Zibdani, plusieurs individus furent arrêtés. Mme. Burton ayant elle-même reconnu l'innocence des détenus, allait demander leur mise en liberté. Que fit Hanna Azar? Il s'empressa de demander de l'argent aux prisonniers, leur promettant la liberté; ce que M. le Consul ayant su, au lieu de renvoyer un drogman dont la perversité morale était incontestable, il se contenta de lui défendre de se présenter devant moi.

En revanche, Azar hante les tribunaux du matin au soir, se charge d'affaires suspectes étrangères au Consulat, fait de faux rapports au Consul qu'il excite et qu'il irrite, maltraite les membres, leur en impose, s'abritant derrière l'impunité que lui assure son titre, pressure les habitants des tribus et des villages voisins de sa propriété, leur intente des procès sans fondement pour des dévastations chimériques, leur réclame des sommes importantes à titre d'indemnité pour des dégats imaginaires, et finit même par les accuser de vouloir attenter à ses jours.

Azar, par son ingérance, continue auprès de l'autorité, a fini par soulever contre lui les clameurs de tous les tribunaux et de tous les bureaux du Vilayet et du Mutessariflik. Il a fait verser la mesure. Jusqu'à ce jour je calmai les tribunaux du Mutessariflik, et je conseillai la patience à ceux du Vilayet. Cette patience aussi a été épuisée. Un cri unanime s'élève contre cet homme qui brave nos lois et toutes les convenances. J'ai longtemps temporisé; je ne saurai plus prolonger ma longanimité; prévoyant qu'un incident fâcheux ne peut manquer de surgir; vu la position que j'occupe et la responsabilité qui incombe sur moi, j'ai été forcé de donner l'ordre à ce que Hanna Azar ne soit plus reçu comme drogman auprès de l'autorité.

Votre expérience des affaires, acquis dans une série de longs travaux, l'esprit de justice et de droiture qui vous distingue, la connaissance que vous avez de ce qu'un drogman peut faire lorsqu'il est mauvais, vous feront approuver, j'en suis convaincu, la mesure extrême que la force des choses m'a forcé de prendre. L'autorité n'a aucune espèce de confiance en Mr. Hanna Azar, et quand bien même M. Burton viendrait à être remplacé, Hanna Azar est de nature à créer de nouveaux embarras au Consul nouveau venu et à l'autorité. Vous désirez, sans doute, comme moi, que la bonne entente règne entre le Consulat de Damas et le Vilayet. Elle est impossible tant que Hanna Azar subsistera comme drogman. C'est un obstacle à la paix et à la concorde. Ma conscience me dit que je devais le supprimer, et c'est ce que j'ai fait.

Le Consul de Damas a d'autres interprètes; ses affaires ne souffriront pas, d'autant plus que Hanna Azar ne se chargeait point d'une affaire pour la mener à bonne fin, mais pour en envelopper le cours d'un réseau de difficultés, de malentendus, et de complications.

Veuillez agréer, etc.,

(Signé) RACHID.

M. Eldridge, Consul-Général de S.M. Britannique à Beyrouth.

[No. 1.]

Foreign Office,
June 14th, 1871.

Sir,

I am directed by Earl Granville to call upon you to furnish by the earliest opportunity a full explanation of the circumstances adverted to in the telegram from the

Governor-General of Syria to Aali Pasha, of which a copy is herewith enclosed, communicated to his Lordship by the Ottoman Ambassador at this Court.

I am at the same time to acquaint you that serious complaints in regard to your general proceedings have been made by the Porte to Her Majesty's Government, and I am to add that his Lordship wishes that from the time of receipt of this despatch until further instructions reach you, you should not quit the seat of your Consulate, the city of Damascus.

I am, Sir,
Your most obedient humble Servant,
(Signed) ODO RUSSELL.

Captain Burton, &c., &c.,
Damaacus.

[Separate.]

H.B.M.'s CONSULATE, DAMASCUS,
July 21st, 1871.

MY LORD,

On Saturday, July 8th, 1871, I had the honour to receive your Lordship's despatch, No. 1, of June 14th, 1871, containing these words:

"I am to add that his Lordship wishes from the time of the receipt of this despatch, until further instructions reach you, you should not quit the seat of your Consulate, the city of Damascus."

At the time of receiving this despatch, my family and myself were suffering from the excessive heat, and from the unusually sickly season of Damascus. The Greeks of Nazareth had been suffered to return home, in order that their *procès verbal* might be revised and terminated. The Consular Corps and the Presbyterian Missionaries had been gone for some time. Convinced that I had done nothing to incur your Lordship's displeasure, and feeling certain that when the truth came before you you would not expect me to consider myself under a kind of arrest at my Consulate in the hot and fœtid air of a Damascus July. I telegraphed to Her Majesty's Ambassador at Constantinople requesting permission to proceed to my summer quarters. I should here explain that the British Consuls in this country have since the establishment of the Consulates, kept two houses, one in the city, and the other within an easy ride of four or five hours, and that messengers constantly ply between the two. After waiting ten days in vain for an answer from Constantinople I received the permission, and I was compelled on the 19th instant, with the view of avoiding serious illness, to comply with the advice of my medical man, and to transfer myself to summer quarters at Bludan. A copy of his certificate shall, if it be judged necessary, at once be forwarded to your Lordship. I trust that the step will not be viewed in any other light but as an act of necessity, and that the explanations forwarded to your Lordship will explain the surprise and the mortification experienced by me when I found that the transparent machinations of the Governor-General of Syria had been successful.

I have the honour to be,
My Lord,
Your most obedient humble Servant,
(Signed) RICHARD F. BURTON,
H.B.M.'s Consul, Damascus.

No. 27. Copy to F.O.

DAMASCUS,
July 19th, 1871.

To Sir Henry Elliot, Constantinople.

SIR,

In several of my despatches (especially in that of June 9th, 1871, marked confidential) I had the honour to inform your Excellency that Rashid Pasha, Governor-General of Syria, had filled all the important posts with his friends and retainers. After the "Belká Expedition" of early 1869, he obtained from the Sublime Porte additional powers, and before the year had ended he dismissed many functionaries, and he promoted and decorated those placed in their stead. Since that time he has carefully excluded from office all except his own nominees. The following list of names and appointments proves the correctness of my statement, and it may explain the popular report that Syria is ready to join what is now called the Quintuple Alliance, and to declare her independence as soon as Egypt moves. The important Governorships (Mutasarrifliks) of Hums (Emesa) and Hamah (Epiphania) are now in the hands of Holo Pasha. This officer, originally a soldier in the Bashi Buzuks, was promoted by Rashid Pasha. Of Bedawi origin, he can command the active aid of his kinsmen the Mawali, the Subáa, and other clans, which may be able to bring 3,000 lances into the field. His brother, Mahmud Bey, has been made Governor of Mazyad in the Nusayri (Ausayrii) mountains. Tripoli is under Vesi Pasha, an old favourite of the Governor-General's, by whose orders he plundered the Bedouin tribes about Hums and Hamah. This post was held by Abd-el-Kadi Pasha, who, being a man of independent character, has been moved successively from Tripoli to Beyrout, from Beyrout to Hums and Hamah. He is now, I believe, at Damascus.

At Baalbek As'ad Effendi, an adherent of Rashid Pasha, has taken the place of Saleh Bey, lately promoted to a Pashalik.

Beyrout has been committed to Raoof Pasha, another dependent of Rashid Pasha. His movements are controlled by M. Delenda, a Smyrniote Greek, intituled "Ma'amur Politika" (political chief). This person is said to have been brought up in Paris with Rashid Pasha, and he is held to exercise an influence the reverse of wholesome.

The Mutasarrif of Damascus is Ibrahim Pasha, an officer who gained but little credit as a member of the commercial tribunal in this city. He was, however, promoted by Rashid Pasha to a Pashalik, and to the government of the Hauran, and thence he was translated to the important post of Damascus. He is controlled by the Governor-General's interpreter, a Greek, whose true name is Petros Didymos, but who is known as Bahjat Effendi, and who is looked upon by all as the active partizan of the powerful Greco-Russian party. His influence at Damascus is all for evil.

The Mutasarriflik of the Hauran Plain has been given to Mohammed Bey El Yusuf, whom I have mentioned in my despatches No. 13, of June 27, 1871, and No. 17, of July 4, 1871. This young man, a Kurd of wealthy family, succeeded in ruining the house of MM. Finzi and Barbour at St. Jean d'Acre.

The Gharb'el Bukáa (Western Cœle, Syria) is under Mustafa Effendi, an old inspector of the Douane at Damascus; he owes all his advancement to Rashid Pasha.

Sayda (Sidon) has been reduced to a Kaimakam; the actual holder is Shakir Bey, formerly a tom-tom player. He was promoted by Rashid Pasha chiefly because he is on bad terms with his distinguished brother Kamil Pasha.

Sur (Tyre) is under Nejib Bey, also a Kurd and appointed by Rashid Pasha. This officer refuses to obey blindly, therefore he was transferred from Baalbek, and it is most probable that presently he will be recalled.

The Mutasarriflik of St. Jean d'Acre is under Rushdi Effendi, formerly Daftardar (1st Comptable) of the Velayet. He was removed, it is said, from Damascus on account of his irregular practices, and after a year he was transferred to this important place.

Hayfa (Caiffa) is under Ashry Bey, son of Vesi Pasha, a young man whose bad conduct to the Protestant missionaries and others at Rasheyya caused him to be removed to another and a better post. Rasheyya is a turbulent place, with a large, mixed population of Druzes, Greeks, Moslems, and a few Protestant converts, and has for Kaimakam Ashraf Effendi, who married the daughter of one of the Governor-General's concubines. His bad conduct caused him to be dismissed from Muallakah.

Hasbeyya, also on the slopes of Hermon, and the most important settlement in the Wady Taym, tenanted by Druzes, Moslems, Greeks, and Protestants, is under the Kaimakam Khurshid Agha, a well-meaning man, but incapable of independent action, and wholly under the influence of Rashid Pasha.

Safat, where there is a large colony of Jews under British protection, is governed by the Kaimakam Abd-el-Kadir Bey Azmeh Zadeh, a man of good family, but almost incapacitated for business by his habits of intoxication.

Tiberias is also inhabited by Jews under British protection, Moslems, and Christians. In a despatch of July 6th, 1871 (No. 47), I have remonstrated with the Governor-General for permitting the Greek Bishop of Nazareth, Mgr. Niphon, to buy a synagogue and a cemetery belonging to the Jews during the last 400 years. Shukri Effendi is the Kaimakam lately promoted by Rashid Pasha from Baysan (Scytropolis), in the Ghor, or Jordan Valley, Nazareth, where we have a mission and a school, is governed by Kurshid Agha, formerly pipe-bearer to Rashid Pasha. The state of this town is described by me in my despatch No. 7, of June 7th, 1871, and by the Rev. Mr. Zeller, a copy of whose letter I enclosed to your Excellency is my despatch No. 20, of July 12th, 1871.

The important district of the Belká, whose *chef-lieu* is Nablus—one of the most turbulent of Syrian towns—is under the well-known Kurdish Chief Mohammed Said Pasha Shamdin. This officer, who owes all his promotion to Rashid Pasha, is a man of great wealth and influence. His only daughter is married to Mohammed Bey el Usuf, Governor of the Hauran. He can command at least 10,000 sabres in the city of Damascus and its environs, and therefore he has been created a Pasha.

Another Kurd who lately was a Bashi-Buzuk, and who now commands the Hajj or Meccan Caravan—a very lucrative post—is Ahmed Agha Bozo, promoted to a Pashalik by Rashid Pasha. The Ottoman Government, knowing the perfidy and the violence of its Kurdish subjects, has hitherto made a rule of not raising them to high distinction. Rashid Pasha has departed from this wise precedent, and the popular voice declares that he does so because he looks forward to benefit by their unscrupulous partizanship.

The emoluments attached to the Hajj were transferred in 1869 from Shaykh Findi el Faiz of the Beni Sakr to Mohammed Doukhy Shaykh, of the great Anizeh clan Wuld Ali. The latter is a man of the worst character. To the rapacity and other vices of the Bedouin he adds the craft and the *savoir faire* of the citizen. His chief merit is his readiness to commit any crime: he can also bring into the field some three thousand lances of his own, and if time be allowed him to intrigue amongst the Anizeh he would probably swell the number to thirty thousand.

In order to invest his adherents with greater prestige, Rashid Pasha has, it is said, proposed and succeeded in raising all the Mutaserrifs to the rank of Pasha. This move is wholly in his own favour, and in case of a rise in Syria his influence would be paramount.

I can supply, if it be deemed necessary, a list of the Great Tribunals of Appeal that sit at Damascus; it will show that amongst them there is not one member who pretends to independence. At present, indeed, these Majlises may be said not to exist. A message from Rashid Pasha to the President, conveyed by Bahjat Effendi, is of more avail than a Firman of the Sublime Porte; and justice is paralysed throughout the land.

The Syrian police is wholly in the hands of the Mir Alai Mustafa Bey, an officer whose exceeding bigotry prevents his being decently civil to any Christian. His second in command, Ismail Agha, an active and intelligent officer, lately died under highly suspicious circumstances. The British Consulate of Damascus is bounded on the west by a house of dubious fame, belonging to a Turkish woman who is intimate with the Governor-General's harem; and the latter, to the great scandal of the city, returned her visits. Ismail Agha detected this person in a shameless intrigue: he was dismissed with disgrace, and he presently died. His place has been taken by the Bimbashi Abdullah Aga, who emulates the fanaticism of his chief. The Yazbashi Serúr Aga, a very useful officer, remains unemployed: he is hated by Mustafa Bey because in 1860 he saved a Christian boy from being made a slave in his Colonel's house, and because he is looked upon as a friend to the British Consulate. The police arrangements are deplorable throughout the province, and the Government pays for thirty where perhaps ten are employed. The people complain that crime has never been so general; and under the circumstances we cannot be surprised.

This state of things in Syria results directly from the Consul-Generals' residing in Beyrout and not in Damascus—the head-quarters of the Vilayet. Instead of exercising due supervision over political matters, they are relegated from the centre to the edge of the Province. The Consuls-General are unable to obtain anything like correct information, and some, indeed have never visited Damascus. They are entirely dependent upon their Dragomans; and they never see Rashid Pasha except when he visits the harbour town for recreation. Of course the Ottoman authorities highly approve of an arrangement which reduces English influence and legitimate Consular interference to the lowest expression.

A report has lately been spread that the Villayet of Syria will be divided into three. The northernmost will consist of the present Mutusarrif-lik of Tor on the Euphrates, to which will be added the rich and fertile districts about Hums and Hamah. The central will be the heart of the present province, and the southern will be represented by the harbour towns from Sidon (Sur) to Gaza (Ghazzeh), with Jerusalem for head-quarters. This project is highly to be commended, for many reasons, especially because it tends to preserve the unity of the Ottoman Empire. It renders concerted action in favour of Russia impossible, and it will prevent Syria from siding as a strong and united power with Egypt should the latter have the temerity to strike a blow for independence.

There are two main reasons which compel Russia to take a vital interest in this corner of Asia. The first is the pilgrimage to the Holy City, which through the Greek Church moves the world from Finland to Abyssinia. The second is the unwillingness of the great Northern Empire to see Syria become the highway of British India.

Such, Excellency, is the present condition of Syria, which, situated as it is in proximity to Egypt, and united with the latter by political sympathies and by ancient interests, ought never to have been subjected to the dangerous and unscrupulous autocracy of Rashid Pasha.

I have the honour to be, Sir,
Your most obedient humble Servant,
(Signed)   RICHD. F. BURTON,
H.M.'s Consul, Damascus.

[SEPARATE.]

HER BRITANNIC MAJESTY'S CONSULATE, DAMASCUS,
July 24, 1871.

MY LORD,
The intelligence that Her Majesty's Consulate at Damascus has been reduced—in fact, is to become a second-class appointment—induces me to submit the following lines to your superior judgment.

The capital of Syria, owing to increased wealth, to the influx of population, and to the establishment of Majlisses, which make it their head-quarters, has doubled its prices in the last 15 years. House rent is now £60 to £80 per annum, and it must soon rise to £100. A Consular Dragoman will, in the present day, spend some 300 to 350 napoleons a year, where his father lived as well upon 120.

An underpaid Consul who cannot afford from his private means an outlay equal to his official income, will now occupy a false position at the residence of the Governor-General of the Grand Courts of appeal and of other high officials. And this is precisely what is desired by that Ottoman party which hates European influence because it is an obstacle to their freedom of maladministration. Its one great object is to keep the Consulates-General relegated to the port of Beyrout—to the edge as opposed to the centre of the Vilayet, to a place of minimum political importance never visited by the Governor-General except when making holiday.

With the second-class Consulate transferred to Beyrout—a harbour town comparatively unexpensive because no establishment need be maintained—an underpaid official would be removed from the many temptations that would beset his path at Damascus. The transfer of the Consulates-General and the Vice-Consulate to the Capital is a step which, as every resident in Syria well knows, has long been called for by European interests. It will, perhaps, be distasteful to the Consuls-General who find Beyrout a safe and civilized dwelling-place in the immediate neighbourhood of the sea and " the mountain " (Lebanon). These functionaries—of course I do not include my immediate superior—have lately been using all their interests to establish at Damascus Vice-Consuls subject to themselves. Thus they have proposed a measure at once most agreeable to the local authorities, whose jealousy of European influence is ever on the increase, and fatal to the beneficial influence which Europe ought to exercise upon Syria.

A dozen years ago the Consul-General might plead that at Damascus he would be separated by two days of rough riding from the seaboard, and consequently from free and regular communication with the home authorities. Now all is changed. There is a telegram office which sends messages in European languages; there is a post-office which will presently learn to forward correspondence unviolated, and there is a day coach throughout the year, with a night omnibus in the hot season. No plausible reason at present exists for the Consul-General to reside at Beyrout, except his personal convenience, and no public servant will allow any weight to such a consideration. Many of the Consuls-General may feel inclined to urge objections against being transferred to Damascus, but should the representative of Great Britain be directed to make the capital his head-quarters, all will be compelled at once to do the same under pain of injuring the interests of their Governments.

In the days when the French road did not exist, a cause for placing the Consuls-General at Beyrout was found in the fact that they were also accredited to the Governor of the Lebanon as well as to the Governor-General of Syria. But the former functionary now transacts business not at Beyrout, which belongs to Damascus, but at Baabdah, during the winter, and in the summer at Ibtiddin, a place far less accessible from Beyrout than Damascus is. A second-class Consulate could do all that is wanted with the Governor of the Lebanon, which is a Mutasarrif-lik (department) not a Vilayet (province). Finally, the distances are so inconsiderable, that the Consul-General could at all times reach Baabdah in twelve hours and Ibtiddin in twenty-four hours from Damascus.

The present, I venture to submit, is the moment when Syria claims increased attention from England. The Euphrates Valley Railway, after being discussed since 1845, has now come before a Committee of the House of Common. It will be opposed by the Government of Syria secretly, but with all its strength; and the opposition of the local authorities will be supported by the Sublime Porte and by Russia. These two powers are the last to desire an English highway from the Levant to the Euphrates, and without the most energetic action on our part they will inevitably be successful.

The first step requisite to clear the way for a Euphrates Valley Railroad is to increase our Consular establishment in Syria and Palestine, a step which has already been taken by France, Russia, Austria, and even Persia. They have placed representatives at all the most important points, a secure method of extending legitimate European influence by bringing to light and checking the malpractices, the peculation, and the abuse of justice which eat into the prosperity of the province. The measure is generally unpopular with our Consuls-General and Consuls, because it always adds to their correspondence, and it occasionally causes trouble with the local authorities. Such considerations need hardly be noticed.

I have the honour respectfully to submit the following plan for extending our Consular jurisdiction throughout Syria and Palestine, and I would invite your Lordship's attention to the fact that it will not require an increase of expenditure.

The Consular corps of Great Britain is at present represented by a Consul-General at Beyrout; by Consuls at Damascus and Jerusalem; by unpaid Vice-Consuls at Lattakia, Tripoli, Sidon, and Jaffa, and by Consular agents at the port of Tripoli, and at St. Jean d'Acre.

The Vice-Consulates and the Consular agencies might be left *in statu quo* until vacated by the actual holders. They should then be replaced by unpaid Consular Dragomans, a step which might at once be taken with advantage, chosen from the wealthiest and the most influential natives, and Protestants, who in many towns are rising to distinction, should be especially preferred. There is nothing derogatory in the title of Consular Dragoman which the French Foreign Office confers upon some of its most respectable *employés*. The solid gain of the change would be that whereas in choosing a Vice-Consul or a Consular agent, we are compelled to take non-subjects of the Porte, and thus we are often unable, as at the important centres of Hums and Hamah, to find suitable persons who are not already employed by other nations; we can bestow temporary protection upon any] Ottoman subject, and make him a Consular Dragoman. The only objection which might be offered is that the number of Dragomans attached to the Consulate-General, the two Consulates, the four Vice-Consulates, and the two Consular agencies in the province is limited by the regulations to four, three, and two respectively. These, however, form a total of 23, and the list is never filled up. The Consul-General, for instance, employs only two; the Consul of Jerusalem one. Moreover, this is a minor matter which can easily be settled. The Persian Consul (General?) at Damascus is allowed an unlimited number.

The Consular Dragomans should be permitted to fly their flags without expecting a salute, which at the inland posts cannot be returned, and they should be restricted to an establishment consisting of one Interpreter (Sous-Dragoman or Elève-Dragoman) and two Kawasses or Janissaries. They should communicate through their Consuls with the Consul-General, and the latter should visit them in person, or if unable himself to make the tour of inspection, by deputy, at least once every two years. This is a precaution of such importance that H.M.'s Foreign Office would be justified in defraying the actual travelling expenses of the Consul-General.

The places were Consular Dragomans are required are :—

1. Hums.
2. Hamah.
3. Baalbak and the Northern Bukáa (Cœlesyria).
4. Zachleh (on the Eastern Slopes of the Lebanon) and the Southern Bukáa.
5. Safet; which has a large colony of Jews under British protection.
6. Tiberias; also with a Jewish colony.
7. Nazareth; where there is a Protestant mission and a school that urgently want protection, this being a turbulent town.
8. Nablus; also the seat of a Protestant school, and, like Nazareth, a turbulent town.
9. Tyre; a port again rising to distinction.
10. Salt; the Chef-lieu of the Belká, where an English clergyman is actually residing.

Hums and Hamah might, if judged proper, be placed under a single Consular Dragoman. It would, however, be far better to station an official at each of these great centres, in view of the immense changes which will be introduced to their vicinity by the newly-established Vilayet of Tor, by the settlement of the Bedouin, and by the Circassian colonization.

Thus Syria will again be made to feel British influence—an influence which of late years has so declined, that the Consular Dragoman of 1850 had more authority than the Consul of 1871. The province will by this measure be prepared for an event that shall give her new life—the laying down of the Euphrates Valley Railroad. Thus, too, we shall counterbalance the present preponderating influence of Russia, whose progress through the Greek Amreh is rapid and sure, and we shall give to Protestantism that support which in Syria and Palestine it so much needs.

That the local Government, as now constituted, will offer the sturdiest opposition to a hange which tends to establish British interests—political, commercial, and social—upon the soundest footing, my personal knowledge of its policy does not permit me to doubt; but the opposition will be factious and destitute of reasonable cause. It must therefore succumb to the first serious effort on the part of H.M.'s Government. My acquaintance with the province, derived not from hearsay but from travel and actual inspection, will enable me to submit, if required to do so, a list of persons best suited for the post of Consular Dragomans, and—however your lordship may see fit to dispose of me—I wish nothing more than to see carried out the measures which I have ventured to propose for the welfare of Syria.

I have the honour to be,
My Lord,
Your most obedient humble Servant,
(Signed)   RICHARD F. BURTON.
H.M.'s Consul, Damascus.

CASE No. 7.

RECALL FROM DAMASCUS.

On 16th August, 1871, I was much surprised by receiving a note from M. Jago, H.M.'s Vice-Consul at Beyrout, informing me that he had been ordered by Mr. Consul-General Eldridge to take charge of H.M.'s Consulate at Damascus. I at once rode into Damascus, when I was more surprised to find a despatch from Her Majesty's Secretary of State for Foreign Affairs ordering me at once to return to England. The reason given was that I had become unpopular with the Moslems, who were supposed to be fanatical enough to want my life. After making over charge of the Consulate I went down to Beyrout, where I found a steamer for Liverpool, and sailed on 20th August. I have, since my return, been exonerated from any fault or shortcoming by H.M.'s Secretary of State for Foreign Affairs, and I have been informed that I am not recalled on the first ground, but on account of H.M.'s Consulate, Damascus, coming under the reduction.

I am still residing in England, hoping that I may receive compensation for my heavy losses, and that Her Majesty's Foreign Office will be pleased to do me the justice of entering into the details of my case.

I beg also to state that the Turkish Government, a month after my departure, recalled the officer who obtained my recall. Moreover, that *his* successor has carried out all my suggestions, and that H.M.'s Government have been pleased to express their approval of what he has done, whilst my own successor has found no cause to complain of anything I, have done, nor to alter anything in the Consulate as it was left by me.

The despatches relating to my recall are:—

From Mr. Jago to Captain Burton, 15th August, 1871.

Mr. Consul-General Eldridge to Captain Burton, August 14th, 1871.

Earl Granville to Captain Burton, U. F. S. to Mr. Consul-General Eldridge, July 22nd, 1871.

Captain Burton's reply to Earl Granville, London, October 16th, 1871.

Captain Burton to Earl Granville, enclosing a letter from the Rev. W. Wright, October 2nd, 1871, and one from Mr. Tyrwhitt Drake, October 1st, 1871.
Earl Granville to Captain Burton, October 25th, 1871.
Captain Burton's reply, London, November 12th, 1871.

DAMASCUS,
August 15th, 1871.

SIR,

In pursuance of instructions from Her Majesty's Consul-General at Beyrout, acting under instructions from Her Majesty's Principal Secretary of State for Foreign Affairs, I have this morning, Tuesday, arrived here to take over from you the charge of H.M.'s Consulate in this city, and to carry on the duties of that office temporarily as Acting-Consul until some other arrangement can be made.

I am also the bearer of a sealed despatch to your address, which I am requested to deliver personally to you.

I have the honour to request that you will be good enough to come to Damascus as soon as possible, to enable the instructions which I bear to be carried out without delay.

I have the honour to be, Sir,
Your most obedient Servant,
THOS. JAGO.

Captain Burton,
    H.B.M.'s Consul at Damascus,
        at Bluden.

ALEIH, MT. LEBANON,
August 14th, 1871.

SIR,

In consequence of instructions which accompanied the inclosed despatch I have instructed Mr. Vice-Consul Jago to proceed without delay to Damascus, to take charge of Her Majesty's Consulate in that city as Acting-Consul.

You will therefore, in obedience to the instructions addressed to you by Earl Granville, proceed at once to give over all the archives and affairs of the office to that gentleman upon his handing to you this despatch.

I have the honour to be, Sir,
Your obedient Servant,
G. JACKSON ELDRIDGE,
Consul-General.

Captain Burton,
    H.M.'s Consul, Damascus.

[No. 3.]

Under Flying Seal, to Consul-General Eldridge.

FOREIGN OFFICE,
July 22nd, 1871.

SIR,

You are informed by a despatch written to you on the 19th of January, 1869, by direction of the late Earl of Clarendon, that very serious objections had been made to your appointment as Her Majesty's Consul at Damascus, and that though his Lordship was willing to allow you to proceed to that post on receiving your assurance that the objections were unfounded, you were warned that it would be necessary that you should be recalled if the feeling stated to exist against you on the part of the authorities and people of Damascus should prevent the proper discharge of your official duties.

I regret to have now to inform you that the complaints which I have received from the Turkish Government in regard to your recent conduct and proceedings, render it impossible that I should allow you to continue to perform any Consular functions in Syria, and I have accordingly to desire that you will, on receipt of this despatch, hand over the archives of Her Majesty's Consulate at Damascus to the person whom Mr. Consul-General Eldridge will appoint to carry on the duties of the Consulate until further orders.

You will therefore make your preparations for returning to this country with as little delay as possible.

I am, Sir,
Your most obedient humble Servant,
GRANVILLE.

Captain Burton,
Her Majesty's Consul,
Damascus.

[COPY.]

14, MONTAGU PLACE, MONTAGU SQUARE,
LONDON,
October 16th, 1871.

MY LORD,

I had the honour to acknowledge, simply and without comment, the receipt of your Lordship's despatch (No. 3) of August, 1871, and according to your directions I returned to England with as little delay as possible. It becomes now my duty in a matter not only so serious of itself, but also so important as regards the public interest, to lay the whole case before your Lordship from the time of my appointment to that of my recall. I confidently hope, from your Lordship's well-known sense of justice, that it will be taken into your favourable consideration, and that my Consular career, especially at Damascus, will be found not undeserving of your approbation.

The appointment to Her Majesty's Consulate, Damascus, was conferred upon me by the then Right Honourable the Lord Stanley, on November 30, 1868.

A rumour was at once spread about that the Moslems hated me because I had pilgrimaged to Meccah, and that my life would be placed in danger by their fanaticism. I have been confidently assured, and throughout Syria it is universally believed, that the originators of the report were certain persons, who, fearing lest I should set on foot an anti-missionary policy, and would perhaps favour Moslem against Christian, represented the peril of arousing Mohammedan bigotry by allowing me to take office. They knew as well as I knew that my main difficulty would be the expectations of the Moslems to be the most favoured party at the Consulate. The late Lord Clarendon could hardly help being impressed by these rumours coming from a source so respectable, and he forgot that after my pilgrimage to Meccah I had lived for years in Moslem communities, Arab, African, and Indian—still more fanatical than the Syrian, as the late murder of Mr. Justice Norman will show. I was, however, allowed to proceed to my post with the following proviso:—"If," says the despatch (Separate) of June 19th, 1869, "the feeling stated to exist against you on the part of the authorities and the people of Damascus should prevent the proper performance of your official duties, it will be his Lordship's duty immediately to recall you." My answer (June 21st,

1869) was a direct denial that any such feeling existed, and a promise to act with more than usual circumspection.

Assuming charge at Damascus on Oct. 2nd, 1869, I met, as I fully expected, with the most flattering reception; and I repeated (Oct. 27, 1869) to Lord Clarendon that the chiefs of all parties—clerical as well as secular—had visited and welcomed me: even such men as the Shaykh Abdullah el Halabi, who were considered too bigoted to enter the house of a European, and whose position forbade them to meet me at a hotel.

Having settled myself at the head-quarters of the Ottoman Government in Syria, I at once saw through the state of affairs. Your Lordship will doubtless have means of ascertaining the position held there by Great Britain, and you will probably concur with me that there is a legitimate influence which it should be the duty of every British functionary in the East to secure and to maintain. You will best know how much of our national *prestige* existed when I took charge of the Consulate of Damascus; and I may venture to assert that it has never been higher than at the time of my recall.

During my first year I gained some credit of impartiality, and by advocating honesty in a place "whose atmosphere," to quote the words of a well-known traveller, "has the effect of denationalizing the English character, and of taking from it its impatience of injustice and oppression."

I opposed the imprudent zeal of Mr. Mentor Mott, superintendent of the British Syrian Schools, and in my despatches I duly reported his visits at the capital as dangerous to himself and to the Christian community. My next step, on the other hand, was a demand for the punishment of certain Druzes who had plundered and maltreated Mr. Mackintosh, an English missionary, and Her Majesty's Ambassador at Constantinople was pleased to approve of my proceedings. My next public duty, as your Lordship doubtless knows from my reports, was that of curbing the rapacity of three native money-lenders enjoying British protection. This roused a storm of wrath, which raged for some months, the case being made to assume a sort of religious aspect from the fact of these persons belonging to the Jewish religion. Thus they obtained a support which they otherwise would not have done, although as a rule nothing can be more dissimilar than the followers of Judaism at Damascus and their respected co-religionists of England, France, and Germany. But notwithstanding the fact of their straining every nerve for my recall, they failed in so doing. I have reason to believe that your Lordship honoured my proceedings with your approval, but no communication to this effect reached me. Moreover, I had the mortification of ascertaining that my course of action in these three affairs was not consonant with the views of my immediate senior in Syria.

The circumstances which finally led to my recall date from the beginning of 1871. I was then weary of the succession of promises by word of mouth, in writing and by telegram, with which the ex-Governor Rashid Pasha had met my first requisitions. I declared that it was my duty no longer to countenance delay in settling the claims of British subjects, amounting to about six millions of piastres, and dating in one case as far back as 1863. I then proceeded to bring the most notorious and flagrant cases to the notice of Her Majesty's Ambassador at Constantinople. Rashid Pasha hated nothing more than such references, and ever regarded and spoke of them as overt acts of hostile inclination. From that time I date his repeated attacks, intended, as is well known on the spot, to weary out the superior authorities at the capital, and to induce demands for my return. I need not specify to your Lordship the mode in which such intrigues are usually conducted throughout the Turkish dominions.

In May, 1871, the Governor-General seized the opportunity of a village riot at Nazareth to take the part of the rioters, and to endorse their falsehoods by sending them in a telegram to Constantinople three days before my return to Damascus, and before I could offer a word of explanation. His report (May 16, 1871) charged me with firing upon inoffensive people, and with sending in chains to Damascus sundry innocent persons when he had himself issued the orders. His appeal was forwarded to the late Grand Vizier, Ali Pasha, under the circumstances usual in Syria, and that officer at once ordered my removal.

I exposed the untruths of the telegram, and I had the honour of laying before your

Lordship the testimony of two clergymen of the Church of England, besides other English travellers who happened fortunately to be present, and who thus could testify to the moderation of my conduct under somewhat trying circumstances. The result, however, was a despatch from your Lordship (No. 1, of June 14, 1871), in which I was directed, until the receipt of further instructions, not to quit the seat of my Consulate, the city of Damascus. I need not say that I at once obeyed the order, notwithstanding the extreme heat and unhealthiness, until compelled by illness, and under medical certificate of the sanitary officer employed by the French Government, to follow the rest of the English colony to the mountains.

Rashid Pasha then affected to look upon a visit which I paid to the Hauran Mountain, within sight of Damascus, and included in the limits of that Consulate, as a movement pregnant with evils to his Administration. I went in pursuance of repeated invitations sent to me by the friendly chiefs of Druze villages who had applied for my interest in establishing an English School.

Rashid Pasha at once forwarded to Constantinople a mistranslation of the letter which I addressed to my friends, thus converting an unimportant into a very serious matter. I therefore despatched a true translation to Her Majesty's Embassy, Constantinople, and I am bound to suppose that it reached Her Majesty's Foreign Office.

Your Lordship's despatch (No. 3, of July 22, 1871) recalled me, however, to England, upon the grounds that certain complaints had been made against me by the Ottoman Government, and it was thus virtually assumed that ill feeling on the part of the authorities and the people of Damascus has prevented the proper discharge of my official duties.

The testimonials herewith presented will, I believe, satisfy your Lordship that, during my entire service as Her Majesty's Consul for Damascus, I have been guided by the strictest impartiality in the performance of my duty, and that my conduct has not only received but has, I trust, merited the approbation and support of the most respectable residents of all religions, and of every condition. During my ten and a half years of Consular service, I have been stationed upon the West Coast of Africa, in the Brazil, and in Syria. My first three years were spent in the Bight of Biafra, where I was successful in my endeavours to procure justice for British subjects, and I may fairly boast that, contrary to all precedent, during the proceedings necessary in attaining this object I was not the cause of a single village being burnt, or of a life being taken. Throughout my four years of service in the Brazil I never had a dispute or even a difference with the authorities, and I can confidently refer your Lordship to Her Majesty's Envoy, Mr. Buckley Mathew, C.B., for his opinion as regards the esteem in which I was held, and for the mode in which I performed my duties. Finally, I may venture to assert that in Syria, where I inherited all the most trying and difficult cases from my predecessors, I have left a name which will not readily be forgotten.

Under the circumstances, my Lord, I cannot but express the deep pain with which I received the communication of your Lordship's recall. I venture to trust that the statements and the corroborative evidence which I have the honour of submitting to you will entirely remove the impression apparently made to my prejudice, and that I have no cause personally to regret the consequences of the unjustifiable and unprovoked attack made upon me and upon my servants at Nazareth, or the offensive and hostile steps taken against me by the ex-Governor General Rashid Pasha, and I feel it my duty to my fellow-countrymen to represent the serious consequences to travellers, if such outrages remain unreproved.

I have now the honour to lay before your Lordship various testimonials wholly unsolicited by me, and only recently forwarded after my departure from Damascus. They consist of letters and addresses (each showing the sentiments of a tribe or community or a village) from His Highness the Amir Abd el Kadir, of Algerine fame, from their Eminences the Archbishop of the Syrian Catholics, the Bishop of the Greek Catholics, the Acting Patriarch of the Catholic Armenians of Damascus, and from the Superior of the Latin Convent at Nazareth; from the Presbyterian Missionaries at Damascus (the Rev. Messrs. Wright and Scott), from the Rev. Mr. Zeller, of Nazareth; from Mr. Rattray, an English colonist of *long standing in Syria; from three Druze chiefs—Salim Beg Shams, Ali Beg el Hammádeh, and Hammad Nofal; from the Bedawr Shaykhs Mijwell el Mezrab and Abdo el Hámed; from Shaykh Ahmad, Chief Inspector of the Great Amawi Mosque; from various other personages, and from no less than fourteen villages in the vicinity of our summer quarters.* The names of the latter have not been inserted owing to a report now current that Rashid Pasha has been successful at Constantinople, and is about to return to Damascus, where his vindictive character is greatly feared.

       I have the honour to be,
          My Lord,
            Your most obedient humble Servant,
              (Signed) RICHARD F. BURTON.

To Her Majesty's Secretary of State for Foreign Affairs.

[COPY.]
        14, MONTAGU PLACE, MONTAGU SQUARE,
            LONDON, W.,
(Separate.)   October 21st, 1871.

MY LORD,

  I have the honour to enclose you copies of two letters I have received from Mr. Drake, who was with me at Nazareth, and the Rev. William Wright, relative to their safety in Syria.

  I think your Lordship will like to hear, after the complaint made by the Wali that the fanatical Moslems wanted my life, that I have received letters from Syria, one of which contains the following passage: "Last Friday the Mahommedans had a great pray for you in the Jamia el Amawi, on account of their getting rid of Rashid Pasha, and praying for your return, and blessed you on the right and on the left of the Mosque." The Jamia is the great Mosque of Damascus, the very centre of fanatical Islamism, where no other Christian except myself can enter without a Moslem escort.

  Another letter says, "The Consulate looks as if a death or a bankruptcy had taken place, and the English are hiding their heads." A third letter says, "If you come back, as we all hope you may, you shall have such a reception as no one ever had before; thousands of Moslems, Druzes, Greeks Orthodox, Greek Catholics, Maronites and Protestants, are preparing to come to Beyrout to give you a welcome."

  The Moslems and Christians are fighting about Beyrout, and there has been a great fight in the gardens of Damascus, in which the Zabtiyéhs were disarmed and killed.

  I also wish to inform your Lordship that the report which I mentioned in my despatch (Separate, October 16, 1871), that Rashid Pasha is to return to Damascus is a false one. He is dismissed with disgrace, never to be re-employed, and was not even allowed to remain till the new Wali arrived. The Porte has at last recognized the truth concerning him. I venture to hope that your Lordship will concur with me in thinking that an English officer who could get on well with him, could not at the same time be faithfully serving Her Majesty's Government.

  I would beg leave to inform your Lordship lest there should be any further misrepresentation, that after receiving your order of recall, I mounted my horse, and rode off in ten minutes without returning to my house, where I had removed some of the important despatches in consequence of a warning I received from a private friend of the Wali that he thought of burning my house and Consulate in Damascus whilst I was absent at my summer quarters. After I left, everything in the house was carefully packed up and sent after me to England, but will not arrive for a fortnight. Should there be, as I suspect, any papers belonging to the office, I shall return them immediately on the arrival of my effects.

       I have the honour to be, my Lord,
          Your most obedient humble Servant
              RICHARD F. BURTON.

To Her Majesty's Secretary of State
  for Foreign Affairs,
    the Earl Granville, K.G.

[COPY.]

SALATIGEH, DAMASCUS,
October 1, 1871.

MY DEAR BURTON,

Yesterday, and again to day, Mr. Jago, H.B.M.'s Acting-Consul here, came to me with reference to a telegram received by Mr. Consul-General Eldridge, who was called upon by H.M. Foreign Office to engage the Turkish Government in Syria to look after my safety and that of Mr. Frigh (? Wright). Mr. Jago asked me officially whether I had any *particular* danger to apprehend at this moment. After the attempt made in June by Rashid Pasha—for I feel convinced from what I have heard both from Druzes and Bedawin that it was by his orders that the Ghiat and Shtais were put on my traces—I should have had something to apprehend, but now that that curse of Syria is gone I suppose it is hardly likely. I should have mentioned this to Mr. Jago, but though *morally* certain of the Wali's complicity, I have not the legal proofs in black and white, and though many of the most influential natives have expressed their fears of disturbances to come—in fact, riots took place last week at Beyrout which are popularly supposed to have been instigated by the Wali—yet, as in the former case, I was unable to state this in reply to an official query. You know better than any one how difficult, or rather impossible, it is to get evidence that would avail before a legal tribunal on matters of this sort, convinced though one may be of the facts. Consequently, in answer to Mr. Jago's direct official enquiry, "Do you apprehend any *particular* danger at this moment to yourself?" I was obliged to say that I could not name any. I feel, however, *morally* sure that we shall have some disturbances here, and it is not at all impossible that the Wali may have left orders to hinder the journey into N. Syria upon which I start to-morrow. I have, however, taken the precaution to get a safe pass (buzuldore) from the Serai, and I take two mounted Zabtiyeh with me,

You are at liberty to make what use of this letter you like.

Yours very truly,
CHARLES F. TYRWHITT DRAKE.

Captain R. F. Burton, F.R.G.S.,
&c., &c., &c.

[COPY.]

DAMASCUS,
2nd October, 1871.

MY DEAR CAPTAIN BURTON,

Yesterday Mr. Jago sent for me and asked me if I required any special protection, or if I feared any special danger at the present time. I answered that now that the Governor was removed I did not apprehend any special danger. Mr. Jago said he did not want that answer. Did I apprehend any special danger *now?* I said I considered the ordinary danger was increased by your recall, and that I had private information that the Governor had an animosity towards me. He again put the "danger *now*" question, to which I replied that when going to church in the morning, past the Castle, a soldier came up, and, unprovoked, struck my horse. "That," I said, "is the latest fact I have to report." I told him also that I had spoken to a Turkish officer, who referred me to some high functionary, and that the soldier walked away undisturbed. Mr. Jago proposed to take up this affair, but I refused to allow him to do so, as so doing would only expose our weakness. He then told me that he was officially asked if I needed any special protection—that a telegram to that effect had come from the Foreign Office. I said that a perfectly logical answer to that question was the one I had given—that, inasmuch as his Excellency had gone off the night before, I considered that I was now menaced by no special danger.

It then appeared that (it was only a guess that) I was one of the persons enquired after as the name was spelled "Fright." I declared that I was neither Fright nor Frightened, and that I would not recognize that as my name, but that if he asked me officially if I apprehended danger, I would give my answer in writing, as I would not have words put into my mouth, nor be impaled on the horn of a dilemma. We then agreed that I was not the person. I was glad to be able to escape this, as any special protection would only tend to increase my danger, and would undoubtedly interfere with my work. I had also before my mind the action of a British Minister, in a panic, recalling the best Consul who has been in Syria in my time, to the undoubted lowering of English *prestige* and influence here; and reflecting on the loss that similar action on the part of my masters might entail on the Church, I was exceedingly glad to court the shade. Above all things save me from special Turkish protection.

Thinking, however, that the above telegram may have emanated from your solicitude for us, and knowing privately that the last act of the Governor was to write a very strong letter (strong in inuendoes) with respect to the despatch, and believing that an attempt might be made to injure you on the ground of your raising needless alarm, I send you the above statement of which you may make what use you please.

Yours most truly,
WM. WRIGHT.

P.S.—Mr. Jago told me Drake said he knew no special danger by which he was now menaced. He must have permitted himself to be forced on the dilemma, for *we* know that he has gone about of late a perfect arsenal of locomotion.

WM. W.

[COPY.]

FOREIGN OFFICE,
October 25th, 1871.

SIR,
I have received your letter of the 16th of October, recapitulating, with reference to the cessation of your functions as Her Majesty's Consul at Damascus, the several employments in Her Majesty's Consular service, which you have successfully held.

I do not think it necessary to follow you through that recapitulation, or to enter into any review of your conduct in the post which you last held. I am willing to give you credit for having endeavoured, to the best of your ability and judgment, to carry on the duties which were entrusted to you; but having come to the conclusion, on a review of the Consular establishments in Syria, that it was no longer necessary to maintain a full Consul at Damascus at a cost to the public, including salary and allowance, of £1000 a year, your withdrawal from that residence necessarily followed on the appointment of an officer of lower rank, and at a lower rate of salary, to perform the Consular duties in that place.

I am, Sir,
Your most obedient humble Servant,
GRANVILLE.

Captain Burton,
14, Montagu Place,
Montagu Square.

[COPY.]

14, MONTAGU PLACE, MONTAGU SQUARE,
LONDON, W.,
November 12th, 1871.

MY LORD,
I have the honour to acknowledge the receipt of your Lordship's despatch of October 25, 1871. It is gratifying to me to find that the cause of my recall from Damascus

is not on account of any erroneous impression that ill-feeling existed against me on the part of the authorities or the people of Syria.

This circumstance will render it unnecessary to trouble your lordship with many other testimonials lately forwarded to me from the British protected Jews of Tiberias and Safed, from the Druzes, from the villages about Damascus, and from other sections of the community.

It is, however, my duty to lay before your Lordship the inevitable results of appointing, under existing arrangements, an officer of lower rank and at a lower rate of salary, to perform the Consular duties in Damascus.

In my despatch of July 24, 1871 (Consular changes, "suggestions"), I had the honour to point out the serious detriment to the public service, resulting from Her Majesty's Consulate-General being placed at Beyrout. Whilst in Damascus, the head-quarters of the province, the residence of the Governor-General and of the High Court of Appeal, Her Majesty's Government is represented by an officer of lower rank. It will not have escaped your Lordship's notice that Syria, and especially Damascus, are at present in an abnormal state of excitement; that a religious movement of an unexampled nature is shaking the foundations of Mahommedanism, and that the danger to British subjects and protected persons (I might say to all Christians, native and foreign), threatens to become serious. Until I brought these facts before Her Majesty's Foreign Office, they were, I believe, very imperfectly understood, even at Beyrout.

No wish on my part to obtrude my opinions causes me to bring this state of affairs to your Lordship's notice; but I should be deservedly subject to blame, did I neglect to lay before you the state of affairs in Syria, and to suggest for your consideration the measures by which serious consequences to British influence and to the lives and property of English subjects may be avoided.

With respect to my own future employment, it only remains for me to place myself at your Lordship's commands, in the assured hope that such employment will be of a nature to mark that I have not forfeited the approbation of Her Majesty's Government.

I have the honour to be, my Lord,
Your most obedient humble Servant,
RICHARD F. BURTON.

To Earl Granville, K.G.,
    H.M.'s Secretary of State
        for Foreign Affairs.

CASE No. 8.

TESTIMONIALS FROM SYRIA.

Letters from Syria on the occasion of Captain Burton's departure, showing the feeling of every creed, race, and tongue, Moslem and Christian, with only seven dissentient voices. The latter were—
1. The Wali Rashid Pasha.
2. Mr. Consul-General Eldridge.
3. Mrs. Mentor Mott.
4. Yakoob Stambouly.
5. Ishaak Tobi. } Three British-protected Jew money-lenders.
6. Daoud Harari.
7. M. Niffon, the Greek (Orthodox) Bishop of Nazareth.

Conclusion. A short *résumé* of Captain Burton's stewardship in Syria.

---

1. Allah, favour the days of your far-famed learning, and prosper the excellence of your writing. O wader of the seas of knowledge, O cistern of learning of our globe, exalted above his age, whose exaltation is above the mountains of increase and our rising place, opener by his books of night and day, traveller by ship and foot and horse, one whom none can equal in travel.

To His Excellency Captain Burton—

But afterwards, verily we wondered at the suddenness of your departure, and we deeply regretted our not being present in the city when you honoured us with your farewell visit, and truly this greatly affected us. But as the thing was (to be), so we imagine that we had seen you from our personal friendship. This has been written and intrusted to the hands of your excellent Lady, manifesting our sorrow at your departure. We hope that you will keep a friendly remembrance of us as merit the excellencies of your qualities, of which the best is your zeal and devotion to the service of your country. We only hope that everything will turn out to you as happily as can be. It is our personal friendship to you which dictates this letter.

(Signed)   Your Friend,
ABD EL KADIR.

Danzig, Jemad el Tani 22.
A. H. 1288.

DAMAS,
Le 15 Sept., 1871.

Monsieur le Consul,

C'est avec surprise et regret que nous avons appris votre départ inattendu pour l'Angleterre ; et cette surprise a été d'autant plus sensible qu'on avait répandu le bruit que vous alliez nous quitter pour toujours.

Probablement ces bruits proviennent de vos ennemis ; mais quoi ! à Damas vous n'aviez pas d'ennemis ; tout le monde vous était ami. Vous étiez aimé, cheri, estimé, et presque adoré par toutes les classes de la société, même par les Musulmans ; parce que vous étiez devenu le protecteur des opprimés et le défenseur de la justice. Vous aviez su, par votre complaisance et votre extrême délicatesse, capturer le cœur des honnêtes gens et reconcilier tous les intérêts. Il n'y avait que les gens pervers et corrompus, qui se gênaient de votre présence et cherchaient votre éloignement. Les insensés ! Ils ne veulent pas comprendre qu'en agissant de la sorte, ils ne font que suivre l'exemple des fils de Jacob, qui, voulant empêcher Joseph de devenir roi, l'ont vendu à l'esclavage ; et c'est précisément pour l'avoir vendu qu'il est devenu roi, et ainsi ils ont été, sans le vouloir, l'instrument de la volonté divine.

Quoiqu'il en soit, nous regrettons vivement votre départ et celui de Madame Burton, qui était devenu la mère des pauvres, et nous aimons à espérer que le sage et prevoyant Gouvernement de Sa Majesté Britannique ne privera pas Damas d'un si digne représentant, qui a mérité dans le pays le titre glorieux *El Moustakim* (homme impartial).

Ainsi nos yeux sont tournés vers vous, Monsieur le Consul, nos vœux vous accompagnent et nos sympathies vous suivent par tout où vous serez. Nous prions le bon Dieu de vous combler de ses bénédictions, et de vous donner toutes sortes de prospérité et de bonheur.

Agréez, Monsieur le Consul, cette expression collective de notre sincère amour et notre extrême attachement à votre estimable personne.

Fr. DOMINIQUE AISLA, (L.S.)
　Pressidente e lure delta Ferre Sainte.
　　JACOB GEOHARGI, (L.S.)
　　　Vice-Général du Patriarche des Arméniens Catholiques.
　　　　JEAN, (L.S.)
　　　　　Vice-Général du Patriarche Arménien Orthodoxe.

A Monsieur le Capt. Richard Burton,
Consul de S.M. Britannique à Damas, actuellement à Londres.

---

[3]

DAMAS,
Le 8 Septembre, 1871.

Monsieur le Consul,

Grand a été notre étonnement, et profonds ont été nos regrets, lorsque nous avons appris votre départ subit pour l'Angleterre. Et ce départ nous a été d'autant plus sensible, qu'on a de suite répandu le bruit que vous ne reviendriez plus à Damas.

Ce sont probablement vos ennemis qui ont à dessein répandu cette fausse nouvelle. Mais quels ennemis ! Vous ne deviez pas en avoir, puisque vous étiez aimé, chéri et estimé de toutes les classes de la société.

Quoiqu'il en soit, si vous deviez, ce qu'à Dieu ne plaise, ne pas revenir au milieu de nous, nous regretterions toujours vivement votre absence et celle de Madame votre épouse, qui était, pour les pauvres de cette ville, une véritable providence. Nous aimons donc à espérer encore que le Gouvernement de Sa Majesté Britannique ne privera point Damas d'un homme qui le représentait si bien, et qui a su, en si peu de temps, s'attirer l'estime de tout le monde.

En attendant, soyez persuadé, Monsieur le Consul, que nos vœux et nos prières vous accompagneront partout où il plaira à Dieu e vous appeler. Je le prierai aussi de vous combler de ses plus abondantes bénédictions, et de vous faire prospérer dans toutes vos entreprises.

Agréez l'assurance de la plus haute considération avec laquelle j'ai l'honneur d'être, Monsieur le Consul,

Votre tout dévoué en N.S.,
(L.S.) GREGOIRE JACOBE HELIANI,
Archevêque Syrien Cath. de Damas.

---

[4]

From Damascus. Aylul 1, 1871.

To His Excellency the Consul, abounding in honour and in respect, whose praiseworthy qualities and remarkable gifts and superior graces and purity of heart, with all other peculiar manifestations of excellency with which he is adorned and with which he has been gifted by Allah, and which draw our hearts to him in love, and cause us so deeply to regret his departure after we have been upon such friendly terms.

I was indeed desirous of expressing my affection to you before we separated, in order to bid adieu to you in due form; but unfortunately we had no opportunity so to do. Very great was our sorrow when we heard from your excellent lady that she intended to leave us this week. May her journey be prosperous to you both, and may you both increase in every worldly gift; and may you rise by her good aid and excellent qualities to the height of fame and to spiritual and material greatness. And the Arab saying has proved true (a wise man), "Shamm has met (the wise woman) Tabakah." We have begged her to offer to you our respects, and explain to you the excess of our love to you, praying the Lord to prosper her journey, and that you may both return to us at once whenever the Holy Spirit shall please. Let us rejoice in seeing you both once more, and enjoy the benefits which you have both conferred upon us. Our desire is that we may again meet and renew our friendship, and thus obtain fruition of all our desires, and ensure a continuance of our heartfelt affection. For that reason I offer myself as your servant, even in the name of the Lord Jesus Christ.

Yours prayerfully,
(Signed) MACARIUS, Acting Patriarch in Damascus and the Hauran.

[5.]

NAZARET,
A 6 Emb., 1871.

(L.S.) Illmo. Signore Console.

Sesi per mezzo del Signor Zeller sendi il desiderio di V.S. che demandava dai me una dichiararione del fatto successo, ma paro in francese, simile a quella spedito a V.S. iu Italiano.

Senza nessuna dificolta, e con piacere sarèi stato pronto a scriverla ma V. Signoria ben sa che qui in convento non ci hanessuno che scrive il francese, e volendola fare, sarei costretto a chiamare uno di fuori, e chi trovare da poterci fidare? ed essere sicuro, se senza vedere niente, sequitano a parlare contro di noi e della vostra Signoria che ne sara se sendano de quarta lettera. Io, Signor mio, o creduto pui opportuno di non andane sogetto a nessuno, V. Signoria potra prevalersi di queste mie in Italiano, credo bene che in Inglaterra, non pochi sono quelli che sanno leggere l'Italiano, e perciò la potra far tradurre in francese, e cosi si evita ogni occasione a questi di partare di più e contra V.S. e contra di noi, che come oi disse tuttora si parla.

Solo vi e di più in questa mia che la venuta in Nazaret del Bascia e del Mamur di Damasco, non fualtro di fare a loro modo, e non colla Giústizia e perciò il Procuratore di V.S si vidde costretto, di fa la protesta por due volte e tutte le due volte fu suspento e non accettato. Allora il Procuratore di V.S. non vedendo altra Strada, ho pure [dato] autorita da presendarsi per far accettare la protesta at Pascia, si presento al convento, e scritto la terza Protesta. Io per mezzo di un mio frate la presento at Pascia ma il Pascia net vederla rimase attonito, non potendola rifiútare la presa, e voltatosi at Mamur di Damasco, che li era al fianco, li disse. Ecco prendetela che voi siete la causa di tutto questo, e percio io non so niente, vedetevela voi. Ed il Pascio dopo di aver Stato per 17 giorno in Nazaret, quando era sul punto di partire mi mando la risposta della Protesta, che V.S. gia ne Sara del tutto informato.

Ecco quando mi ho creduto in dovere di notificare alla Sria. Vortra mentro passo a riverirla unito alla Signora con tutto rispetto ho il bene di raffermarmi.

D. V. S. Illma.,
(Signed)   JR. ANGELO MARTINEZ, Guardiano.

---

[6]

DAMASCUS,
August 23rd, 1871.

DEAR CAPTAIN BURTON,

We were painfully surprised a few days ago by the intelligence that a despatch had been received from the Foreign Office calling upon you to resign your position as British Consul in Damascus. We are quite at a loss to understand the motives for such a procedure. We can scarcely suppose that any one was bold enough to charge you with corruption in your official capacity. We have never known of a solitary reflection being made on your integrity, but have heard repeated testimony to the purity of your Consulate; and we can ourselves witness that your first official act was to replace dishonest by honest Dragomans.

On the other hand, it seems to us highly probable that the very integrity which should have been your highest claim to the confidence of your superiors has proved the cause of your removal by raising against you the bitter enmity of all, whether Turkish official or English *protégé*, whom your honesty disgusted or disappointed. Especially we have reason to believe that your straightforward course provoked the hatred of the Wali of Syria. This functionary, at once corrupt, treacherous, and incapable, prefers a Consul who is pliant to his will, and who knows how to shut his eyes on his rapacity, or even to be a sharer in his spoliations—what wonder that he should watch his opportunity to have removed a man whose conduct was a marked contrast to and a tacit reproach on his own.

We conjecture that he caught hold of the affair of Nazareth, and sought so to colour it as to injure you with your own Government. It was easy for the Wali to represent you as having become unpopular with the people of Syria in consequence—just as easy as for him now to make it believed at Constantinople that he is himself a most popular Governor, though the contrary is notoriously the case. Still, we feel greatly surprised that an English Minister should be deceived by his representations, and remove from a position he worthily filled a faithful servant of his country.

We think our testimony as English missionaries and subjects should go for something; it is that of men who were strongly prejudiced against you on your first coming to Damascus, who were bound to you by no tie of sect or of party, but who have admired the manly, vigorous, and upright course you have pursued while here, and who deeply regret that qualities such as yours should be lost to the land for whose moral and spiritual improvement they labour.

We are, Sir, most sincerely yours,
(Signed)   WILLIAM WRIGHT, A.B.
JAMES ORR SCOTT, M.A.

[7]

NAZARETH,
September 7th, 1871.

MY DEAR CAPTAIN,

I received both your letters, and also one from Mr. Drake. You can easily imagine how astonished we were when we heard what course the Foreign Office had taken in your affairs. When the Greek Bishop first spread these news here I flatly contradicted him, till I heard from Mr. Drake. It seems your return to England is necessary in order fully to expose the doings of the Wali of Damascus, who evidently has powerful friends. To-day I received the enclosed letter from the Superior of the Latin Convent, and hope the same will contain the statements you require.

An investigation about the attack made upon some of the workmen at the church was ordered by the Wali, but led scarcely to any result, and gave me so much trouble, that I would in future much rather abstain from complaining. These kind of investigations are only calculated to make a foreigner odious and ridiculous.

I shall be very glad to hear from you, if it is only by a line, and hope you may be able to obtain justice in England.

Believe me,
Dear Captain Burton,
Yours very truly,
JOHN ZELLER.

In great haste.—

I have not heard what trick the Wali played you at St. Jean d'Acre. By next post I will write to you to London. It is scarcely necessary to say how much I regret your sudden departure.

---

[8]

EL KHORABEH ANTI-LEBANON
18th August, 1871.

DEAR CAPTAIN BURTON,

I have just heard of your departure for England, but can hardly realize the fact.

My wife and myself are deeply grieved at the news; and, indeed, we have cause for regret, not only on account of losing friends, but for our personal safety. Having settled down permanently here amongst somewhat dangerous neighbours, we felt our chief security lay in your presence at Damascus, knowing the esteem and respect with which all the Moslems regard you. Of course I except those who are employed by the Wali; and every one knows that the animosity of the Wali and his party arises from the fact that you are aware of the bribery and corruption which pervade the whole system of administration, and which has grown worse in his time than it was under his predecessors. I do not believe any one of the Consuls in Damascus, except yourself, dared to do anything but what the Wali pleased, right or wrong. In the fourteen years of my residence in Syria, I never knew the English name so much respected as during the last twelve months. It is, however, selfish on our part to regret your departure, since both Mrs. Burton and yourself were probably glad to leave such a pestiferous hole as Damascus.

With our united kind regards,

Believe me, yours very truly,
JOHN SCOTT RATTRAY.

---

[9]

To his Excellency the Superior in Energy, the Elevated in Nature, Consul of the Great Government of England. May Allah increase his prosperity with all good gifts.

After inquiring about your honourable self, and committing you for ever to the charge of the Almighty King, I have the honour to state that, to my deepest regret, you are recalled from the city of Damascus, and are about to proceed to England, leaving us a prey to sorrow and trouble. We therefore supplicate Allah that your Excellency will return without loss of time. All our people are grieving sadly, because your presence at Damascus was a safeguard and a protection to us. We entreat the Lord, who has ordained this separation, that we may again have the joy of meeting, and that your enlightened heart will not forget us. And may Allah prolong your days, Effendi.

        (Signed) SELIM (BEG SHAMS).

Jemadi el Aksin,
  25 A.H. 1288.

---

[10]

Translation of Letter from Ali Beg el Hammádeh, Governor of the Druzes in Lebanon.

To the high in mind and generous in manner, the Excellent Bey. May Allah prolong his days. After presenting the usual compliments, and all due respect and prayers for your life and prosperity, it is our duty to inquire after your well-being and your present state. Secondly, since you left us going on the way of peace, you have filled our hearts with sorrow and regret; you have grieved our souls after the joy and pleasure we enjoyed. Such is the effect of your leaving this place, and of taking from us the light of your exalted countenance, we ever pray the Almighty once more to favour us with your return to this place, and gladden our souls and joy our hearts, for He is Almighty. We are ever awaiting your Excellency, and we hope from the All-powerful that this may soon take place. Praise be to Allah, your fame and reputation, your good gifts and qualities, are witnessed by all, great and small. May the Lord ever increase your prosperity and guide your ways and direct you to the highest dignity, and preserve you in joy and happiness. This is the object of writing to you, in hopes of your speedy return, and we shall be honoured by any orders that you may have to give us. All our brotherhood and tribes send to your Excellency their best wishes and enquiries, and know that we are ever awaiting to see you. May the Almighty prolong your days.

        (Signed) ALI BEG EL HAMMADEH.

Jemadi, 15 A.H. 1288.
Ab. 31, A.D. 1871.

---

[11]

From * * * * Chief Druze of the Village of . . . . . .

To the exalted in rank and dignity, His Excellency the Consul Bey. May Allah prolong his days! After many prayers to the Almighty Creator that your life will be long in the land, and your honour and prosperity ever increase and be exalted, we have to inform your Excellency, that having heard of your intended departure, we waited upon the Lady, and we felt in despair when we heard the truth. We pray to the Almighty that the news may not be true, considering the kindness and goodness which you have bestowed upon us, and which has made us eternally grateful. Therefore we supplicate the Creator that things will not long endure in the present state. The reason of our writing is to know the truth of things, and to express the grief with which we have heard of your departure, and may Allah ever preserve you!

        (Signed) HAMMAD NOFAL.

Aylul 12, 1871.

[No. 12.]

Letter from Shaykh Mijwel el Mezrab.

After sending most affectionate greetings, and the great affection we offer your Excellency it was our great misfortune that we did not see you when you came to our house, and we are very sorry for it; and after that we heard of your going to England, grief and sorrow came heavily upon us because we have never seen any one equal to your Excellency in this country, for all those related to England are deeply indebted to you—and all the denominations, Moslem and Christian, were fully satisfied with your Excellency, and they are all very sorry at your leaving; but we ask the Lord of Mercy to send you back to us in good health, and to let us meet you soon. From us and our brothers who send their greetings, and from all our Bedawin who send their best salaams, and whatever you wish us to do tell us to do it, and peace be with you.

(Signed) (L.S.) MIJWEL EL MEZRAB,
Chief of Mezrab Tribe.

Jemadi 7, A. H., 1288.

[No. 13.]

From the Bedawi Shaykh Abd el Hammad to His Excellency the Consul Effendi of the Great English Government, etc., etc.

After sending our best greeting, and offering up many prayers for you, the dealer in good advice and justice, and after hearing of your departure, I was sorely grieved, and may Allah ruin the house of the man who caused it! But if it please God you will soon return and overcome those that were jealous of you. I know that all those under your protection are very sorry for you, as you have been very good to them. All creeds and denominations pray for your return to this land, and curse the other man, hoping for his speedy ruin. Allah is merciful.

(Signed) ABD EL HAMMAD.

Jemadi 19, A. H., 1288.

[No. 14.]

To the Master of Dignity and Prosperity, of Science and Dignity, always the Object of our Hopes, sent to us by the Most High and Merciful God, Amen!

After sending our duties and compliments to your noble person, I have the honour to state that I am still standing in the same truthful love that was between us, and in the affection which was mutual, and in ever blessing and praying for you to the Most High, supplicating Him that your star may always rise brighter, and pour upon you its beneficent rays of largesse and generosity. The love of this your servant is too deep to be expressed by the pen, and it dates from the days when the disembodied souls met in hosts innumerable during the beginning of time. I doubt not that your enlightened heart will feel for me as I feel for you, and that no one may expel me from your memory. The excess of my affection impels me thus to write to you, hoping from the Lord that we may presently meet and renew our affectionate intercourse. May He prosper your return to us in the happiest state, and defend you from all calamities.

(Signed) AHMAD MUSALLIM,
El Ashráf at Damascus.
(Chief of the Great Mosque El Amawi.)

Jemadi 15, A. H., 1288.

[No. 15.]

Damascus to London.

Aylul 8, 1871.

To His Excellency M. Burton, Consul of the Noble English Government in Damascus, &c.

After asking about your valuable health we felt great sorrow at your leaving us, and we always speak well of your good name and of your justice, and we hope that you will reach London in safety, and that you will send us news of your safe arrival, and this we hope from your kindness, and that you will soon return to Damascus, for day and night we are looking out for your return in peace to this place, because in your days we experienced peace and quiet, and we met with nothing but good at your hands. It is not only we, but all the community, which is grieved at your leaving, on account of what they saw of your just conduct and steadfastness to the truth. And your lady's leaving is also a great grief to us, because she is going to England, and we hope that you will let us know of her joining you in safety and happiness, and we beg God Almighty that we may soon see you both again in happiness and good fortune. These are my wishes, and may God Almighty spare you.

(L.S.)   ABD ER RAHMAN.

[No. 16.]

To His Excellency.

Sir,

After sending our best compliments and our love, which we do not measure, we heard that your Excellency went away, and a great grief came upon us—firstly, because your Excellency is separated from us; and, secondly, that we did not see you before your leaving, which would have been a satisfaction; and, thirdly, because you did not send the news to one who truly loves you. But in your great kindness you told no one of your going that they might not trouble themselves.

By my life we never saw any one like you, and we never heard of any one who acted so well as you did in the way of mercy. And we pray God Almighty to let you return soon, and to renew for us the happiness that was, for He is merciful, and will compassionate us. Amen.

(Signed)   MUSTAFA ABD EL RAHMAN,
Kalib of the Mutaserrif of Damascus.

[No. 17.]

From the Sayyid Mohammed,

To His Excellency Captain Burton, the Consul of H.B. Majesty's Government at Damascus.

After inquiring about your precious health, I have the honour to declare that your departure has been to us the greatest of sorrows, and we ever are praising your excellent ways and qualities. We hope that you have happily reached London, and will let us know of it, in order that our hearts may take rest about your health. And we hope from your kindness that you will let us know of your return to Damascus, as we expect you night and day in health and well-being. During your time we enjoyed every happiness, and we saw from you nothing but good. Not only we, but all the people are grieving at the separation, considering how much of goodness in official matters they saw from you and your preserving the paths of right. We equally regret the departure of your excellent lady to join you, and we hope that she will travel in peace and safety. We also pray to Allah that both of you may presently return to us in health and prosperity; and may Allah prolong your days.

(Signed)   SAYYID MOHAMMED.

Aylul 8, 1871.

[18]

From Hasan Ayyus Aba Shadid,
To His Excellency our Lord the Sayyid Bey of H.B. Majesty's Government at Damascus.

After kissing your hands, your servants would state that they have heard with great regret of your departure for England, and we intended to have come and kissed your honourable hand. We pray the Creator that we may soon be blessed with the sight of you; and we ever take refuge under the wing of the Lord. We hope from your kindness of heart that it will not forget its servants, and we supplicate Allah to grant to you the greatest of victories, and crown you with a crown which shall last for ever, and peace be with you according to our desire; and our services are ever at your disposal.

(Signed) HASAN AYYUS.

Jemadi el Tani,
10, A.H., 1288.

---

[19]

From Shahadah el Halabi and Kasim el Halabi,
In the Maydan quarter of Damascus.

To His Excellency the Consul Bey of the British Government, may Allah prolong his days, Amen!

We your servants entreat with heartfelt prayers that your Government may increase in power and grandeur, and that the Creator may shower upon it his choicest blessings and adorn it with all good gifts. Thus may it happen, Amen, O Lord of the (three) worlds! Accept our supplications for your Excellency's welfare, and take pity upon us, and prolong your kindness to us and your protection to us. And we shall ever expect and pray that we may again see you in the best of health; and we entreat the beneficent Lord that you may obtain all your desires in your official position to the fullest extent. And your servants will never cease to pray for your obtaining all your wishes.

(Signed) SHAHADAH.
KASIM.

Jemadi 22, A.H., 1288.

---

[20]

Translation of Letter from certain Moslem Divines, Merchants, and others at Damascus.

From the day that Captain Burton came as English Consul to Damascus till now, we saw no faults in him, and he did not listen to any false reports, but acted in truth, and what was not truth he rejected it. He never received any bribes (bartíl) from any one, Any business that was just and legal he did it, but that which was bad and worthless he left alone. And we saw no bad in him, and he loved the Mahommedans and those who were under him. And there never came from him anything but truth, and he always walked with justice and hated none but the liars.

MOHAMMED AWAR,
BIKRI ABDER TAHAN,
EL AKKAD,
ABDU EL HABAL,
HASAIN EL AMARI,
ABD EL WAHED ES SOURRAF.
SHEIKH MOHAMMED ALI,
MOHAMMED SALEH,
(From the Mosque el Amawi).

[21]

Translation of Letter from ———

11th day of Jemadeh, 1288.

To His Excellency, &c., the Consul of the great English Government.

After asking after your Excellency's health, we hope to God that all is well, we address your Excellency; for the moment we heard that your Excellency had gone to his country, great sorrow came upon us by reason of the great kindness your Excellency has always shown us. For you always acted with goodness to us and our property, and in your time the truth prevailed and falsehood did not succeed. May God spare you for us, and return you to us in safety. Amen.

Signed and sealed by your Excellency's servants, all the people of ———, great and small.

       Sheikh MOHAMMED ALI,
        MOHAMMED HAMMED,
        KASIM HAMUD,
        HUSEYN HAMUD,
        IBRAHIM EL GHAU,
          and many others.

[22]

Translation of Letter from ———

To His Excellency, &c., the Consul of the great English Government.

The cause of our writing is first to inquire after your health, and we ask God Almighty to protect you from all injury and harm, and to return you to us in safety that you may protect us from all hurt, as you did before; for the moment you left, our mind was distracted, and many thoughts came to us. We ask the Lord of the Universe and His Prophet not to take you away from us, but that you may protect us from all enemies and injuries, as you did before; for you are good to all who are in difficulties and protect them. May God make your days long in the name of every prophet who worships the Lord of the Universe. Amen.

Your Excellency's servants, the men of ———
(L.S.)   Seal of the Sheikh Ali Yehyeh.   (L.S.)   Sheikh Mohammed Yehyeh.

[23]

To His Excellency the Consul of England, &c., at Damascus.

From the Village of ———

To His Excellency the Bey-Consul for the Government of England in Damascus, may His Honour live. Hoping to gain your merciful favour and (please) your noble disposition.

When the news reached us that your Excellency is going to your country, great sorrow and heartache came upon us, because we were slaves for your Excellency's service, asking God Almighty in his glorious Eternity, the Lord of Heaven, to return you to us in triumph, the giver of good news of help from the Lord of Universe, and wherever you go may the Apostle of God help you in the name of the Lord of Universe, and may the Lord hear our prayer for your return, and may He spare you for ever. Amen.

For your Excellency's servants the inhabitants of ——— under the Government of Baalbek.

  Signed and Sealed by your Excellency's faithful Servant,
   11th Jemadeh, 1288.   MUSELLIM AYYUB,
   (August 25, 1871.)   (L.S.)   Official Seal.

[24]

Translation of Letter from ———

To His Excellency, &c., the Consul of the exalted English Government, and may God spare him.

You, our just Lord, whose hand is strong, why is it that you have acted thus and left us. This has all come from our bad fortune, for you were for us a shield to protect us from all harm and injury, and preserve us from shame, for only in your time have we always enjoyed rest, for you have guarded our property, and do not allow our religion to be mocked, and you allow no one to cheat us. But what are we now to do, O Sir? For this order did not rest with us, but the order is with Him to whom it belongs, and He is the Lord Almighty, and we ask from Him in our first prayers that you may return to us in safety, and our longing for you is like the longing of a man to be in heaven with the Lord Almighty because of your great kindness to us; (we swear) thrice by the name of the most excellent God (that we hope you will) return to us soon, and if you do not come we will witness against you on the Judgment Day of God Almighty, for it is your duty to do good to the sons of Adam, and may you be spared for ever. Amen.

We beg of you to excuse us in taking such a liberty as this, but because our hearts are burning with fire on account of your leaving us, we hope that you will not blame us.

Signed and Sealed by the Servants of your Excellency, the people of ——— collectively.

(L.S.) Seal of the Sheikh,
SULEYMAN MURAD.

---

[25]

Translation of Letter from people of ——— and ———

To His Excellency Mr. Burton, Consul of the Honourable English Government, may God Almighty spare him.

After kissing your noble hands with all honour and dignity, we address your Excellency, we, your servants, the Moslem Sheikhs of ——— and ——— (wo villages) We have heard that your Excellency has gone to the land of England. Please God that this news may turn out for good, because we, the Moslems, are your slaves, and without the help of your Excellency to us we should be utterly ruined, because your Excellency is kind and loves the truth for all people, and especially for us the Moslems you honour our religion and love truth and mercy an advocate of justice. We are hoping to God Almighty that He will send your Excellency to us again in a short time, for without your Excellency's help we shall be left destitute. We beg of your Excellency that you will have compassion on us and return in peace and soon, and may God grant that your Excellency may remain with us, and may your life be prolonged.—11th Jemadeh, 1288 (25th of August, 1871).

The Mukhtar of the villlage of
    ALI HUSAYN VASIF.
The Khatib of ——— and of
    HUSAYN EZED DIN.
The Sheikh of the village of
    ALI ABDER RAHMAN.

---

[26]

Translation of Letter from ———

We, the Sheykhs, the Beys, and the Elders of ——— collectively, are sending this to Damascus, and state that two years ago we were honoured with becoming neighbours of Captain Burton, Consul of the English Government at Damascus, and during his residence for the summer in Bludan, which is near our village, we did not find from him anything but justice and truthfulness both to Mahommedans and Christians; and we offered our duty and services to him, and thanked him for his kindness to us, and, hoping that he will overlook all our shortcomings, we address this letter to him for his kindness to us.

11th Jemádeh, 1288 (26 August, 1871).

(23 Seals in all.)

[27]

Translation of Letter from Sayyad (descendants of the Prophet) living at ———
To the Bey, the English Consul, &c.

After kissing the hands of your noble Excellency, we, the Sayyad of . . . heard the news that your Excellency is recalled to England, and great sorrow and grief came over us, and we, the Sayyad, were thinking of coming over and kissing your Excellency's hand; but the reason we did not is that your Excellency went away to that land. We ask God Almighty to show us the light of your countenance in health, and not to prevent us from kissing your Excellency's hand, and your servants always hide under the wings of their lord; and we hope from God that you may not stay away from us, and may God make your days happy and well-being for us, and may you ever be victorious,

Signed and sealed by your Servants,

The Sayid,	The Sayid,	The Sayid,
ALI ZAIN.	AHMET ALI IBRAHIM.	HOSEYN SAYID.
		ALI YUSUF.

[28]

Literal Translation of Letter from Moslem Sheihks at ———

To reach with honour His Excellency and Highness, &c., &c., &c., the Consul of the English Government living at Damascus.

To your Highness and Excellency the Officer of England, may your life be prolonged and preserved.

After enquiries for your Excellency, we hope from God Almighty that you may be always in happiness. We have heard the news that your Excellency is journeying in peace to your country. We were deeply grieved for the departure of your Excellency, but hope from God Almighty that he will soon show us your face again, because your Excellency is an advocate of justice, and especially for the Mahommedan religion, and loves all those who are dependent upon your Excellency, because your Excellency is beloved especially by the Moslems. May your life be long.

7th day of Jemádeh, 1288 (August 21st, 1871).

Your Servant,	Your Servant,
ALI SHUMMAT (Sheik of the town).	ALUSA KAMALED DIN.
Your Servant,	Your Servant,
MUSTAPHA DAKDUK.	HASAN KASIM AHMED.

Literal Translation of Letter from Moslems of ———

To His Excellency the Bey, Consul of the Honorable English Government.

We address this petition to your Excellency, we your Servants the Mohammedan Sheiks of . . . . and . . . . because we have heard that your Excellency is gone to England, and we are in deep sorrow, which we cannot express to your Excellency, but we hope from the mercy of God Almighty that He will have pity on us and return your Excellency to us in peace, because there is no Consul except your Excellency who loves uprightness and mercy *(and acts with them)* to us, the poor. And without the compassion your Excellency shewed to the poor in the last year, half the world would have died from hunger or in prison, and now all the world cries to God to return your Excellency to us; for we are very cast down without your Excellency. Your Excellency's commands will be commands.

10th day of Jemádeh, 1288.

Sealed and signed by Six Shaykhs.

[No. 30.]

Translation of Letter from Moslems of ———

To His Excellency, our Master the Consul of the Honourable English Government in Damascus. May his life be spared.

After kissing your Excellency's hands, and because we your servants had the news that your Excellency is gone to England, a great sorrow came upon us, and we thought that we would be honoured with kissing your noble hands, asking God Almighty that He will not prevent us from seeing your Excellency in a short time, and we your servants always hide ourselves under the wings of their lord. May God call us together to see your Excellency soon. We pray your Excellency will not forget your servant, but order him to fulfil your bequests. We ask God that your Excellency may triumph exceedingly, and that you may receive a crown from God which will never fail you, and peace be with you as much as our longing to you is. We send your Excellency our service. May your life be preserved. Amen.

Your Excellency's Servant, who kisses your hand,

(L.S.) HASAN AGERS ABU SHEDID

10th day of Jemádeh, 1288.

[No. 31.]

From the Village of ———

To His Excellency the exalted, the beneficent, the great, the glorious, the honoured Consul Bey of the Great Government of England at Damascus. May he ever prosper!

After kissing your honourable hands, and expressing our prayers for your being blessed by Allah the Almighty King, and for your being raised to honor and dignity over us, it is our bounden duty to write enquiries about you, and to congratulate our souls by the tidings of your Excellency's return to our parts. This return to us would be the greatest of blessings. It is our duty, one and all, to kiss your hands, and now our Brother, Abu Ibrahim Mohammed, wishes to kiss your Excellency's hands, and we both beg to offer you all our services, Sir.

(Signed) by the Shaykh and Notables of the Village of

Jemadi el Akhir 18
A. H. 1288

[32.]

Letter from the Village of ———

To his Excellency the Consul Bey of the Great Government of England. May he and they ever prosper.

Your servants pray with the strongest prayers that the light of your Government may ever shine, and that its honour and majesty may increase, and that the Lord will prolong the days of your Sovereign, and adorn her with perpetuity of rule. Amen! We hope that your Government will take pity upon these your servants, and extend its protection over them for all time, whilst your servants ever expect and look forward to the honour of serving you to their utmost. And they will ever pray, sir, for your speedy return.

Signed by two Shaykhs.

Jemadi, 20 A. H. 1288.

130

[33.]

From the Druzes of the Village of ———

To his Excellency the Dew of great Qualities, the Exalted in Mind, the generous and beneficent Consul Bey of the Great Government of England. May he ever be preserved in welfare and dignity.

After sending what is due and proper to your honourable self and your exalted qualities, offering our respect which passes all bounds, and expressing our gratitude to your glorious Government, may it never cease to be robed in honour, and dignity, and prosperity for ever and ever. We, your faithful servants the Druzes resident at . . . . have the honour to forward this petition to your Excellency's portal, because we are always obedient and subject to your high orders, and to the orders of your great Government. May its dignity ever endure! and its protection will ever be extended to its servants, especially to those who are faithful to it. With one mouth and heart we raise our voices to the Most High, hoping from his goodness that he will strengthen the pillars of your great Government with dignity and victory, enfolded in the cloak of Majesty and enjoyment. And may your Excellency ever be kept in health and happiness; and we hope from the generous kindness of your Governmen, that you will be able to keep your eye upon us. All this induces us to expect the support of your faithful slaves' reputation, and they will do, sir, all that you wish from them.

Signed by six Shaykhs.

Jemadi 20 A. H. 1288.

---

[34]

From the Druze Village of ———, near Damascus.

To his Excellency, &c.

After sending our compliments and greeting to the honourable and merciful person offering all our respects to your noble Government, which is covered with glory, and happiness, and good fortune for ever, and offering to your Excellency, as your slaves, this paper to your merciful hands, the Druze community, natives and strangers in and near Damascus, because we are your Excellency's obedient and trusty slaves, and the same to your noble Government, &c., the strength of the people, and because we belong to it, and we are but mortals, and grief and sorrow have come into all our hearts, and we all with one voice pray to the Highest beseeching his mercy that he will strengthen your noble Government in glory and happiness, and that you may be dressed in robes of honour and attain good fortune, and that you may be spared to us in health and happiness. And we hope that through your Excellency's kindness we may find favour with you; and we write this to show our obedience to you, and we are ready for any service that we can do for you.

(L.S.) Government Seal of Sheikhs and Village of ———
(L.S.) Sheikh Abbar Zayn el Din.
(L.S.) Sheikh Yusuf Shaan.
(L.S.) Sheikh Hosayn, A.K.L.
(L.S.) Sheikh Khalil ibn Mohammed.
(L.S.) Sheikh Hosayn el Khotib.

20 Jemádeh, 1288.

To His Honourable Excellency. To Captain Burton, the Honourable Bey.

May God spare him for ever. After the asking for your noble health, hoping from God that you are happy is the reason I wrote that letter. You have departed, leaving us the sweet perfume of charity and noble conduct in befriending the poor and supporting the weak and oppressed, and your name is large on account of what God has put into your nature. And our nation is troubled at missing your face in the accustomed place. O be pleased not to forget us from your good mind, because we are now under your shadow.

The Shaykh and People of a Druze Village in the Mountains.

September 25, 1871.

To his High Excellency.

May God spare him. Kissing your hands and feet, we your servants the Druzes of K———— and A————, belonging to W————, from the people of noble Damascus, after asking after your welfare, and may God make all your time good. We are always your servants and unceasing, and ask the Holy Highest that he will spare you to us, and we hope that your Holiness and noble Excellency may always throw your mantle over us. And we are still more than ever your faithful servants, because you came to us and looked upon us with honour, and we are full of gratitude therefore. Hoping from God that you may be sent back to us, your servants hope that you will still protect them with our honourable and respected lady. May God spare her, and leave her for us, who are longing to kiss her hands, and God spare you both for ever and ever.

The Shayks, Elders, and People of the above-named Villages.

September, 1871.

To his Excellency and Highness the Consul of England.

May God spare him for ever.

After kissing your noble hand and asking after your health to rest our minds, we are always praying for your return, and we are ready for everything you want, and you have honoured us with a word and visited us in the Lebanon, and we are calm and happy, resting in you for all things. We are all kneeling to pray that you may be spared to us, and may God preserve your noble health.

Shaykh . . . . . . , an Amir of the Druses of the Lebanon.

September, 1871.

To His Excellency the English Consul Bey.

May God spare him for ever. After kissing your noble hand and praying you may be spared in every happiness, and from the time you departed you left our nation in great sorrow, and we ask the Holiest to send you back to us in prosperity and good health to be over us. If you deign to ask for your servants we are well, but uneasy at your departure, and asking God always to spare you to us, and send you back to us, because we are most thankful and proud to be your servants, for you have been most kind to us, and we send our loving salaam to the noble Lady, and ask her to look after us, because we are your servants, and whatever you want, Highness speak, and your servants will obey,

SHAHAD EL HALALI,
Druzes.

Sept. 14, 1871.

Extracts from private letters showing the sentiments of the people in Syria on most of the affairs which took place:—

Anent Jews.

BAHIA, October 8th, 1874.

I hope you got well over your differences with those lying Jews, and that you were eventually backed up by the Minister at home. What a pity that the English name should be so little considered in Syria, when you could so easily bring it into repute and make it respected, if only backed up at home. Many thanks for your and Mrs. Burton's extreme kindness to me in Damascus, which I shall never forget.

&c., &c.,

C. H. WILLIAMS.

Anent Nazareth.

Damascus, February 8th, 1872.

I have delayed in order to give you good news. The Nazareth affair is decided in your favour. I congratulate you most heartily, for the *justice* of your cause won it for you, and not any intrigue or indirect influence. You owe nothing to me or anyone else in the matter.

A CLERGYMAN.

From a Greek Orthodox Deacon, Damascus.

September 14, 1871.

Vous étiez le protecteur de tous les Chrétiens, étant toujours ami du Moslem, vous étiez le mien, sans vous les Chrétiens de Damas et de toute la Syrie sont étouffés, sont foulés aux pieds par les Turcs barbares. Sans vos secours et votre courage, les Chrétiens n'osent plus paraître au gouvernement et se plaindre, car ils craignent d'être pendus comme le pauvre C—— dans la Mosquée de Damas. Sans la presence du Capitaine Burton, tout est immobile. Comment faire pour vous voir, faut-il que je vienne jusqu'à Londres vous exprimer de vive voix tout ce que je ressens pour vous. Vous êtes pour jamais mon protecteur, mon plus grand ami, mon père, mon frère, mon esperance, mon tout; ici tous les braves gens vous désirent, vous chérissent. Tous vos protégés élèvent les mains au ciel jour et nuit, souhaitant votre retour. Quand à moi, jespère plus que tous, que le bon Dieu, qui connaît toute votre justice et toutes vos actions, vous rendra dans quelque mois comme notre Consul-Général.

From the Jews of Tiberias and Safed.

Captain Burton, at the request of the Jews, visited their two cities of Tiberias and Safed. They wrote letters to Her Majesty and Her Majesty's Government, petitioning to be placed under Captain Burton's jurisdiction. In reply, Mr. Consul-General Eldridge received orders, almost a year ago, to inspect and report on the above-named cities, but his health has only just permitted him to carry out his instructions.

To Captain Burton.

We beg to inform you, that at the report of your departure for London we prayed to our Heavenly Father that He be with you and grant success in every way. Amen.

Mr. Solomon Pekus has told us that you kindly promised to do during your stay in London all you can in our favour; that the Keris el Jehud in Tiberias should be restored unto us; that you took with you the petition we sent you and the document signed by the elders of the Mohammedans in that city, which states that the above-named *Keres el Jehud* belongs to the Israelites, and promises to investigate the matter. May the Lord reward you fully, and may he grant that you will return safely to Damascus. We hope that you will remain faithful to the promise repeatedly given us that you now, having the best opportunity, investigate the matter in order to help us to possess our right: to deliver the prey out of the hand of the robber; to restore unto us the above-mentioned inheritance of our forefathers, including the piece of land used for washing the dead. We are quite sure you will not fail to carry out our wishes. Meanwhile, Sir M. Montefiore will receive a letter from us in which we request him to assist you in the matter; and he will certainly do so, as none of us are able to write English. We have been compelled to address you in Hebrew.

Hoping a favourable answer,

We are, &c., &c.,

From Daoud Zalzal, Beyrout.

Parlez moi des agréables nouvelles de votre retour ici, plutôt pour notre satisfaction et et notre bonheur que pour vous; cette à votre connaissance que l'affaire F——— a été reglée à l'aimable.

J'ai regretté tant votre départ sans vous avoir fait des adieux. Je ne puis me consoler que dans l'espoir de vous revoir bientôt. Je forme les vœux les plus sincères pour avoir ce bonheur. Donnez-moi bientôt cette bonne nouvelle. Je m'estime heureux d'avoir obtenu vos bonnes grâces ; ce sont ces sentiments de justice qui m'ont fait obtenir des avantages.

From a Christian house of note in Beyrout.

Sir and my Lord,

Offering you my greeting, I cannot tell you my grief because I have not seen you, and have heard of your departure suddenly, which I can never forget. I cannot comfort my thoughts or hope in God except to hope you will return here. May your flag be hoisted above all on that day I ask God. I ask God's blessing to spare you, and he is above all strength or worldly power, and from what is in my heart I wish I was in your service, anywhere, on any conditions; but what hurts me more than all is, that though the eye can see the hand is short. Begging of you to receive my trouble from my heart, faithful until death to your noble person, all honour should be given to it. Hoping you will not eject me from your kind thoughts, and that you will condescend to honour me with any services you may want, wherever it is. I am ready for that, and always thinking and saying, "Oh, if ever I shall succeed to obtain your friendship, be under your noble excellency's protection." God is just, and he will do what he will, and send you back to this country, and I am waiting for that alone with all my heart.

From a Missionary house in the Beyrout district: "The news of your departure has been to me a tremendous shock; I cannot get over it. It is too much. With you yesterday, and to-day you are gone; I am grieving sadly. I need not say you have heartfelt sympathy. Glad I should have been had you been allowed to carry out your plans and wishes. It would have been for the benefit of mankind, and the advance of Christianity. But truly we are shortsighted and know not what a day may bring forth. I shall follow you with deep interest, and shall always want to know how and where you are. Won't you write to us? We shall so miss you. It won't be any great loss to you leaving Damascus, I daresay, but it will to those you leave behind. Nobody else could manage like you in the emergencies to which we are always subject in this country. Our warm sympathy and best wishes for a pleasant voyage to dear old England, and a speedy return to Damascus. I cannot believe that you are gone for ever, and hope for all our sakes you will be spared to come back and fill your post as Consul with all honour."

From a Missionary, Damascus, 12th June, 1872.

If I might give you my advice, I should say do not injure your prospects for a sentiment. The world has far better work in store for you. There are lots of brave and plucky things to be done in the world yet, and none are so fitted as you to do them. This Government must have been astonished to find how blameless you must have been, not counting on the unscrupularity of your few opposers. Mr. Green (your successor) is said to resemble you. I hope he may in his acts.

From an Engineer, Aleppo, November 7th, 1871.

I was glad to hear of your signal victory over the great Rashid, though he got up all sorts of petitions and forwarded them to Constantinople. The Grand Vizier knew better, and sent orders to the military authorities to turn him out if he did not vacate peaceably. There were public prayers in your behalf in the great Mahomedan Mosque, and Turks as well as all well disposed Christians wish you back again.

A Clergyman who was in Syria, now in Lincoln's Inn Fields, November, 1871.

It must be highly gratifying to you that everybody is with you, and testifying from so many and such independent sources, the appreciation of your efforts to uphold the dignity of the position you held in the midst of much intrigue and difficulty, and in a country where deceit and fraud hold their own. That our Government may be led to adopt a course of sturdy principle, and not allow themselves to be subject to mere diplomatic intrigue in this matter is everybody's earnest hope.

An English Colonist in Syria.

December 19th, 1871,

We have heard of the projected change in the Consulate arrangements, but unless you are to be Consul-General nobody gains anything by the arrangements—none that anybody can perceive.

February 1st, 1872.

A line to tell you that H.B.M.'s, his Consulate-General in Beyrout has lately announced that it is its Royal will and pleasure that no more letters should be directed to its care, so you must change our address here. Expect more massacres like 1860. Everything is going to the bad altogether. Every dog has his day, and I suppose ours is now come.

A Consul . . . . . .

Sept. 30, 1871.

Comment? Vous avez été rappelé? Et par les intrigues du Wali? C'est à ne pas y croire; mais souvent c'est la récompense qui est échue à ceux qui, comme vous, se conduisent bien. Les Turcs se fichent des Européens bien plus qu'on ne le croit; ils ne craignent que les Russes. Peut-être le Wali réussira avec ses projets d'indépendance.. Fuad Fasha n'en fut pas si loin. Dites moi si vous pensez retourner en Syrie. Sous tons les rapports comme je serais content de vous avoir de nouveau comme collègue. On ne trouve pas toujours comme vous dans notre carrière. Adieu! Adieu! une bien chaude poignée de main.

CONCLUSION.

I have now respectfully to submit that, having given a clear account of every unpleasantness that came upon me owing to my necessary peculiar and unpleasant duties, that I should like to say a few words on my own account to those whom duty or kindness may lead to read my case. By the above remark I mean that I ventured on my career in the important and highly interesting post of Damascus most anxious to serve my Country and to please my Government. I found, on taking charge (and as I knew more and more of the country), a peculiar state of things, in which no man calling himself a gentleman and an Englishman, and no man with any pride in the good name of his Government, could sit down at his ease before he had effected a radical change. I knew it would be a difficult task, and that a sea of intrigues and enemies, with all their spites, falsehoods, jealousies, and unscrupulous manœuvres, would arise up and rage about me; but I also knew my own capacity and my knowledge of the East; I was persuaded that a just and right-minded Government would stand by me and support me, and even thank me for my work when it was accomplished. I was not aware that the East was so little known or understood in England. To those who have said that I made too much of my post, and have mistaken the duties of Consul and Governor, I can only repeat that the jurisdiction of the Consul of Damascus is very great, extending to Bagdad on the east and down to Nablus on the south. Damascus is the heart and capital of Syria, the residence of the Wali, and the head-quarters of the Army and Police, the Chief Tribunals which represent our Parliament, Chambers, Judges, and Courts, and all business institutions and transactions, besides the Religious Head-quarters and focus of Mahometanism; and the Consul of Damascus has all the real work to do. Dependence on Beyrout is a moral impossibility, as Damascus work requires prompt and decided action, and no loss of time; and an order which might apply to Beyrout would be totally inapplicable at Damascus, and would probably only proceed from the advice of some Dragoman interested in the case. Upon the Consul devolves the responsibility of the post for Bagdad, and the protection of commerce and travellers in the desert, and he may, through personal influence, quiet the Bedawin. Therefore, the Consul-General should live at Damascus, or six months in Damascus and six at Beyrout, with a Vice-Consul under him at both places, and he should visit the whole of Syria within, say, every two years. Less cannot be made of the post of Damascus, unless England wishes to abandon Syria altogether, which would be even better than occupying the *triste* position she does now.

I quote from an author who has lived long in Damascus:—

"Whoever lives in Damascus must have good health and nerves, must be charmed with Oriental life, and must not care for society, comforts, or luxuries, but be totally occupied with some serious pursuit. Should he be a Consul—an old soldier is best—he must be accustomed to command with a strong hand. The natives must be impressed by him, and know that he can fight if attacked. He must be able to ride hard, and to rough it in mountain or desert, in order to attend to his own work, instead of sending a Dragoman or a Kawass, who, probably, would not go, and, if he did, might be bribed. He must have the honour and dignity of England truly at heart, and he should be a gentleman to understand fully what this means—not a man risen from the ranks, whose mind might be pre-occupied by trading, and who might be bullied or bribed. He should speak Arabic, Persian, Turkish, and Hindostanee as well as English, French, and Italian, so as not to take the hearsay of his Dragomans. He must be able to converse freely with Arabs, Turks, Bedouins, Druzes, Kurds, Jews, Maronites, Affghans, and Persians, and understand their religions and prejudices. He must have his reliable men everywhere, and know everything that goes on throughout the length and breadth of the country, and then test its truth. He must have a thorough knowledge of Eastern character; he must keep a hospitable house; he must be cool, firm, and incorruptible. He must not be afraid to do his duty, however unpleasant and risky; and, having done it, if his Chiefs do not back him up—*i.e.*, his Consul-General, his Ambassador, and the Secretary of State for Foreign Affairs—the Turkish local authorities know he has done his duty at his own risk. They admire, fear, and hate the individual, but they despise his Government, whilst they fawn and cringe to it, and thus the interests of England and English pride get trampled in the dust." I am quoting the words of an author who knows the land, and who will one day be a great authority. I know all these things above-named, and I did them. Had I been spared there for one more year, nay, six months, my work would have been well done and Syria would have been a happy land. Soubhi Pasha the new Wali of Syria, Mahmoud Pasha the new Grand Vizier of Constantinople, would have appreciated my exertions. Had Lord Stratford de Redcliffe been Ambassador at Constantinople; had Lord Dufferin been the Commissioner; had Colonel Rose (Lord Strathnairn) or Mr. Consul-General Richard Wood been at Beyrout, the Foreign Office would have heard nothing but my praise. These gentlemen knew the East. Those to whom I was accountable are men of another stamp and policy.

The interference of Great Britain and Austria in the affairs of Syria, and the expulsion of Ibrahim Pasha, were movements highly applauded at the time, but now universally condemned in the country where they can best be judged. Mohammed Ali, Viceroy of Egypt, would inevitably, without that fatal *contretemps*, have entered Constantinople, and his progressive measures would have regenerated the effete empire. Russia knew this well. She was prepared to resist it by force, but she found the two Powers ready to do her work for her. She must have laughed loud and long at Lord Palmerston's peculiar diplomacy.

Presently, England suspecting that she had committed herself, and perhaps satisfied with the amount of attention and expense bestowed upon a distant country which offers few commercial attractions, withdrew herself as much as possible from Syria and her affairs. The first step was to make way for rivals. Whilst France and Russia, Austria and Egypt, established weekly or fortnightly lines of steamers amply subsidized, connecting all the Levantine ports, and showing their flags with imposing regularity England was literally nowhere on her own element, she ranked even behind Egypt. Thus, tacitly yielding up her supremacy in the waters of the Levant, she threw away, or rather she gave to others, the carrying as well as the commission trade, as early as 1845. Mr. Macfarlane (vol. i., p. 25) foresaw the evil consequences of this tactic. "In ten years," he wrote, "there will hardly be an English vessel carrying a cargo to the Levant, or bringing home a cargo from that part of the world." He was fatally right—all our little remaining *prestige* has been preserved by individual energy and probity. The sturdy Englishman is not easily taught to give "foreigners" the precedence, even in foreign lands.

The next step was to show practically that any Consul was good enough for Syria. Colonel Rose and Mr. Richard Wood are the only names remembered in the land with something more than respect. It is not surprising that the French, who chose such men as M. de Lesseps and M. Outrey, not to speak of the late Baron Rousseau, carried the day in every disputed question, even in such private matters as the Sarcophagus of Asmunazar, and completely defeated us by land. This was partly the work of the party popularly called "Peace-at-any-price." Our Consuls were ordered not to acquire legitimate influence, either for themselves or for their nations. Virtually they were commanded to like being despised.

In 1860, England, much against her own wish, underwent a temporary revival of her old popularity and pre-eminence in the Levant. The honourable and high-principled bearing of Lord Dufferin, appointed by Lord John Russell to sit upon the Syrian Commission which followed the massacres of June and July, bore fruit. Whilst some of his colleagues were bribed, and others were bullied, and all were outwitted by Fuad Pasha, he made himself conspicuous by his justice, his delicacy of feeling, and his open-handed charity. Whilst the Christian commission openly sided with the murderous Maronites against the murderous Druzes he held the scales carefully balanced, and he never became an advocate except in the cause of humanity. But he unhappily proposed to erect in Syria a Vice-royalty after the fashion of Egypt, and who should he propose for Viceroy, by a curious fatality, but Fuad Pasha? This astute personage was the last nominee in the world that should have been named. His love of breeding discussion and dissension between Druze and Christian, and his secret support of the Moslem, had directly caused the Syrian Massacres of 1860. True to her policy, the Porte sent Fuad Pasha to punish the offenders whom he had taught to offend, and of course the English public, ignorant and incurious of things Oriental, wondered how the Turkish statesman was so tender to his own tools. The proposal of Fuad Pasha for Viceroy was rich in bad results. As long as he lived Syria was never quiet; he stirred up all manner of troubles in order to remind the world that he was the man to put them down.

On the other hand, the French party proposed for their Viceroy the Algerine Amir Abd el Kadir. The ex-hero is a devout, learned, and humane man—in fact, a good Moslem; but he is unfitted by nature and education to work in such a hot-bed of intrigues as Syria. However, in the massacre of 1860, the British Consul's life was preserved by *his* Algerine Guard (the Turkish one was treacherous), and he slept on a mat across his own threshold, lest some unhappy Christian might be driven from his shelter. The Amir affects a kind of semi-independence, keeps up an *imperium in imperio*, and looks forward to being "King of Arabistan." He became a kinglet, ruled his Algerines, and asserted supreme authority in the Mosque. He is still the "Báshat el Magháribeh," Pasha of the Algerines, as opposed to the other Pasha, the Governor-General.

Loudly enough and naturally, too, the Porte protested against being dismembered. She shrewdly suspected that the "Syrian Vice-royalty" scheme came from the higher powers in England. Orientals are not apt to recognize independence of action in subordinate functionaries. Still she believed in Lord Palmerston, after whose death Ottomans began to think that their Sultan had lost his only influential friend in Great Britain. This feeling has been greatly increased amongst the educated classes since the abolition of the Black Sea Treaty. The Turks are now turning, as might be expected, towards Russia. It is the recoil of the bow.

Since 1865 our downfall in Syria has been complete.

The best measure—and there is no *instantia crucis* more decisive—of our utter loss of influence is the accumulation of long-pending and systematically-ignored claims for which British *protégés* have implored settlement, but in vain. One of these dates from 1863. In another case an English Consular Dragoman has been ousted from his village, in order to make way for a French Dragoman. And the measure of a nation's *prestige* in the East is now, has ever been, and will always be, the treatment of its protected subjects by the native authorities.

A strong man in Syria would have arrested all these wrongs at the outset; but then we had not a strong man. Our Consuls-General and Consuls possessed little interest, and less support at home; they had orders not to be troublesome—not to *faire des affaires*. The Governor-General of Syria, Rashid Pasha, was more than a match for the whole corps. In some cases he winked at irregularities which he could use as weapons, meanwhile satisfying himself with treating the official as a kátib, or clerk. In other cases he wheedled the enemy by promises never meant to be kept. But at all times and on all occasions it was " *Gare à vous* if you refer questions to Constantinople!" Hence it gradually became the fashion to finish off every despatch with praise more or less fulsome of Rashid Pasha.

When I had settled myself at head-quarters (Oct. 1869) my experience in the four quarters of the globe enabled me at once to see through the state of affairs. But I was powerless to act. A malicious rumour had been spread, evidently for the purpose of crippling my career, that the Moslems hated me because I had pilgrimaged to Mecca, and that my life would be in danger at Damascus. The vague report found a speaker in the Rev. Dr. Barclay, late of Jerusalem. This gentleman, believing that I had set on foot an anti-missionary policy, and would perhaps favour Moslem against Christian, enlisted the sympathies of Exeter Hall, not by telling the truth—this is not the way of Syria—but by representing the peril of arousing Mohammedan fanaticism by allowing me to take office. He knew as well as I knew that my main difficulty would be the expectations of the Moslems to be the most favoured at the Consulate. Lord Clarendon could hardly help being impressed by rumours coming from a source so respectable. He ignored, as Englishmen are now too apt to do, that England can still, by the power of her ancient name, impose upon the East in a matter of the kind, and he allowed me to proceed to his post, but under protest : " If the feeling stated to exist against you on the part of the authorities and the people at Damascus should prevent the proper performance of your official duties, it will be his Lordship's duty immediately to recall you." (Separate, F.O., June 19, 1869.) So I fought the battle of reform, where all my strength was needed, with pinioned arms.

During my first year I gained some local credit by impartiality and active humanity in a place " whose atmosphere has the effect of denationalizing the English character, and of taking from it its impatience of injustice and oppression." I opposed the proselytizing and the tract-distribution of the Superintendent of the British Syrian Schools; and I reported his visits to the Foreign Office as dangerous for the Christians, although well aware that I was thrusting my hand into a hornet's nest. My proceedings could not be blamed, and the only unpleasant remark made was that a copy of a certain letter ought to have been sent, if it had been received, which it had not. I punished certain Druzes who had plundered and maltreated an English missionary; and I curbed the rapacity of certain Jewish money-lenders under British protection, who would have converted me into a kind of bailiff for tapping on the shoulder insolent peasant debtors. This aroused a storm of wrath which raged for months. The Israelites strained every nerve to secure my recall, but my cause was too good. The Foreign Office approved of my proceedings, but did not communicate to me their approval. In these trials, so far from being assisted, I was systematically opposed by H.M.'s Consul-General at Beyrout. Mr. Eldridge asked me in private not to report the proselytizing superintendent, not to punish the Druzes, not to interfere with the Jews; and because I required positive orders on paper to that effect, he ranged himself in the foremost ranks of my opponents.

Early in 1871, though well knowing the difficulty and the danger of the struggle, I was compelled to oppose some of the evil doings of Rashid Pasha, the Governor-General, when they crossed or interfered with my Consular duties.

From outward pressure from those in distress, I could no longer countenance delay in settling the claims of British subjects, and I was compelled to report flagrant cases to Constantinople. This was crossing the Rubicon. Rashid Pasha hated nothing more than such references, and has ever regarded and spoken of them as overt acts of hostile inclination; he dislikes them almost as much as paying money to foreign *protégés*.

The Governor-General saw that he was wrong and would be defeated, and he prepared for it, "*more Turco,*" by turning my flank. This manoeuvre was to press for my removal by a succession of trivial complaints, skilfully calculated to weary the Foreign Office and the Embassy. He represented me as a " véritable boute-feu." He seized the opportunity of a village riot at Nazareth, where my servants had been beaten and severely injured by a mob of Syrian Greeks, to take part with the latter, and to endorse their falsehoods by sending them in telegrams to Constantinople three days before I had returned to Damascus, and before I could offer a word of explanation.

He actually succeeded in causing the Foreign Office to confine me to Damascus, at a time when the climate was peculiarly hot and unwholesome (mid-July): I was suffering from fever, and the little English colony was all in summer quarters. He affected to look upon a trip to the Hauran as an event pregnant with evil to his administration, and actually composed a circular from me to the Druzes. I was compelled, in return, to make known Rashid Pasha's maladministration of Syria, his prostitution of rank, his filling every post with his own sycophants, who are removed only when they have made money enough to pay for being restored; his factious elevation of a Kurdish party; his projects against the Druzes; his persistent persecution of Moslem converts to Christianity, in the teeth of treaties and firmans; his open sympathy with the Greeks, and through them with Russia; and, finally, his preparations for an insurrection in Syria, should Egypt find an opportunity to declare her independence. I meanwhile continued to push my demand for the 6,000,000 piastres claimed by British subjects in Syria. My list shows a grand total of eleven, and of these five are important cases. On July 4th, 1871, I wrote to the Foreign Office and to the Embassy, urging that a Commission be directed to inquire into the subject, and to settle the items found valid. I expressed a hope that I might be permitted personally to superintend the settlement of these debts, with whose every item the study of twenty-one months had made me familiar, and another six months would have seen Syria swept clean and set in order. On August 16th, 1871, I was recalled suddenly, on the ground that the Moslems were fanatical enough to want my life. I have proved that to be like all the rest of Rashid Pasha's reports, utterly false. Rashid Pasha was recalled one month later. Some have pretended that he is not in disgrace, but it may be asserted that twenty-four hours' notice and threatened chains may be considered uncomplimentary to a man occupying the position of a viceroy. I am now awaiting the pleasure of Her Majesty's Government, which I trust may be to restore me to such a position as may mark that I have in no way forfeited its esteem and confidence.